Communications
in Computer and Information Science

1245

Commenced Publication in 2007
Founding and Former Series Editors:
Simone Diniz Junqueira Barbosa, Phoebe Chen, Alfredo Cuzzocrea,
Xiaoyong Du, Orhun Kara, Ting Liu, Krishna M. Sivalingam,
Dominik Ślęzak, Takashi Washio, Xiaokang Yang, and Junsong Yuan

More information about this series at http://www.springer.com/series/7899

Ludovico Boratto · Stefano Faralli ·
Mirko Marras · Giovanni Stilo (Eds.)

Bias and Social Aspects in Search and Recommendation

First International Workshop, BIAS 2020
Lisbon, Portugal, April 14
Proceedings

 Springer

Editors
Ludovico Boratto 🆔
Eurecat - Centre Tecnològic de Catalunya
Barcelona, Spain

Mirko Marras 🆔
University of Cagliari
Cagliari, Italy

Stefano Faralli 🆔
Unitelma Sapienza University of Rome
Rome, Italy

Giovanni Stilo 🆔
University of L'Aquila
L'Aquila, Italy

ISSN 1865-0929   ISSN 1865-0937   (electronic)
Communications in Computer and Information Science
ISBN 978-3-030-52484-5   ISBN 978-3-030-52485-2   (eBook)
https://doi.org/10.1007/978-3-030-52485-2

This Springer imprint is published by the registered company Springer Nature Switzerland AG
The registered company address is: Gewerbestrasse 11, 6330 Cham, Switzerland

Preface

The International Workshop on Bias and Social Aspects in Search and Recommendation (BIAS 2020) was held as part of the 42nd European Conference on Information Retrieval (ECIR 2020) on April 14, 2020. BIAS 2020 was expected to happen in Lisbon, Portugal, but due to the COVID-19 emergency and the consequent travel restrictions, the workshop was held online. The workshop was jointly organized by the Data Science and Big Data Analytics unit at Eurecat (Spain), by the University of Rome Unitelma Sapienza (Italy), by the Department of Mathematics and Computer Science at the University of Cagliari (Italy), and by the Department of Information Engineering, Computer Science and Mathematics at the University of L'Aquila (Italy). It was supported by the ACM Conference on Fairness, Accountability, and Transparency (ACM FAccT) Network.

In total, 44 submissions from 17 different countries were received. The final program included 10 full papers and 7 short papers (38% acceptance rate). All submissions were single-blind peer-reviewed by at least three internal Program Committee members to ensure that only submissions of high quality were included in the final program. Individual requests for reviewers were set forth aiming to strengthen the Program Committee, integrating and catching up with both new and accomplished reviewing workforce in the field.

The workshop collected novel ideas to detect, measure, characterize, and mitigate bias in the data and algorithms underlying search and recommendation applications, to provide a common ground for researchers working in this area. The workshop day included demo and paper presentations and a final discussion to highlight open issues, research challenges, and briefly summarize the outcomes of the workshop. The presentations covered topics that go from search and recommendation in online dating, education, and social media, over the impact of gender bias in word embeddings, to tools that enable the exploration of bias and fairness on the Web. The workshop included also a track about social aspects and implications of the above elements, related to recommendation and search, on online users. More than 70 participants were registered to the workshop.

In addition to the demo and paper presentations, the program also included a keynote presented by Prof. Chirag Shah from the University of Washington (USA). Prof. Shah highlighted how bias, especially in relation to search and recommender systems, causes material problems for users, businesses, and society at large. The examples spanned areas of search, education, and healthcare. To find a balance or fairness in the system and address the issue of bias, the concept of a marketplace was introduced, to lead to a more sustainable growth for various industries, governments, and our scientific advancement.

Overall, the workshop was a success, both in terms of number of participants and of interests that emerged during the presentations and the final discussion, creating new relationships and novel ideas in this area. Plans to organize the second edition of the workshop next year were formed. The organizers would like to thank the authors, the reviewers for shaping an interesting program, and the attendees for their active participation during the event.

May 2020

Ludovico Boratto
Stefano Faralli
Mirko Marras
Giovanni Stilo

Organization

Workshop Chairs

Ludovico Boratto — Eurecat - Centre Tecnològic de Catalunya, Spain
Stefano Faralli — Unitelma Sapienza University of Rome, Italy
Mirko Marras — University of Cagliari, Italy
Giovanni Stilo — University of L'Aquila, Italy

Program Committee

Himan Abdollahpouri — University of Colorado Boulder, USA
Luca Aiello — Nokia Bell Labs, UK
Mehwish Alam — FIZ Karlsruhe - Karlsruhe Institute of Technology, Germany
Marcelo Armentano — National University of Central Buenos Aires, Argentina
Solon Barocas — Microsoft Research and Cornell University, USA
Alejandro Bellogin — Universidad Autónoma de Madrid, Spain
Asia Biega — Microsoft Research, USA
Glencora Borradaile — Oregon State University, USA
Federica Cena — University of Turin, Italy
Pasquale De Meo — University of Messina, Italy
Sarah Dean — University of California, Berkeley, USA
Danilo Dessì — FIZ Karlsruhe - Karlsruhe Institute of Technology, Germany
Laura Dietz — University of New Hampshire, USA
Damiano Distante — Unitelma Sapienza University of Rome, Italy
Carlotta Domeniconi — George Mason University, USA
Michael Ekstrand — Boise State University, USA
Francesco Fabbri — Universitat Pompeu Fabra, Spain
Golnoosh Farnadi — Mila, University of Montreal, Canada
Nina Grgic-Hlaca — Max Planck Institute for Software Systems, Germany
Rossi Kamal — Kyung Hee University, South Korea
Toshihiro Kamishima — AIST, Japan
Karrie Karahalios — University of Illinois, USA
Aonghus Lawlor — University College Dublin, Ireland
Cataldo Musto — University of Bari Aldo Moro, Italy
Razieh Nabi — Johns Hopkins University, USA
Federico Nanni — The Alan Turing Institute, UK
Alexander Panchenko — Skolkovo Institute of Science and Technology, Russia
Panagiotis Papadakos — University of Crete, Greece
Emma Pierson — Stanford University, USA
Simone Paolo Ponzetto — Universität Mannheim, Germany

Contents

Facets of Fairness in Search and Recommendation

Sahil Verma[1]($\boxtimes$), Ruoyuan Gao[2], and Chirag Shah[1]

[1] University of Washington, Seattle, WA 98195, USA
{vsahil,chirags}@uw.edu
[2] Rutgers University, New Brunswick, NJ 08901, USA
ruoyuan.gao@rutgers.edu

Abstract. Several recent works have highlighted how search and recommender systems exhibit bias along different dimensions. Counteracting this bias and bringing a certain amount of fairness in search is crucial to not only creating a more balanced environment that considers relevance and diversity but also providing a more sustainable way forward for both content consumers and content producers. This short paper examines some of the recent works to define relevance, diversity, and related concepts. Then, it focuses on explaining the emerging concept of fairness in various recommendation settings. In doing so, this paper presents comparisons and highlights contracts among various measures, and gaps in our conceptual and evaluative frameworks.

Keywords: Search bias · Fairness · Evaluation metrics · Fairness in recommendation · Fair ranking

1 Introduction

Recommendations or ranking candidates for any purpose is an integral part of the technologies we use each day. Each potential candidate is scored with relevance which is used to rank them in a recommendation list. The algorithms used in the underlying software are not only complicated, but they also take clues from the previous actions of the users on the platform. This feedback loop potentially leads to discrimination against future users, for example, women less likely to be shown advertisements for high-paying jobs [3,10].

Left unchecked, such implicit biases can amount to increased stereotypes and polarized opinions. Mitigation of bias in automated decisions is an emerging area in machine learning and related domains. Classification and ranking/filtering are the two important categorizations of automated decisions using machine learning. Fairness in automated decisions has gained significant traction, and many papers published in the recent years have attempted to 1) devise metrics to quantize fairness, 2) design frameworks using which fair models can be produced (according to the fairness desired metric) or 3) modify data to fight bias in the historical data. There have been many works of the kinds mentioned beforehand

L. Boratto et al. (Eds.): BIAS 2020, CCIS 1245, pp. 1–11, 2020.
https://doi.org/10.1007/978-3-030-52485-2_1

in both classification and recommendation settings. A recent work summarized and explained various fairness metrics used in the classification tasks [23]. Unlike classification, recommendations have widely different facets and application scenarios. One of the significant differences lies in the output space, which is very restricted in the case of classification. In contrast, the output space for ranking or recommendation could be the entire list of ranked items. Owing to the sheer abundance of the fairness metrics and their applicability in specific scenarios, understanding their differences and similarities is complicated.

We review papers from major conferences which received submissions related to fairness in ranking and recommendation, including KDD, WSDM, WWW, SIGIR, ECIR, RecSys, IP&M, and FAT*, from 2015 to 2020. We found twenty-two relevant papers that propose new fairness metrics and provide frameworks to optimize models using them. In this paper, we collect and intuitively explain the fairness metrics used in five major recommendation settings: non-personalized recommendation setting, crowd-sourced recommendation setting, personalized recommendation setting, online advertisements and marketplace. Since literature has proposed several metrics for each of the settings above, we present all the metrics but we do not attempt to develop arguments in favor of any particular metric, we rather explain the underlying similarities and differences between them, and show how these metrics affect other dimensions of ranking. We also develop a clear distinction between fairness in various recommendation settings from often related terms such as diversity, novelty, and relevance. We have categorized fairness metrics according to the setting they are applied. The main contribution of this work is intuitive categorization and explanation of *twenty-five* fairness definitions in various recommendation settings and identification of relationships between them.

The remainder of this paper is organized as follows. Section 2 presents the definitions of commonly used terms in the recommendation literature. Sections 3 to 7 delineates the fairness metrics in various settings. Section 8 outlines the conclusions.

2 Dimensions of Search and Recommendation Results Evaluation

We formally define three dimensions for evaluating search and recommendation results – relevance, diversity, and novelty. These dimensions help to gauge the quality of ranking for a search query or recommendation.

- **Relevance** [12]: Search results are relevant if they accurately answer or describe various aspects of the query or recommendation. It focuses on whether and to what extent a search result relates to the given query. For example, it can be considered as the documents containing some keywords in the query, answering the query, or providing information related to the topic of the query. Relevance only considers the match between the query and the results, often disregarding a user's intent.

- **Diversity** [12]: Search results for each query might have several topics. For example, given the query "Lisbon", the topics include geographic and historical facts, tourism information, and the weather. Diversity refers to the constitution of the search results from its various topics. Various metrics have been defined to measure diversity, such as those found in [6,20].
- **Novelty** [12]: Given several relevant results pertaining to a query, novelty requires the presentation of results that deliver considerably different information content than the results already shown. It thus encourages uniqueness in the shown results with a purpose of maximizing information gain.

3   Fairness Metrics in Non-personalized Recommendation Settings

We collect the following metrics from literature to capture fairness in search and recommendations. We consider the setting where a ranker wants to rank a set of candidates that are relevant to a query or for recommendation. The ranker does not account for individual preferences of the consumers of the ranked list. The fairness in this setting addresses how the candidates are ranked. We assume the existence of protected and unprotected groups (binary setting), which are defined by law [1].

3.1   Accuracy-Based Fairness Metrics

Most fairness metrics for recommendations either state the condition for their satisfaction (ideal ranking) or provide a measure of deviation from the ideal ranking. These metrics require a certain proportion of candidates from the protected group in the ranking, or given a ranked list they calculate the divergence from that required proportion in it. Collectively they are called *accuracy-based fairness metrics*.

1. **Statistical/Demographic Parity:** A ranker is said to be satisfying statistical parity if the proportion of candidates from the protected and unprotected groups match the underlying proportion in the top-k rank search results. Therefore statistical parity can be defined at any k length of the ranking. For example, in the image search query, "CEO", if the displayed results show an equal proportion of male and female CEOs, the results are said to satisfy statistical parity. Singh et al. [22] define *exposure* as the resource allocated to a candidate that is computed as a measure of its relevance and position in the ranking. Average exposure to each demographic group also implies statistical parity. If the average exposure to the candidates belonging to different demographic groups is not equal, the ranker is said to violate statistical parity.

2. **Disparate Treatment:** Disparate treatment refers to the unequal treatment of a candidate due to their membership in a protected group [15]. The candidate would have been treated differently if they had belonged to another

group. If the average exposure of different groups is not proportional to their average relevance, then the ranker is said to exhibit disparate treatment [22].

3. **Disparate Impact:** Disparate impact is the practice of not allocating favorable outcomes to protected groups. For searches and recommendations, a click on a candidate is the favorable outcome, which is called as candidate's click-through rate. If the expected click-through rate for members of protected and unprotected groups is not proportional to their average relevance, then the ranker is said to cause disparate impact [22]. Click-through rates for a ranked item can be estimated with the help of several techniques [19].

4. **Search Neutrality:** Search neutrality refers to the search engines' lack of editorial power. It means that the search engine should return results to a query impartially and based solely on relevance. It should not promote/demote or differentiate based on websites [14]. Google, Facebook, and other tech companies have been accused of violating search neutrality to promote websites that pay them for higher rankings [2].

5. **Top-k fairness:** Zehlike et al. [27] describe a ranking as a top-k fair ranking if the top-k candidates in the ranking contain a required proportion of members from the protected group. Given a required proportion, the algorithm they propose ranks candidates in a manner that fairly represents the protected group. Within the protected and unprotected groups, the candidates are ranked by relevance. If the required proportion is equal to the underlying proportion between the populations of the protected and unprotected groups, top-k fairness and statistical parity are equivalent.

6. **Skew@k:** Geyik et al. [13] define Skew@k as the logarithm of the ratio of proportions of the candidates belonging to the protected group in the top-k ranked candidates to the desired proportion of the protected group in top-k ranks. A negative skew implies lower than desired representation in the top-k ranks. Zero skew implies a top-k fair ranking (Definition 5.). Therefore a zero skew with the required proportion equal to underlying proportion would imply equivalence between Skew@k, top-k fair ranking and statistical parity. They also define minskew@k and maxskew@k to extend the metric beyond binary groups.

7. **Normalized Discounted Difference (rND):** Yang et al. [26] point out that establishing statistical parity at higher ranks (e.g., top-10) is more important than establishing it at lower ranks (e.g., top-100). To account for this, they measure set-based fairness metrics at discrete points (e.g., top-10, top-20) and use logarithmic discounts for lower ranks. Normalized discounted difference (rND) computes the difference between the proportion of the protected group members in top-k results and the overall population proportion. If the protected group is proportionally represented, a lower rND value is achieved, which is preferable. If the desired proportion equals to the actual population proportion, then the rND score is correlated with top-k fairness, Skew@k and statistical parity.

8. **Normalized Discounted KL-divergence (rKL):** Normalized discounted KL-divergence(rKL) [26] measures the expected difference between the proportion of the protected group members in the top-k rank and the overall

population proportion. The metric rKL resembles rND, only it is a smoother measure (and therefore optimizable in gradient-based optimization setting) and can be applied to multiple group settings.

9. **Normalized Discounted Ratio (rRD):** Normalized discounted ratio(rRD) [26] takes the difference between the ratio of the protected to unprotected group members among the top-k ranking and the ratio of underlying sizes of the protected and unprotected groups. A score of zero rRD implies zero skew@k rank, top-k fair ranking and a ranking that satisfies statistical parity. The metric rRD is considered to be useful when the protected group is a minority, in which case it resembles rND and rKL values; otherwise, rRD is meaningless.

3.2   Error Based Fairness Metrics

Kuhlman et al. [17] point out that fairness in classification setting has several metrics that are error-based, i.e., they require the classifier to have similar error-rates across the protected and unprotected groups. They claim that those metrics carry value and should be used for measuring fairness in rankings. Unlike a classification task where the error is readily computable, there exists no such error in case of ranking. Therefore, Kuhlman et al. propose to use pair-inversions to measure ranking errors. They assume the existence of a ground-truth rank for each candidate. If a ranker ranks a candidate higher than its ground-truth rank, they call it a false positive case. Similarly, a candidate that is ranked lower is called a false negative case. Each definition that follows has roots in the counterparts described in fairness in classification literature [23].

1. **Rank Equality:** Rank equality has its origins in the metric called *equalized odds*, which requires equal classification error rates (false positive and false negative error) across the protected and unprotected groups. Rank equality error captures the number of times a candidate from a group has been falsely given a higher rank than a candidate of another group; the score is calculated for each such inverted pair. This metric does not penalize the ranking where a candidate from the same group has been falsely ranked higher.

2. **Rank Calibration:** Rank calibration [17] has roots in calibration which enforces equal precision of classifiers across the protected and unprotected groups. It checks how correctly the ranker predicts candidates in each demographic group. Rank calibration error is calculated as the number of times a candidate from one group is falsely ranked higher than candidates of all groups; the score is calculated for each such inverted pair.

3. **Rank Parity:** Rank parity criterion [17] has roots in statistical parity. It requires proportional representation of members from the protected and unprotected groups in the ranking. The rank parity error is computed as the number of candidates belonging to one group that were ranked higher than candidates from another group; the score is calculated for each such inverted pair.

3.3 Causal Approach for Mitigating Discrimination

Wu et al. [25] use a causal graph to counteract bias contained in historical data. They use a score variable (instead of rank) to account for individual qualifications and the path-specific effect technique to capture direct and indirect discrimination based on one's membership in the protected group. Having detected discrimination, each individual's score is modified to remove the bias, keeping the distribution of new scores close to the original distribution. The modified scores are applied to create a fairer ranking.

4 Fairness Metrics in Crowd-Sourced Non-personalized Recommendation Settings

Chakraborty et al. [9] consider the setting of top-k trending recommendations on platforms like Twitter or Yelp which is a non-personalized setting. Generally, recommendations are the top-voted candidates using a procedure that resembles an election (with some differences). Each person on the platform can vote (e.g., via a click) for multiple candidates and that too multiple times.

1. **Equality of Voice:** In the setting described above, trends are subject to manipulations by hyper-active group or campaigners of all kinds. This can lead to a veneer of popularity for a particular candidate. To avoid this situation, Chakraborty et al. propose a "one person, one vote" election procedure in which everyone has an equal say. Each person is asked to specify their preferences across a set of candidates. The first position is assigned to the candidate, which is the first preference of the majority.
2. **Proportionality for Solid Coalitions:** Chakraborty et al. [9] point out that due to the abundance of options, user's votes might get split across irrelevant or redundant alternatives, e.g. if there are three candidates out of which the first two are very close. Assume that 60% of the people are interested in the first two candidates. Due to their similarity, votes would split among them. Thus, even though the sum of the votes across these two candidates is more, a less popular third candidate would emerge as the winner. To avert this, proportionality for solid coalitions requires the diversity of opinions in the overall population should be proportionally represented in the top-k recommendations.
3. **Anti-Plurality:** Chakraborty et al. also propose that if a majority of users dislike a candidate, it should not be in the top-k recommendations. In the previous example, the third candidate, disliked by 60% of the population, would not be recommended.

5 Fairness Metrics in Personalized Recommendation Settings

Beutel et al. [7] consider fairness metrics for personalized recommendation settings. Consider M total candidates, out of which M' are relevant to a query, but only K candidates are useful as part of personalization. Since they are dealing with personalized ranking along with clicking, Beutel et al. also consider the engagement of the user with a recommended candidate. Engagement between a given user and recommended candidate can be estimated. They compare ranked candidates pairwise and define **pairwise accuracy** as the probability that a clicked candidate is ranked above another relevant unclicked candidate.

1. **Pairwise Fairness:** A ranker is said to satisfy pairwise fairness if the probability of a clicked candidate being ranked higher than another relevant unclicked candidate is the same across groups, conditioned on the candidates that have the same predicted engagement score. Pairwise fairness does not eliminate systematic preference between demographic groups. For example, one can rank all candidate belonging to a favored group that are not relevant to the query and give a lower rank to candidates from the other group that are relevant to the query.

2. **Inter-Group Pairwise Fairness:** A ranker satisfies inter-group pairwise fairness [7] if the probability of a clicked candidate being ranked higher than a relevant but unclicked candidate in the other group is the same across pairs of demographic groups, conditioned on the candidates that have same engagement score.

3. **Intra-Group Pairwise Fairness:** A ranker is said to satisfy intra-group pairwise fairness [7] if the probability of a clicked candidate being ranked higher than another relevant but unclicked candidate in the same group is equal across demographic groups, conditioned on the candidates that have the same predicted engagement score.

A combination of Intra-Group and Inter-Group Pairwise Fairness can reduce systematic bias against a demographic group.

6 Fairness Metrics in Advertisement Settings

Chawla et al. [16] present fairness concerns from an entirely different perspective. Thus far, we have described metrics that view fairness from the perspective of a candidate to be ranked or recommended. Chawla et al. describe fairness from the perspective of individuals who are being served advertisements. Individual fairness [23] states that the advertisements shown to two similar individuals should be similar. For instance, qualifications of an individual can characterize the similarity. Nevertheless, the solution to the problem does not lie in showing an equal proportion of advertisements from all categories to similar people, as individuals have needs and preferences.

1. **Envy-Freeness:** Envy-freeness [16, 21] is a complementary notion to individual fairness, in which only a user's preference is considered for advertisements and a user's qualifications (therefore, similarities) are not reasoned. It requires every user to be content with their share of advertisements.

2. **Inter-Category Envy-Freeness:** Enforcing individual fairness for all categories of advertisements is problematic since it does not recognize individual preferences. Inter-category envy-freeness [16] allows each user to specify individual preferences, and the criterion requires that all users interested in a category should be served the same amount of advertisements belonging from that category. For example, two individuals interested in jobs should be shown the same number of job-related ads.

3. **Total Variation Fairness:** Inter-category envy-freeness does not ensure a fair distribution of advertisements within a category. For instance, two equally qualified individuals belonging to different demographic groups can be unfairly shown high-paying and low-paying jobs respectively, while satisfying that metric. Total variation fairness [16] overcomes this limitation by requiring that all subsets of the advertisements from any category shown to two similar individuals must be the same. Consequently, it evades the problem of unfairly showing high-paying job ads to one user.

4. **Compositional Fairness:** Compositional fairness [16] combines inter-category envy-freeness and total variation fairness. Compositional fairness has two requirements: 1) a user's preferences must be recognized, and advertisements served to them belong to their preferred categories only (*envy-freeness*) and 2) within each category, the proportions of advertisements should be the same across all users interested in that category. This lets an advertiser serve advertisements from different categories with varying probabilities to a user (based on their preference). However, the mix of advertisements from each category should be the same across all interested users.

7   Fairness Metrics in Marketplace Settings

Advertisement setting brings us to a discussion related to marketplaces, in which consumers are shown advertisements about products which the suppliers want to publicize. Marketplaces are ubiquitous. Almost all online platforms we interact with serve as a marketplace for consumers and service providers. These multi-sided recommendation platforms have complicated fairness constraints. Historically, most marketplaces have optimized for consumer satisfaction, but given the rising competition among different platforms, the satisfaction of service providers has also gathered attention. For example, Spotify would like to recommend tracks that a particular consumer would find relevant and is likely to listen. But it would be problematic if Spotify only recommends songs from a few popular artists to the consumers because: 1) it gives low exposure to less popular artists, and 2) the consumer may not find the recommendations interesting after sometime. There has been a few recent works discussing and addressing these concerns [4,5,8,11,18,24].

There are several classes of multi-sided recommendation: 1) Multi-receiver recommendation – when a target audience is a group of people rather than an individual, e.g., students on an education platform; 2) Multi-provider recommendation – when several suppliers provide the recommendation content, and the platform needs to choose between them, e.g., Airbnb and Spotify, and 3) Side stakeholder recommendation – when there are parties other than suppliers and consumers involved in the marketplace, the recommendations need to consider their preferences as well, e.g., drivers in the Uber Eats platform.

1. **Consumer Fairness:** A recommendation satisfies consumer fairness [5] it is does not cause any disparate impact on members of protected groups. For example, consumers of all groups should be served the same distribution of job ads.
2. **Provider Fairness:** A recommendation satisfies provider fairness [5] if all the providers have an equal chance of exposure to the consumers. For example, Spotify recommends both famous and less famous artists publishing a specific genre of music to users who prefer that genre.
3. **Side Stakeholder Fairness:** A recommendation satisfies side stakeholder fairness [5] if it takes into consideration the preferences of side stakeholders. For example, fairly distributing consumer orders and commute distance among drivers in Uber Eats.

8   Conclusion

In this short survey, we collect and present various metrics proposed in the emerging literature on fairness in recommendations. Succinct and distinct categorization of fairness metrics would help people understand the landscape and triage missing gaps, consequently fuelling future research. We are already experiencing an adoption of this research in the industry. For instance, Geyik et al. [13], in a first large-scale deployment, enforced fair ranking in LinkedIn search. We envision such deployments to other major search engines in the future.

References

1. Protected Group. https://en.wikipedia.org/wiki/Protected_group. Accessed 20 Jan 2020
2. What is Search Neutrality? https://hackernoon.com/what-is-search-neutrality-d05cc30c6b3e. Accessed 20 Jan 2020
3. Women less likely to be shown ads for high-paid jobs on Google, study shows. https://www.theguardian.com/technology/2015/jul/08/women-less-likely-ads-high-paid-jobs-google-study. Accessed 20 Jan 2020
4. Abdollahpouri, H., Burke, R., Mobasher, B.: Recommender systems as multistakeholder environments. In: Proceedings of the 25th Conference on User Modeling, Adaptation and Personalization, UMAP 2017. Association for Computing Machinery, New York (2017). https://doi.org/10.1145/3079628.3079657
5. Abdollahpouri, H., Burke, R.D.: Multi-stakeholder recommendation and its connection to multi-sided fairness. ArXiv abs/1907.13158 (2019)
6. Amigó, E., Spina, D., Carrillo-de Albornoz, J.: An axiomatic analysis of diversity evaluation metrics: Introducing the rank-biased utility metric. In: The 41st International ACM SIGIR Conference on Research & Development in Information Retrieval, SIGIR 2018. Association for Computing Machinery, New York (2018). https://doi.org/10.1145/3209978.3210024

7. Beutel, A., et al.: Fairness in recommendation ranking through pairwise comparisons. In: Proceedings of the 25th ACM SIGKDD International Conference on Knowledge Discovery & Data Mining, KDD 2019. Association for Computing Machinery, New York (2019). https://doi.org/10.1145/3292500.3330745
8. Burke, R.: Multisided Fairness for Recommendation. arXiv:1707.00093 [cs], July 2017
9. Chakraborty, A., Patro, G.K., Ganguly, N., Gummadi, K.P., Loiseau, P.: Equality of voice: towards fair representation in crowdsourced top-k recommendations. In: Proceedings of the Conference on Fairness, Accountability, and Transparency. FAT* 2019. Association for Computing Machinery, New York (2019). https://doi.org/10.1145/3287560.3287570
10. Datta, A., Tschantz, M.C., Datta, A.: Automated experiments on ad privacy settings: A tale of opacity, choice, and discrimination. ArXiv abs/1408.6491 (2014)
11. Ferraro, A., Bogdanov, D., Serra, X., Yoon, J.J.: Artist and style exposure bias in collaborative filtering based music recommendations. ArXiv abs/1911.04827 (2019)
12. Gao, R., Shah, C.: Toward creating a fairer ranking in search engine results. Inf. Process. Manag. **57**, (2020). https://doi.org/10.1016/j.ipm.2019.102138
13. Geyik, S.C., Ambler, S., Kenthapadi, K.: Fairness-aware ranking in search & recommendation systems with application to linkedin talent search. In: Proceedings of the 25th ACM SIGKDD International Conference on Knowledge Discovery & Data Mining, KDD 2019. Association for Computing Machinery, New York (2019). https://doi.org/10.1145/3292500.3330691
14. Grimmelmann, J.: Some skepticism about search neutrality. Essays on the Future of the Internet, The Next Digital Decade (2011)
15. Heidari, H., Krause, A.: Preventing disparate treatment in sequential decision making. In: IJCAI (2018)
16. Ilvento, C., Jagadeesan, M., Chawla, S.: Multi-category fairness in sponsored search auctions. In: Proceedings of the 2020 Conference on Fairness, Accountability, and Transparency, FAT* 2020. Association for Computing Machinery, New York (2020). https://doi.org/10.1145/3351095.3372848
17. Kuhlman, C., VanValkenburg, M., Rundensteiner, E.: Fare: diagnostics for fair ranking using pairwise error metrics. In: The World Wide Web Conference, WWW 2019. Association for Computing Machinery, New York (2019). https://doi.org/10.1145/3308558.3313443
18. Mehrotra, R., McInerney, J., Bouchard, H., Lalmas, M., Diaz, F.: Towards a fair marketplace: Counterfactual evaluation of the trade-off between relevance, fairness & satisfaction in recommendation systems. In: Proceedings of the 27th ACM International Conference on Information and Knowledge Management, CIKM 2018. Association for Computing Machinery, New York (2018). https://doi.org/10.1145/3269206.3272027
19. Richardson, M., Dominowska, E., Ragno, R.: Predicting clicks: Estimating the click-through rate for new ads. In: Proceedings of the 16th International Conference on World Wide Web, WWW 2007. Association for Computing Machinery, New York (2007). https://doi.org/10.1145/1242572.1242643
20. Sakai, T., Craswell, N., Song, R., Robertson, S.E., Dou, Z., Lin, C.Y.: Simple evaluation metrics for diversified search results. In: EVIA@NTCIR (2010)
21. Serbos, D., Qi, S., Mamoulis, N., Pitoura, E., Tsaparas, P.: Fairness in package-to-group recommendations. In: Proceedings of the 26th International Conference on World Wide Web, WWW 2017, International World Wide Web Conferences Steering Committee, Republic and Canton of Geneva, CHE (2017). https://doi.org/10.1145/3038912.3052612

22. Singh, A., Joachims, T.: Fairness of exposure in rankings. In: Proceedings of the 24th ACM SIGKDD International Conference on Knowledge Discovery & Data Mining, KDD 2018. Association for Computing Machinery, New York (2018). https://doi.org/10.1145/3219819.3220088
23. Verma, S., Rubin, J.: Fairness definitions explained. In: Proceedings of the International Workshop on Software Fairness, FairWare 2018. Association for Computing Machinery, New York (2018). https://doi.org/10.1145/3194770.3194776
24. Wan, M., Ni, J., Misra, R., McAuley, J.: Addressing marketing bias in product recommendations. In: Proceedings of the 13th International Conference on Web Search and Data Mining, WSDM 2020. Association for Computing Machinery, New York (2020). https://doi.org/10.1145/3336191.3371855
25. Wu, Y., Zhang, L., Wu, X.: On discrimination discovery and removal in ranked data using causal graph. In: Proceedings of the 24th ACM SIGKDD International Conference on Knowledge Discovery & Data Mining, KDD 2018. Association for Computing Machinery, New York (2018). https://doi.org/10.1145/3219819.3220087
26. Yang, K., Stoyanovich, J.: Measuring fairness in ranked outputs. In: Proceedings of the 29th International Conference on Scientific and Statistical Database Management, SSDBM 2017. Association for Computing Machinery, New York (2017). https://doi.org/10.1145/3085504.3085526
27. Zehlike, M., Bonchi, F., Castillo, C., Hajian, S., Megahed, M., Baeza-Yates, R.: Fa*ir: a fair top-k ranking algorithm. In: Proceedings of the 2017 ACM on Conference on Information and Knowledge Management, CIKM 2017. Association for Computing Machinery, New York (2017). https://doi.org/10.1145/3132847.3132938

Mitigating Gender Bias in Machine Learning Data Sets

Susan Leavy[✉], Gerardine Meaney, Karen Wade, and Derek Greene

University College Dublin, Dublin, Ireland
{susan.leavy,gerardine.meaney,karen.wade,derek.greene}@ucd.ie

Abstract. Algorithmic bias has the capacity to amplify and perpetuate societal bias, and presents profound ethical implications for society. Gender bias in algorithms has been identified in the context of employment advertising and recruitment tools, due to their reliance on underlying language processing and recommendation algorithms. Attempts to address such issues have involved testing learned associations, integrating concepts of fairness to machine learning, and performing more rigorous analysis of training data. Mitigating bias when algorithms are trained on textual data is particularly challenging given the complex way gender ideology is embedded in language. This paper proposes a framework for the identification of gender bias in training data for machine learning. The work draws upon gender theory and sociolinguistics to systematically indicate levels of bias in textual training data and associated neural word embedding models, thus highlighting pathways for both removing bias from training data and critically assessing its impact in the context of search and recommender systems.

Keywords: Algorithmic bias · Gender · Machine learning · Natural language processing

1 Introduction

Algorithmic bias, as embedded in search and recommendation systems, has the capacity to profoundly influence society. For instance, recommendation systems targeting employment-related advertisements were found to demonstrate gender bias [14]. The gendering of personal assistant technologies as female is also being questioned as constituting indirect discrimination, potentially contravening international women's rights law [1]. With the rise in the use of facial recognition in areas such as border control, along with the issues with variance in accuracy depending on gender and race [6], there is a risk that bias will be incorporated directly into the core public infrastructure of a country. Even legal systems are vulnerable to the influence of algorithmic bias through the use of systems such as *Compas*, where recommendations around parole lengths have demonstrated evidence of racial bias [3].

The source of this kind of bias often lies in the way societal inequalities and latent discriminatory attitudes are captured in the data from which algorithms

© Springer Nature Switzerland AG 2020
L. Boratto et al. (Eds.): BIAS 2020, CCIS 1245, pp. 12–26, 2020.
https://doi.org/10.1007/978-3-030-52485-2_2

learn. Given the ways in which sentiments regarding race and gender ideology can be deeply embedded in natural language, uncovering and preventing bias in systems trained on such unstructured text can be particularly difficult. This paper focuses on algorithmic gender bias, and proposes a framework whereby language based data may be systematically evaluated to assess levels of gender bias prevalent in training data for machine learning systems. The framework is developed by accessing potential bias prevalent in articles in a popular UK mainstream media outlet, *The Guardian*, over a decade from 2009 to 2018. This is contrasted with biases uncovered in a corpus of 16,426 digitised volumes of 19th-century fiction from the British Library. This paper demonstrates how bridging AI and research in gender and language can provide a framework for potentially gender-proofing AI, and contributes to ongoing work on the systematic mitigation of algorithmic gender bias.

2 Related Work

Strategies to test for algorithmic gender bias have involved evaluation of system accuracy and learned associations in machine learning technologies that underlie many search and recommendation systems [9]. Implicit Association Tests (IATs) were found to be effective in uncovering gender bias in the 'common crawl' corpus, a large collection of text sourced from the web [8]. Stereotypical representations of gender were also identified in an analysis of an embedding model trained on Google News content [5]. Evidence of 100 years of gender bias in relation to employment and associated adjectives was uncovered by applying word embedding techniques to text sourced from the Corpus of Historical American English, Google Books, New York Times, and Google News [11]. The introduction of concepts of fairness to machine learning and modifying learned associations in algorithms have been used to address gender bias [29]. Disassociating biased relationships between entities in word embedding models has reduced stereotypical associations between, for instance, gender and types of employment [5]. However, studies have shown that implicit gender bias persists despite these de-biasing methods [12]. The modification of training corpora prior to learning of gender bias has been explored through the provision of training data where the gender of entities in the corpora are swapped and has been proven to reduce gender bias in predictions [30]. Building on these approaches, this paper explores the opportunity to incorporate findings from research in the gender theory and feminist linguistics which has sought to uncover the features of language that encode gender bias, in order to develop scalable methods to systematically identify bias in training data.

2.1 Uncovering Gender Bias

The crucial influence of language in shaping and reinforcing gender in society is explored within the field of feminist linguistics identifying language features that encode bias [18]. For instance, premodified terms such as 'female lawyer' or 'female police officer', are interpreted as highlighting their existence as contrary to societal expectations [25]. Similarly, terms such as 'career woman' or 'working mother' don not have popular equivalents for men [23]. How language change reflects underlying changes in prevalent gender ideology in society is demonstrated by the increasing use of 'they/them' rather than 'he/him' and 'humanity' rather than 'mankind', and the replacement of 'Mrs' and 'Miss' with 'Ms' [4]. Such shifts in language use indicate the potential for language corpora to preserve and potentially perpetuate outdated concepts of gender.

Of particular relevance in the context of AI-supported recommender systems ans web search is the tendency shown in the media to refer to adult women as 'girls' [25]. Women have also been shown to be more associated with derogatory, sexual and negative descriptions [4,7,21]. Associations between women, beauty and lack of agency have also been identified as encoding gender bias [10,18].

Measurements of the presence of women in text has shown to be an effective measure of potential gender bias [2,24]. More subtle measures of potential gender bias could also be considered. For instance, conventions regarding how binomials are ordered in English dictates that the most powerful is named first (e.g. doctor/nurse, teacher/pupil). However, gender is the most important determiner of order, thus revealing a concept of social order assigning more power to men [19,20,28].

In devising methods to identify gender bias in algorithms, studies have incorporated researchers' or crowd-sourced interpretations of what constitutes gender stereotypes [5,11,26]. Building on this, this paper proposes a framework whereby language-based training data may be systematically gender-proofed to mitigate bias in machine learning algorithms.

3   Methods

Given that early studies of bias in the representation of women focused study of literature, we analyse a set of over 16,000 volumes of 19th-century fiction from the British Library Digital corpus [15]. This corpus was selected due to the well-documented evidence of stereotypical and binary concepts of gender in 19th-century fiction [13], and therefore represents a useful source of baseline data, allowing methods to be tested and refined, and subsequently generalised to other corpora. To investigate evidence of gender bias in contemporary corpora, this research analyses a decade of articles from the UK newspaper, *The Guardian* including every article published online between 2009 and 2018, as retrieved from The Guardian Open Platform API[1].

Word embeddings refer to a family of machine learning approaches that yield numeric, low-dimensional representations of words based on lexical co-occurrences. We focus on these models in our work, as they are widely used as a building block for further downstream analysis in many language processing tasks [27]. These approaches have also been successfully used to uncover patterns

---

[1] https://open-platform.theguardian.com.

of stereotypical gender-based associations [5, 8, 11]. Following these approaches, we investigate conceptual relationships in the texts using embedding representations. The conceptual relationships examined for evidence of gender bias were informed by a framework based on feminist critiques and analysis of the use of language. This framework focused on linguistic features that encode gender bias, and was used to inform both the development of thematic lexicons and the selection of features from the corpora, specifically:

- Presence of women in text
- Gender-specific terms (e.g. career woman)
- Premodified terms (e.g. female lawyer)
- Androcentric terms and misuse of gender neutrals
- Negative or stereotypical associations

The particular word embedding variant used in this work is a 100-dimensional Continuous Bag-Of-Words (CBOW) *word2vec* model [17], trained on the full-text volumes of the 16,426 fictional texts from the British Library corpus. *Word lexicons* can used to represent concepts of gender and themes related to bias. In our work, lexicons are constructed by defining an initial small set of seed terms, and expanding this set using related words as determined by similarities derived from the embedding model. Contemporary thematic lexicons which were used to examine gendered associations within the text were based on *The General Inquirer* dictionaries[2]. Given the consistent findings within gender theory of the portrayal of women in texts as passive, emotional and defined in the context of family relationships, the themes focused on involved the General Inquirer semantic categories pertaining to emotion, family and terms that convey activity. The semantic category pertaining to moral judgement and misfortune (vice) is also explored to capture an idealised concept of femininity that is evident in Victorian literature and examine changes within contemporary culture.

The relationships between conceptual lexicons in the corpus were visually explored using the Tensorboard tool[3]. Relational patterns were then analysed by calculating cosine distances between terms within the embedding model. These were depicted visually to highlight differences in how terms in lexicons representing gender were related with other concepts in the text. Rule-based information extraction was also used to evaluate the volume of representations of men and women in text and to extract particular linguistic features, such as the ordering of binomials.

4   Findings and Analysis

This research demonstrates an approach for developing metrics for bias in data sets informed by feminist linguistics and gender theory, in order to mitigate algorithmic bias. We see that gender bias was uncovered in neural word embedding models trained on both historical and contemporary data-sets thus presenting scalable techniques for automatically assessing data sets for evidence of bias.

---

[2] http://www.wjh.harvard.edu/inquirer.
[3] https://www.tensorflow.org.

4.1   Presence of Women in Text

The presence of women in data sets is a simple but highly effective metric of bias in the Guardian as measured by the proportional occurrence of male and female pronouns was distinctly lower than that in the corpus of 19th-century fiction (Fig. 1a). While a higher representation of women is arguably to be expected in the 19th-century volumes, it is also lower also than an analysis of the New York Times which found female representation of 28% in 2008 [24]. Only 20% of gendered pronouns in the year following that in The Guardian were female. However, there has been a steady increase to 30% female representation in The Guardian by 2018 (Fig. 1b). Based on an evaluation of gender bias by the metric of volume of coverage alone, The Guardian appears to be more biased than 19th-century British fiction, pointing towards the need for further semantic analysis of the texts.

4.2   Gender-Specific Terms

The premodification of terms can introduce a gender dimension to concepts that can often convey stereotypes and imply information about gender that is biased. In the 19th-century for example, there was a prevailing idealised concept of femininity that saw certain attributes as distinctly female (e.g. female nature). This is reflected by the fact that the term 'female' appears 2.5 times more frequently than the term 'male'. This also points towards 'male' being considered the default in many contexts, and 'female' the exception that should be named (see. [22]). Following this rationale, the lowering of proportional use of the term 'female' to 56% in 2009 suggests a lessening of gender bias. However, this figure increases to 60% in 2018, potentially due to a greater level of gender discourse in the media during this year, demonstrating the importance of take context into account when attributing gender bias to a particular collection of texts.

Gender-Specific Occupations. The context of gender premodification was analysed and classified according to those pertaining to occupations, characteristics and references to the physical body. The volume of terms related to

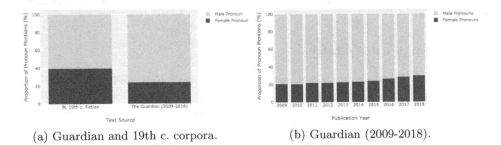

(a) Guardian and 19th c. corpora.   (b) Guardian (2009-2018).

Fig. 1. Presence in of women in text, as reflected by pronoun usage in The Guardian and 19th-century British fiction corpora.

occupations that are specified by gender notably increased by the end of the decade from 2009 in The Guardian. This increase is not, however, exclusive to women, and demonstrates a potential new dimension in the analysis of gender bias in language. In 19th-century fiction, male premodified occupations were rare and the three examples found referred to roles that both men and women undertook (see Table 1).

In 2009 in The Guardian, occupations specified as male were primarily related to occupations that were often shared or roles predominantly held by women. For example, 'nurse' is primarily a female occupation, so a male nurse is identified, through premodification, as an exception. However, by 2018 there is a dramatic increase in premodified occupations that are stereotypically male. For example, 'doctors', 'footballers', 'executive' are premodified as male in 2018. A similar increase is evident in the use of terms that are specified as female. Overall, however, occupations that are conceptually associated with both genders equally, denoted by the terms being premodified equally by both genders (e.g. 'writer', 'journalist'), remain a small proportion of the gender-specific terms that were used. A potential cause for the increase in the occupations specified by gender may be media discussion of workplace equality. Therefore, a calculation of gender specified occupations may not reflect gender bias, but the presence of feminist discourse arguing for gender equality. These finding suggest that a more reliable measure of gender equality is the number of occupations that are equally premodified by gender, where neither is considered the default gender for a given role.

Gender-Specific Characteristics. By extracting characteristics that are specified as female from the British Library corpus, we captured the Victorian associations of women with 'loveliness', 'weakness' and 'modesty' (see Table 2). This contrasts with female 'empowerment', 'power', and 'talent' in 2009 in The Guardian. However, those associated with men in 2009 reflect stereotypical concepts of violence and dominance. There was a striking increase in the use of premodified characteristics by 2018 with the introduction of terms that echo feminist discourse.

These findings demonstrate that, even though mentions of gendered characteristics in relation to men and women may occur in the context of articles critiquing stereotypes, depending on the application of a machine learning algorithm, these associations may still be learned and may perpetuate the very stereotypes the articles propose to disrupt. For instance, the association in the 2018 Guardian data between female 'hysteria' and 'fragility' and male 'privilege' might not reflect bias on the part of the authors, yet uncovering these associations systematically demonstrates how gendered character traits could be learned by a machine learning algorithm from such a training corpus.

Gender-Specific Physical Terms. The corpus of 19th-century fiction, as expected, reflects abstract and potentially metaphorical references to gender-specific physical aspects of the human body (Table 3). In The Guardian corpus these descriptions are more direct. However, in 2018 there is a notable increase in the number of terms premodified by both 'male' and 'female'. This further supports the proposal suggested in relation to occupations, that a solid indicator of bias may be a relatively higher rate of terms that are equally premodified for men and women.

Table 1. Premodified occupations in order of frequency

Corpus	Male premodified	Female premodified
British Library	**servant**(s) **domestic**(s) **attendant**(s)	**servant**(s) **attendant**(s) warrior(s) **domestic**(s) slave(s) art(ist(s)), novelist(s) detective(s) sovereign(s) warder labour missionary(ies) singers(ing) highwayman writers employment teacher(s) philosopher doctor poets assistant forger students cook politician industry occupation proprietor warders (**28 unique terms**)
Guardian 2018	**writers artists actors** players **employees artist authors writer mps** actor player athletes **directors models politicians stars** presenters critics model **journalists officers** director doctors **dancer dancers staff** co-stars footballers athlete football **officer** author executives **teacher** applicants **celebrities** comedians journalist musicians novelist scientists **star workers** academics **boss** comic doctor investors **police** presenter **teachers bosses** ... (**145 unique terms**)	**artists staff directors candidates employees** students **writers artist** athletes director **politicians workers** president **journalists** governor film-makers footballers doctors **authors** doctor **stars** musicians chief presenters scientists **writer** composers **police teachers** coaches employee jockeys singer **officer** mayor candidate journalist performers pilots student comics singers entrepreneurs **officers** cast jockey reporter athlete chef chefs engineers **politician** senator ... (**263 unique terms**)

4.3   Trends in Use of Androcentric Generics and Gender Neutrals

The term 'mankind' is often used as a gender-neutral term. However, research dating back to the 1970's demonstrates that such terms are not perceived as inclusive [16]. As expected, androcentric gender neutrals were commonplace in 19th-century but also appears surprisingly often. The use of gender-neutral terms such as 'chairperson' and 'statesperson' is negligible. While the proportion of female MPs in the UK is 30%, the fact that the gender neutral term 'statesperson' is not applied to them but 'statesman' is commonly used, suggests that the role remains conceptually male. The use of contemporary gender-neutral terms therefore would indicate levels of gender bias in a corpus.

Table 2. Premodified characteristics

Corpus	Male premodified	Female premodified
British Library	violent(ce), mind, **character(s)**, **young**, beauty, **intellect**, youth (**7 unique terms**)	heart(s), **character(s)**, mind(s), loveliness, education, influence, nature, charms, virtue, curiosity, vanity, ailments, delicacy, excellence, **intellect**, heroism, **young**, instinct, taste, innocence, soul, purity, propriety, grace, perfection, weakness, affection, finesse, modesty, ingenuity, monster, sympathy, tactics, errors, old, pride, dignity, honour, spirit (**40 unique terms**)
Guardian 2009	voice bonding dominated attention **characters** voices grooming dominance violence **character** domination primary **brain** ego gaze heroes **power** behaviour life preserve bravado chauvinist elite performance privilege rage (**26 unique terms**)	**characters character** talent empowerment emancipation perspective adolescence **power** soul stereotypes action acts **brain** (**14 unique terms**)
Guardian 2018	**gaze characters** privilege sexual lead **voice** dominance voices entitlement dominated **behaviour** character supremacy perspective **desire** identity rage winner culture fantasy leaders mental performance pleasure pride aged ego genius leads authority literary psyche aggression misbehaviour perpetrators political problem energy environment life queerness anxiety approval attitudes chauvinism chauvinist domination fantasies glance grooming ... (**123 unique terms**)	**characters** representation empowerment character voices experience **voice gaze** aged power solidarity identity **desire** agency narrator autonomy superhero ambition presence artistic representatives strength senior state anger **behaviour** liberal narratives women achievement brain creative energy equality imagination objectification resistance social wits brains creativity fantasy freedom friendly gender hereditary independence love relationship ... (**92 unique terms**)

Table 3. Premodified physical references.

Corpus	Male premodified	Female premodified
British Library	**figure**(s) **eye**(s) **sex** heart **head hand**	**figure**, form(s), **sex**, beauty, **hand(s)**, attire(d), **head(s)**, face(s), **eye(s)**, breast, shape, lips, tongue(s), bosom(s), flesh **(16 unique terms)**
Guardian 2009	beauty **sex genitalia sexual** figures body fertility figure hormone psyche **(10 unique terms)**	sexuality genital **sexual** body form **genitalia sex** beauty face anatomy faces figure vocals orgasm **(14 unique terms)**
Guardian 2018	**body infertility sex bodies suicide fertility figure genitalia beauty figures form** gender makeup face clothes clothing eyes faces hormone hormones orgasm sperm anatomy flesh gay hair health hormonal libido physique reproduction reproductive suicides **(33 unique terms)**	genital **body** sexuality **form** sexual **beauty** orgasm **sex bodies figure genitalia** pain **figures** flesh reproductive anatomy biology face masturbation genitals same-sex **suicide fertility** gay hormones cancers faces health breast contraceptive hormone **infertility** nipples bodily breasts orgasms pregnant skin sterilisation **(39 unique terms)**

4.4   Gendered Associations: Negative or Stereotypical Descriptions

Conceptual associations between gender and particular themes were assessed with neural word embedding. Conceptual lexicons based on the General Inquirer that were analysed included emotion, terms denoting family, action and vice (described as an assessment of misfortune or moral disapproval).

4.5   Gender and Emotion

The analysis of cosine similarity of terms within the word embeddings uncovered distinctly stereotypical associations of gender and emotion for the BL corpus, as we might expect from 19th-century fiction. The top 20 terms denoting emotion associated with men and women were extracted and the levels of association for both the historical and contemporary corpora presented in Fig. 2. Overall, women were associated with emotion substantially more than men ('women' with 0.101 vs. 'men' 0.056 mean cosine similarity). In contrast, in The Guardian corpus the overall association of men and women with terms denoting emotion was almost equal ('women' 0.078 vs. 'men' 0.089 mean cosine similarity).

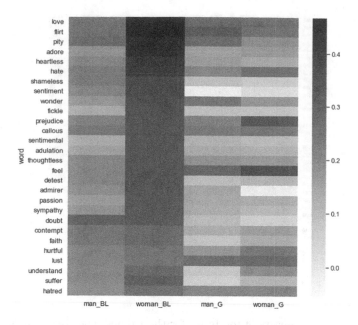

Fig. 2. Emotion: Similarity of top terms for the BL and The Guardian corpora.

4.6   Gendered Action

The association of terms denoting action in the corpus of 19th century support the theory that men were portrayed in more active and women in more passive terms (Fig. 3. Men are most closely associated with terms including 'leader', 'warrior', 'advocate', 'campaigner', 'fighter', and 'commander'. This contrasts distinctly with the kinds of actions women were associated with, including 'love', 'flirt', 'adore', 'idolize', and 'pretend'. These distinctive associations did not continue in The Guardian corpora, but present more subtle differences and reflect contemporary issues, as indicated by the level of co-occurrence of terms like 'harass' and 'liberation' with 'women' in 2018 (Table 4).

4.7   Character Descriptions and Gender

The concept of vice for women in the 19th-century was particularly gendered, and this is reflected in the top terms from the General Inquirer lexicon that are associated with women in the corpus of British fiction (Fig. 4). Here we see that women are most associated with terms referring to silliness and moral failings. What is unexpected, however, is that among all the themes, the levels of association of individual words seems to have remained the most consistent.

The terms relating to concepts of vice that are associated with men and women in the The Guardian reflect distinct patterns (Table 5). Those associated with women echo contemporary media discourse on sexual violence. While terms pertaining to relationships, including 'divorce', 'unfaithful', and 'adultery', are

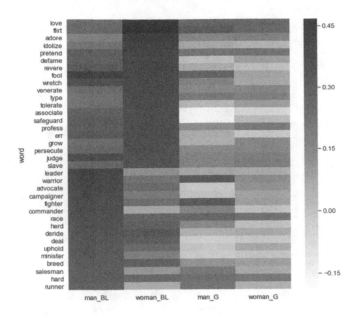

Fig. 3. Action: Similarity of top terms for the BL and The Guardian corpora.

Table 4. Action lexicon: Gendered associations in The Guardian corpora.

Female	
2009	Intercourse divorce groom nurse molest dress violence skin wear cuddle driver participant drink obedient articulate actor abuse antagonistic seeker murder
2018	Representation intercourse abuse actor violence skin speak wear liberation assault articulate driver nurse dress aspire violent humiliate harass behavior

Male	
2009	Driver stab boxer killer cuddle groom hug love occasion nurse lying guard actor compliment fan stroke wear crowd murder stood
2018	Driver compliment warrior figure fuck saw stab alive humiliate fan actor boxer guess killer reason occasion wear gone motivation

associated with women, there are no equivalents associated with men. Terms denoting vice associated with men largely pertain to judgements of character (e.g. 'drunk', 'crazy', 'selfish', 'madman', 'idiot', 'arrogant', 'cruel', 'stupid').

4.8 Gendered Associations with Family

Gender bias is evident in the gendered associations present in the neural word embedding model pertaining to 19th-century fiction with terms denoting family. Men in this corpus had little association with concepts of family, when compared

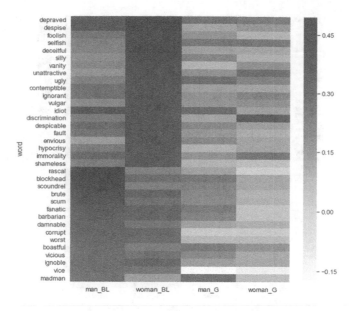

Fig. 4. Vice: Similarity of top terms for the BL and The Guardian corpora.

Table 5. Vice lexicon: Gendered associations in The Guardian corpora.

Female	
2009	Divorce discrimination loveless adultery drunk insecure indecent violence unfaithful stigma suicide sick cruel illness depraved selfish vile ignorant abuse
2018	Stigma discrimination abuse trauma violence insecure suicide sick inferior depression adultery assault blindness ordeal unjust coercion violent unsure condescending vulnerable

Male	
2009	Drunk misfortune ordeal vain idiot arrogant cruel stupid vile mad naive forgetfulness damned foolish ugly unbelievable awful loveless fanatic murder
2018	Drunk crazy selfish madman rascal horrible arrogant stupid suicide idiotic inferior foolish audacity idiot ungrateful guilty assault adversity unlucky badly

to women (see Fig. 5). Evidence suggests that this has changed in contemporary culture, with overall associations appearing equal. However, women are distinctly more frequently associated with the status of parenting, as 'mother' or 'childless'.

4.9   Ordering of Binomials

Women were listed after men in examples of gendered binomials in 87% of cases appearing in the corpus of 19th-century British fiction. The cases analysed involved listings of wife, husband, girl, boy, son, daughter, man, women,

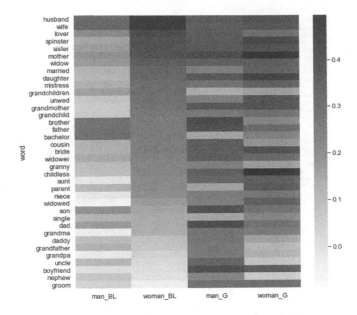

Fig. 5. Family: Similarity of top terms from BL Corpus with The Guardian.

men, women. Listings were captured using a rule-based extraction process where excerpts containing both terms were identified and evaluated. In The Guardian news articles, this occurred 78% in 2009, dropping to 74% in 2018. Listing husbands before wives was the most persistent case, remaining at 87% and 84% respectively for the 2018 and 2009 collections, suggesting the concept of marriage is most closely tied with power relations. This finding of a relationship between power, gender, and the ordering of binomials suggests that augmenting ordering in training data may prevent the learning of underlying structures in language denoting a societal conception of the most powerful.

5   Conclusion

The findings of this research demonstrate how methods from machine learning, used within a framework informed by feminist linguistics and gender theory, can be used to evaluate levels of gender bias within natural language training corpora. A corpus of 19th century fiction along with a contemporary data set comprising every article published online in The Guardian newspaper over the decade between 2009 and 2018 was examined. The methods developed in this research uncovered gendered patterns in the corpus of 19th-century fiction that reflected Victorian concepts of gender while analysis of The Guardian uncovered linguistic patterns that capture contemporary concepts of gender. The emergence of feminist discourse in the media is also evident through gendered associations captured in word embedding uncovering an intriguing finding concerning how critiques of gender stereotypes could in fact generate stereotypical associations in neural embedding model. The systematic approach for capturing gender bias outlined in this paper is scalable and may be applied to a broad range of corpora, presenting new pathways for automatically assessing levels of bias in training corpora for search and information extraction systems.

Acknowledgements. This research project was supported by the Irish Research Council (IRC) and Science Foundation Ireland (SFI) under Grant Number SFI/12/RC/2289_P2.

References

1. Adams, R., Ni Loideain, N.: Addressing indirect discrimination and gender stereotypes in AI virtual personal assistants: the role of international human rights law. In: Annual Cambridge International Law Conference (2019)
2. Ali, O., Flaounas, I., De Bie, T., Mosdell, N., Lewis, J., Cristianini, N.: Automating news content analysis: an application to gender bias and readability. In: Proceedings of the First Workshop on Applications of Pattern Analysis, pp. 36–43 (2010)
3. Angwin, J., Larson, J., Mattu, S., Kirchner, L.: Machine bias risk assessments in criminal sentencing (2016). ProPublica https://www.propublica.org
4. Baker, P.: Sexed texts: language, gender and sexuality. Equinox (2008)
5. Bolukbasi, T., Chang, K.W., Zou, J.Y., Saligrama, V., Kalai, A.T.: Man is to computer programmer as woman is to homemaker? debiasing word embeddings. In: Advances in Neural Information Processing Systems, pp. 4349–4357 (2016)
6. Buolamwini, J., Gebru, T.: Gender shades: intersectional accuracy disparities in commercial gender classification. In: Conference on Fairness, Accountability and Transparency, pp. 77–91 (2018)
7. Caldas-Coulthard, C.R., Moon, R.: 'curvy, hunky, kinky': using corpora as tools for critical analysis. Discourse Soc. **21**(2), 99–133 (2010)
8. Caliskan, A., Bryson, J.J., Narayanan, A.: Semantics derived automatically from language corpora contain human-like biases. Science **356**(6334), 183–186 (2017)
9. Dixon, L., Li, J., Sorensen, J., Thain, N., Vasserman, L.: Measuring and mitigating unintended bias in text classification. In: Proceedings of the 2018 AAAI/ACM Conference on AI, Ethics, and Society, pp. 67–73. ACM (2018)
10. Frith, K., Shaw, P., Cheng, H.: The construction of beauty: a cross-cultural analysis of women's magazine advertising. J. Commun. **55**(1), 56–70 (2005)
11. Garg, N., Schiebinger, L., Jurafsky, D., Zou, J.: Word embeddings quantify 100 years of gender and ethnic stereotypes. Proc. Natl. Acad. Sci. **115**(16), E3635–E3644 (2018)
12. Gonen, H., Goldberg, Y.: Lipstick on a pig: debiasing methods cover up systematic gender biases in word embeddings but do not remove them. arXiv preprint arXiv:1903.03862 (2019)
13. Ingham, P.: Language of gender and class: transformation in the Victorian Novel. Routledge, London (2002)
14. Lambrecht, A., Tucker, C.: Algorithmic bias? an empirical study of apparent gender-based discrimination in the display of stem career ads. Management Science (2019)

15. Leavy, S., Meaney, G., Wade, K., Greene, D.: Curatr: a platform for semantic analysis and curation of historical literary texts. In: Garoufallou, E., Fallucchi, F., William De Luca, E. (eds.) MTSR 2019. CCIS, vol. 1057, pp. 354–366. Springer, Cham (2019). https://doi.org/10.1007/978-3-030-36599-8_31

16. Martyna, W.: What does 'he' mean? use of the generic masculine. J. Commun. **28**(1), 131–138 (1978)

17. Mikolov, T., Chen, K., Corrado, G., Dean, J.: Efficient estimation of word representations in vector space. arXiv preprint arXiv:1301.3781 (2013)

18. Mills, S.: Feminist Stylistics. Routledge, London (1995)

19. Mollin, S.: Revisiting binomial order in english: ordering constraints and reversibility. Engl. Lang. Linguist. **16**(1), 81–103 (2012)

20. Motschenbacher, H.: Gentlemen before ladies? a corpus-based study of conjunct order in personal binomials. J. Engl. Linguist. **41**(3), 212–242 (2013)

21. Pearce, M.: Investigating the collocational behaviour of man and woman in the BNC using sketch engine. Corpora **3**(1), 1–29 (2008)

22. Perez, C.C.: Invisible Women: Data Bias in a World Designed for Men. Abrams (2019)

23. Romaine, S., et al.: Communicating Gender. Psychology Press, New York (1998)

24. Shor, E., van de Rijt, A., Ward, C., Blank-Gomel, A., Skiena, S.: Time trends in printed news coverage of female subjects, 1880–2008. Journalism Stud. **15**(6), 759–773 (2014)

25. Sigley, R., Holmes, J.: Looking at girls in Corpora of English. J. Engl. Linguist. **30**(2), 138–157 (2002)

26. Swinger, N., De-Arteaga, M., Heffernan IV, N.T., Leiserson, M.D., Kalai, A.T.: What are the biases in my word embedding? In: Proceedings of the 2019 AAAI/ACM Conference on AI, Ethics, and Society, pp. 305–311. ACM (2019)

27. Tang, D., Wei, F., Yang, N., Zhou, M., Liu, T., Qin, B.: Learning sentiment-specific word embedding for twitter sentiment classification. In: Proceedings of the 52nd Annual Meeting of the Association for Computational Linguistics (Volume 1: Long Papers), pp. 1555–1565 (2014)

28. Vefali, G.M., Erdentuğ, F.: The coordinate structures in a corpus of new age talks: 'man and woman'/'woman and man'. Text Talk-An Interdisc. J. Lang. Discourse Commun. Stud. **30**(4), 465–484 (2010)

29. Zhang, B.H., Lemoine, B., Mitchell, M.: Mitigating unwanted biases with adversarial learning. In: Proceedings of the 2018 AAAI/ACM Conference on AI, Ethics, and Society, pp. 335–340. ACM (2018)

30. Zhao, J., Wang, T., Yatskar, M., Ordonez, V., Chang, K.W.: Gender bias in coreference resolution: evaluation and debiasing methods. arXiv preprint arXiv:1804.06876 (2018)

Why Do We Need to Be Bots? What Prevents Society from Detecting Biases in Recommendation Systems

Tobias D. Krafft[(⊠)][iD], Marc P. Hauer[iD], and Katharina A. Zweig[iD]

Algorithm Accountability Lab, Technische Universität Kaiserslautern,
Kaiserslautern, Germany
krafft@cs.uni-kl.de

Abstract. Concerns about social networks manipulating the (general) public opinion have become a recurring theme in recent years. Whether such an impact actually exists could so far only be tested to a very limited extent. Yet to guarantee the accountability of recommendation and information filtering systems, society needs to be able to determine whether they comply with ethical and legal requirements. This paper focuses on black box analyses as methods that are designed to systematically assess the performance of such systems, but that are, at the same time, not very intrusive. We describe the conditions that must be met to allow black box analyses of recommendation systems based on an application on Facebook's News Feed. While black box analyses have proven to be useful in the past, several barriers can easily get in the way, such as a limited possibility of automated account control, bot detection and bot inhibition. Drawing on the insights from our case study and the state of the art of research on algorithmic accountability, we formulate several policy demands that need to be met in order to allow monitoring of ADM systems for their compliance with social values.

Keywords: ADM systems · Recommendation systems · Black box analysis · Bot detection · Black box audit

1 Introduction

With new machine learning techniques, more and more decision-making is delegated to machines. Therefore, the potential societal impact of so-called *algorithmic decision making systems* (**ADM systems**) and the information and power asymmetries that they can entail increases accordingly. Among these ADM systems, we count all recommendation systems that filter and rank news and messages on search engines and social media, such as news feeds, or time line curating systems. An entire field of research has emerged that deals with the question of how to safeguard an accountable use of such ADM systems. This field of *algorithmic accountability* (Diakopoulos 2014) encompasses various theoretical,

L. Boratto et al. (Eds.): BIAS 2020, CCIS 1245, pp. 27–34, 2020.
https://doi.org/10.1007/978-3-030-52485-2_3

technical, legal, and civil society approaches to contribute to a responsible and transparent handling of algorithmic decision processes.

An important method to monitor some characteristics of an opaque ADM system and to reduce information asymmetries without acquiring insight into the actual decision structures of the ADM system (for example via code audit) is called a *black box analysis* (Diakopoulos 2014). When conducting this form of testing, the appropriateness of the ADM system's results is assessed by running various experiments on the system (e.g., varying the input, observations under different conditions) without looking into its code, the implemented decision rules or its statistical model that produces the results.

In recent years, many people started using certain social media platforms as their primary, possibly even sole source of information and news. Websites like Facebook and Google have become power intermediaries between information sources and readers. This has led to a discussion about the rights and responsibilities associated with this position of large tech companies and information intermediaries (Dreyer and Schulz 2019).

One aspect of this discussion is whether television channels which host a Facebook page can fulfill the principle of neutrality (§11/2 of the *German Interstate Broadcasting Agreement*[1]) on the platform Facebook given the nontransparent behavior of its News Feed algorithm. In collaboration with the *Rhein-Neckar Fernsehen* (RNF)[2] we probed the usefulness of black box analysis by examining whether Facebook displays an unduly polarizing or a balanced selection of news to the subscribers of the respective pages. In this analysis we were faced with two main obstacles, one of which was the very limited access to information and the other the quick banning of our fake accounts (bots). Our results suggest that while bot detection and selective bot inhibition are fundamental to a trustworthy usage of social network platforms, this case study shows that at least for some questions, society might need privileged access in form of fake accounts.

2   Black Box Analyses

Black box analyses as a form of systematic auditing allow for the evaluation of the overall appropriateness of an ADM system, including indirectly observable effects (Diakopoulos 2014). This requires access to interfaces through which the reviewing entity can observe the system as a black box and inspect which outputs are generated based on which inputs. Although this method does not enable a researcher to understand the ADM system completely - since it does not peak inside the black box - it can nevertheless reveal undesired behaviour of an ADM system's results - whether it was intended or not. Hence, this approach is rather superficial and hardly intrusive. It does not inspect the way in which the ADM system has been configured and *how* it produces outcomes, as it does not go beyond what is commonly called *instrumental* or *outcome accountability* (Patil et al. 2014).

---

[1] Rundfunkstaatsvertrag.

[2] A regional, private television channel in Germany: https://www.rnf.de.

Although the details of a black box analyses are highly application-specific, they roughly follow the same five steps (see Fig. 1). Depending on the access to

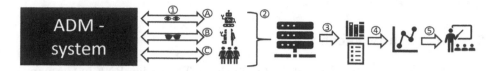

Fig. 1. Conceptualized process of a black box analysis. The numbers represent the different fields in which errors can occur.

the system, requests with previously defined input variables are automatically sent to the system and the results are collected (1 A). This audit form is called **Scraping Audit** (Sandvig et al. 2014). Researchers issue queries to a platform, observe its reactions and make a statistical evaluation of them. These queries might be very simple and can be issued by either using an application programming interface (*API*) or a browser control system like Selenium[3]. Either way, the automated access does not try to impersonate human behaviour, so that queries can be submitted at a very high frequency and/or can act in a for human atypical manner, as long as the interface allows this (Sandvig et al. 2014). If this form of auditing does not work, e.g. because the specific usage behaviour is part of the required input variables (like human typing or clicking), the automated query must pretend to be a real user before or during the data collection. This can be done, for example, by simulating an organic user behaviour (1 B). This form of audit, in which a computer imitates human behaviour, is called **Sock Puppet** or **Bot Audit** (Sandvig et al. 2014). It is similar to a Scraping Audit, but aims at impersonating realistic user behavior. By simulating human interaction, including personal characteristics, the behaviour of the platform towards its actual users can be captured. Since actual human behaviour is part of the input to the ADM system, there is normally no API over which these inputs can be submitted. A third approach is the so called **Crowdsourced Audit** (Sandvig et al. 2014) which makes use of actual users of a platform, by either letting them enter queries, or by interposing an algorithm that pretends to be the actual user that is logged in[4]. Finding enough users that agree to participate is a major obstacle of this kind of audit— as is the possible self-selection of these users into the auditing procedure[5]. No matter which form of auditing is chosen, it is always followed by a central data collection (2) as well as a processing of the collected results which are fed into data cleaning (3). Data analysis methods (4)

---

[3] https://selenium.dev/.

[4] Even when no login is needed, this approach yields a great advantage in certain cases, for example, when geospatial data like the IP address might be relevant (Krafft et al. 2019).

[5] Self-selection refers to the self-enrollment in these kinds of studies. It almost always biases the sample such that it is not representative of all users of a system.

can then only be applied to structured and verified data sets. The last step is the presentation of the results of the data analysis (5). All these steps involve their own challenges. This paper focuses on the intricacies and challenges encountered in the first stage.

3   Case Study Facebook

In a private conversation, a member of the private TV station RNF in Germany told us that the followers of their Facebook account complained about the selection of news issued by the RNF in their time line. Some of them expressed the feeling that they only got to see news of the "Blood & Crime" type, while the RNF has a wide range of regional and global news, from the weather forecast over municipal to police and societal news.

The first question was whether and, if so, to which extent followers of RNF's page see only a part of the news content. The second question was how such a selection developed in time: Did followers at the beginning see a fair sample of all news, maybe weighted by the frequency of the corresponding category? Was it then influenced and more selective by the way in which the followers interacted with the content? A follower who is interested in all categories but—inadvertently—clicks more on the "Blood & Crime" news might induce a positive feedback cycle with the recommendation system that increasingly prioritized those news and suppresses news from other categories.

3.1   Page Owner Perspective

We obtained full access to the Facebook account of the RNF, but still could not answer any of the questions mentioned above with the information provided directly to the account. The type of information provided by Facebook is highly aggregated and does not allow to track the delivery of single news items to followers. It was thus clear, that we needed to do a black-box analysis.

3.2   Appropriate Forms of Audit

For the black box analysis of Facebook, we examined the three audit approaches previously introduced, and evaluated their feasibility. In general, we wanted to see whether the filtering and ranking of the news items by the personalized recommendation system would change the fraction of news in each category in a user's News Feed, e.g., towards a heavy fraction of "Blood & Crime" news. At the time of the study, there was no API available, which we could have used to address that question. Extended API access can be granted by Facebook, for example to support the solution of research tasks, but a corresponding request remained unanswered. We also ruled out a Crowdsourced Audit in which we would ask users to open up their accounts to us. We would then have been able to scrape the RNF news from their News Feed, however, the privacy problem would have been massive without any possibility of filtering only those news items from the otherwise very personal stream of messages. For the same reason, crowdsourcing of only political ads in Facebook is impossible today which heavily impedes the analysis of how political elections might be influenced by those ads. In general, any Crowdsourced Audit is highly problematic on Facebook as long as there are no fine-grained filtering approaches that enable a selective access to a user's News Feed.

Based on these considerations, we concluded that: To respect the privacy of real users and without access to information via the page owner's account or a suitable API, we needed to implement a Sock Puppet Audit. To make initial validations in a pre-study, we generated 30 fake accounts by hand based on email addresses from various providers. Each account has been manually set up to follow only the Facebook group of the RNF. Every day, our software logged in with each of the accounts, scrolled through the respective News Feed and saved the displayed posts in a database. The software was developed in a way that the behavior was as realistic as possible to avoid bot detection (Yang et al. 2014). After the first day it already became obvious that even accounts that have been created in a seemingly identical fashion are treated differently in terms of selection of posts for the respective News Feed. For the next days none of the News Feeds displayed the same posts in the exact same order. After three days the selection of posts didn't match for any two News Feeds at all, independent of their order. From the fourth day on, bot detection could not be avoided and thus, several of our Sock Puppets got banned every day because we could not provide a telephone number for account verification—after 10 days none of them remained. As a result, further analyses were neither qualitatively nor quantitatively feasible.

While it might have been possible to create even more realistic bots by, e.g. faking telephone numbers or by hiring real people to navigate our fake accounts, the effort necessary to ask this simple but important question on Facebook's News Feed recommendation system is exceedingly high. To assess the appropriateness of personalized recommendation systems and to ensure algorithmic accountability even through non-intrusive procedures, such as black box analysis, society needs a reliable, efficient, and not too costly access. In the following, we will quickly sketch the general scope of this demand.

3.3 Broader Scope

While the RNF case study provides a sketch of the problems of black box analyses in one important question, namely the question of news diversity, this is by far not the only application where society needs to analyze personalized recommendation systems. Other applications are:

1. Webshops with dynamic prices like Amazon or Trivago have the option of offering personalised prices on the basis of recommendation systems. This involves the risk of personalization based on protected characteristics and thus of discrimination.

2. Do headhunters on career platforms like LinkedIn, Xing, Monster, Stepstone or others get a personalized selection of possible candidates? Might this lead to a biased selection towards a certain gender or ethnicity over time? This would be problematic because national law in many countries regulates a fair access to job opportunities.
3. Analysis of the personalized roll-out of political ads on Facebook, Instagram or Twitter. A biased roll-out might hinder democratic processes, as indicated by the Cambridge Analytica scandal (Schneble et al. 2018).

The last section sketches possible solutions on the political actions that need to be taken in order to give society the ability to reveal illegal, illegitimate or unethical biases in recommendation systems.

4   Demands for a Legal Framework for Black Box Analyses

For monitoring black box systems, privileged, legally guaranteed and continuous access is needed. In order to make this possible, politics must intervene and create a legal framework for black box analyses. This section points to the requirements of such necessary accesses. Many problems with opaque systems can be countered with provisions that establish transparency and allow for the scrutiny of ADM systems. Such provisions should be demanded if a sufficiently great danger to democratic values is possible. The following demands address the obstacles that currently hinder an inspecting instance in trying to reveal illegal or immoral behaviour of recommendation systems.

I. Set Up of a Suitable Machine Interface (API)
There are two perspectives on the monitoring of recommendation systems in which granting suitable API access is useful.

The first requirement concerns the users of the recommendation systems. In our case study for example, a preferable solution to the problem would be a more comprehensive access to relevant information for page operators on Facebook. We found that the existing API does not give insights into what posts are displayed to whom in their respective News Feed. As demanded by van Drunen, Helberger and Bastian, it must become clearer how user behaviour affects selection (van Drunen et al. 2019). Still, it is important to comply with data protection and privacy regulations such as the General Data Protection Regulation (GDPR). Some aggregation of user data may therefore be necessary.

Another option is privileged access for accredited researchers/auditors acting on behalf of the state or a regulating instance. Some questions such as which political party orders which kind of advertisement for which target group can only be answered by accessing the system-wide or aggregated information of the recommendation system. Facebook's disclosed information platform for political ads, which actually should answer those questions, is currently under criticism for not revealing all relevant information[6].

---

[6] https://www.propublica.org/article/facebook-blocks-ad-transparency-tools.

II. Allow Conditional Use of Bots

A platform that makes use of a recommendation system must allow the automated control of accounts by accredited scientists. This may include the use of bots, at least as long as it is assured, that user manipulation by such bots (for example by enforcing trending topics) is prevented. Bots that are specifically authorized by the platform operator raise yet another problem, since it is important that they are treated equally to a human user. Independently, to allow representative monitoring of such a platform, there needs to be a way to automatically generate a large number of bots for scientific purposes.

III. Provide Selective Access for Normal Users

An insightful monitoring method for opaque systems needs, as already presented, the active participation of users of the system via Crowdsourced Audit. One obstacle to such participation, however, is the issue of data protection. As stated in the case study, it is not possible for Facebook users to share only parts of their News Feed for the purpose of analysis. There is only full access to the account or none at all. In addition, the API access to the News Feed has been discontinued, which means that access is only possible by reading it from browser sessions. A selective access would therefore be necessary to create a low-entry threshold for such an audit. An important aspect in this regard is the possibility of anonymization or pseudo-anonymization, which could be achieved by allowing adequately configuring access. Scientific analyses would then be significantly simplified.

IV. Legal Certainty for Automated Audits

The attempt to examine a recommendation system for researching activities without any criminal intent must not be criminalised by the terms of use or other legal regulations. Platform terms of service are often written to prohibit the automated downloading of any information from a Website, even if that information is public. For instance, exploiting security vulnerabilities to raise public awareness may result in legal consequences by the US Computer Fraud and Abuse Act (CFAA)[7]. The same legal basis would currently apply if a scientist performs a black box analysis. These are two very different kinds of actions which should be treated differently, and scientists should be allowed to carry out research within a secure legal framework when examining such systems for unaccountable behaviour. Otherwise, there is no possibility to level existing information and power asymmetries.

Of course, the above-mentioned demands raise questions of objectivity, because the platform operators are aware of the required and provided access. This would allow the platform to issue unequal treatment vis-à-vis the reviewing agency, similar to what happened with the Dieselgate affair, where cars recognized that they were in a test stand and then operated differently than under normal conditions (Bovens 2016). Another important aspect to consider is the risk of an abusive use of ADM systems by the state. It may ultimately be the state that is enabled to tap into and understand all black boxes that intervene

---

[7] https://www.wired.com/2013/03/att-hacker-gets-3-years/.

into the public sphere. Great care must thus be taken not to create a set of instruments that would allow total surveillance of citizens. Rather, the state should enable other stakeholders to independently ensure the accountability of ADM systems. Only this way it is possible to achieve a balance between the interests of the platforms and the interests of society as well as to avoid a concentration of possibly unaccountable power.

Acknowledgement. We wish to thank Ralph Kühnl for presenting us the issue of the perceived unequal roll-out of content from Facebook pages and his trust to give us access to the Facebook account of the Rhein Neckar Fernsehen.

References

Bovens, L.: The ethics of dieselgate. Midwest Stud. Philos. **40**(1), 262–283 (2016)

Diakopoulos, N.: Algorithmic accountability reporting: On the investigation of black boxes. Tow Center for Digital Journalism (2014)

Dreyer, S., Schulz, W.: Künstliche Intelligenz, Intermediäre und Öffentlichkeit. Technical report, Alexander von Humboldt Institut für Internet und Gesellschaft & Leibniz-Institut für Medienforschung (2019)

Krafft, T.D., Gamer, M., Zweig, K.A.: What did you see? a study to measure personalization in google's search engine. EPJ Data Sci. **8**(1), 38 (2019)

Patil, S.V., Vieider, F., Tetlock, P.E.: Process versus outcome accountability. The Oxford handbook of public accountability, pp. 69–89 (2014)

Sandvig, C., Hamilton, K., Karahalios, K., Langbort, C.: Auditing algorithms: Research methods for detecting discrimination on internet platforms. Data and discrimination: converting critical concerns into productive inquiry, 22 (2014)

Schneble, C.O., Elger, B.S., Shaw, D.: The cambridge analytica affair and internet-mediated research. EMBO Rep. **19**(8), e46579 (2018)

van Drunen, M., Helberger, N., Bastian, M.: Know your algorithm: what media organizations need to explain to their users about news personalization. International Data Privacy Law (2019)

Yang, Z., Wilson, C., Wang, X., Gao, T., Zhao, B.Y., Dai, Y.: Uncovering social network sybils in the wild. ACM Trans. Knowl. Discov. Data (TKDD) **8**(1), 1–29 (2014)

Effect of Debiasing on Information Retrieval

Emma J. Gerritse[✉] and Arjen P. de Vries

Institute for Computing and Information Sciences, Radboud University,
Nijmegen, The Netherlands
emma.gerritse@ru.nl, a.devries@cs.ru.nl

Abstract. Word embeddings provide a common basis for modern natural language processing tasks, however, they have also been a source of discussion regarding their possible biases. This has led to a number of publications regarding algorithms for removing this bias from word embeddings. Debiasing should make the embeddings fairer in their use, avoiding potential negative effects downstream. For example: word embeddings with a gender bias that are used in a classification task in a hiring process. In this research, we compare regular and debiased word embeddings in an Information Retrieval task. We show that the two methods produce different results, however, this difference is not substantial.

Keywords: Query expansion · Word embeddings · Bias

1 Introduction

Word embeddings have been used for many downstream Natural Language Processing (NLP) tasks lately. They are a method of presenting words in a high dimensional vector space, learned by applying machine learning on large text corpora. It has been shown that these embeddings can be very useful in many tasks, hence their wide-spread usage. However, this method is not without any critique. One of the most influential critique papers demonstrates gender bias in pre-trained word embeddings derived from Google News [1].

The authors of that work claim that having a gender bias in word embeddings can be damaging for downstream tasks like information retrieval. Imagine the scenario where a user wants to retrieve documents of people working in a male-dominated field, like computer science. If the embeddings of male names are closer to the embedding of computer science than the embeddings of female names, it could be that John's page gets a higher ranking than Jane's, even when the contents of their pages are otherwise similar.

While this scenario would be very alarming, to our knowledge no experiments have shown this to happen in a practical setting. That is why, in this research, we investigate this. We empirically show the difference in retrieval outcomes when performing a retrieval task with or without debiased embeddings.

© Springer Nature Switzerland AG 2020
L. Boratto et al. (Eds.): BIAS 2020, CCIS 1245, pp. 35–42, 2020.
https://doi.org/10.1007/978-3-030-52485-2_4

For this, we perform a retrieval experiment on TREC Robust. We incorporate biased and debiased embeddings for query expansion, using a method based on [2]. We compare the difference in expanded terms, and also the difference in the effectiveness measurements obtained for the different embeddings.

2   Related Work

Word embeddings are a vector representation of vocabulary. To compute these vectors, many methods have been proposed. One of the best-known methods is Word2Vec [7]. This method works by training a neural network that predicts words considering their context. The Skip-Gram variant of the method predicts a word's context from its observation, while the Continuous Bag of Words variant predicts the word occurrence from its context. Of the two variants, the Skip-Gram is used most widely. The resulting word representations (called word embeddings) have been successfully used in a range of NLP tasks, including sentence classification [5] and text classification [10].

Word embeddings can be used for document retrieval as well. In [2], query terms are expanded with terms found by using word embeddings. The idea here is that you can use the embedding space to find words similar to the other words in the query. This paper shows that using locally trained word embeddings will always perform better than globally trained embeddings for document retrieval. The retrieval is done by combining the expanded terms with a language model. An updated language model is computed for the language model p_q of the query q. This expansion, p_{q+}, is combined with p_q by a linear combination:

$$p_q^1(w) = \lambda p_q(w) + (1 - \lambda)p_{q+}(w) \qquad \lambda \in (0,1) \qquad (1)$$

p_{q+} is computed in the following way. Let U be the embedding matrix of size $|D| \times k$. Let q be the $|D| \times 1$ vector describing the query. Then the query expansion can be computed by taking the top k terms from the resulting $|D| \times 1$ vector $UU^T q$. This is identical to computing $\operatorname{argmin}_{w' \in U} \sum_{w \in Q} w \cdot w'$.

While very useful, word embeddings have also triggered controversy. Pre-trained embeddings have been shared by researchers to be easily used, however, researchers have exposed inherent biases. In [1] for example, the pre-trained word embeddings trained on Google News by [7] are shown to exhibit common gender stereotypes on well-known analogy tasks. One of the appealing examples of analogies in [6] is $\overrightarrow{king} - \overrightarrow{man} + \overrightarrow{woman} = \overrightarrow{queen}$; it looks like word embeddings capture semantic linguistic knowledge! In [1] however, it is shown that less desirable analogies *also* exist in the embedding space, like $\overrightarrow{computer\_programmer} - \overrightarrow{man} + \overrightarrow{woman} = \overrightarrow{homemaker}$ (a particularly shocking example for the computer science field, where many researchers actively try to overcome such prejudices and work toward a better gender balance). They found many more examples for similarly biased analogies, and then asked mechanical Turkers to rate the level of bias in these examples. It turns out that many of these analogies have some degree of gender bias, which is why they propose two methods (hard and soft debias) to remove this bias.

This paper has lead to quite some discussion among academics. The paper [8] points out that the method of detecting biased analogies might not be fair, because of the way the GENSIM packages handles these analogies. The analogy function in this package can never return one of the input words, for example in the example given above, when giving 'king', 'man' and 'woman' as input, these three words can not be given as output. When removing these constraints, it turns out that many of the analogies discussed in [1] do not hold anymore. Most noticeably, without this constraint, the result of the analogy $\overrightarrow{computer\_programmer} - \overrightarrow{he} + \overrightarrow{she}$ is $\overrightarrow{computer\_programmer}$.

Further exploration of the validity of biased analogies is reported by [3]. Here, robustness of analogies is defined in the following way. If for example $\overrightarrow{king} - \overrightarrow{man} + \overrightarrow{woman} = \overrightarrow{queen}$, then the reverse should also hold: $\overrightarrow{queen} - \overrightarrow{woman} + \overrightarrow{man} = \overrightarrow{king}$. If the reverse does not hold, the analogy is not robust. Several of the analogies in [1] were tested. Most importantly, the title-giving analogy is not robust: the answer to $\overrightarrow{computer\_programmer} - \overrightarrow{he} + \overrightarrow{she}$ is indeed homemaker. But when computing the reverse, the answer to the analogy is $\overrightarrow{homemaker} - \overrightarrow{she} + \overrightarrow{he} \approx \overrightarrow{carpenter}$. It seems illogical that these analogies are not always robust, since they are often denoted with an '=' sign instead of an '≈' sign. However, it is important to consider that the embedding space is very sparse. Analogies are computed in GENSIM by finding the closest word-vector to for example the result of $\overrightarrow{computer\_programmer} - \overrightarrow{he} + \overrightarrow{she}$. Looking at the results, it seems that the closest neighbour can still be relatively far away in the embedding space. In this example, $\cos(\overrightarrow{computer\_programmer} - \overrightarrow{he} + \overrightarrow{she}, \overrightarrow{homemaker}) = 0.57$ while with a robust analogy the result is $\cos(\overrightarrow{king} - \overrightarrow{he} + \overrightarrow{she}, \overrightarrow{queen}) = 0.73$. Because the answer to the analogy is relatively distant, it is not surprising that the reverse sequence of operations would identify a different word-vector as the most similar result. This process of reversing the analogy can be repeated until the results are robust. For the home maker example, the analogies converge at $\overrightarrow{carpenter} - \overrightarrow{he} + \overrightarrow{she} \approx \overrightarrow{seamstress}$, and for this analogy is robust. While this analogy is still biased, it seems less severe than the *computer programmer* and *homemaker* combination.

Analogies also seem to depend heavily on the choice of words. When computing the analogy for $\overrightarrow{programmer}$ instead of $\overrightarrow{computer\_programmer}$, the result of the analogy is $\overrightarrow{programmers}$. Then when you look at the convergence of the analogy, it results in the names of two random people. This may be because of the sparseness of the embedding vectors, and because of the constraints of the analogies as discussed in [8].

Finally, people observed that the debiased word vectors still encode some degree of bias: biases can be recovered from the data. The authors of [4] first show that clusters of word embeddings, using k-means to assign the most biased words to two clusters, still align with the given gender with an accuracy of 92.5% for the debiased version. They also trained a Support Vector Machine to predict whether a word was a male or female word, and with an accuracy of 96.5% they were able to recover the gender information, even when debiased. So it seems that debiasing only superficially covers up the bias. This result can be seen with debiasing methods applied before and after computing the embeddings.

3 Method

3.1 Debiasing Word Embeddings

In this paper, we investigate the effects of the hard debiasing method described in [1]. We give a description of the method here, but for exact details, we refer the reader to the original paper.

Debiasing the word embeddings works as follows. First, define a gendered set consisting of words with a clear gender component (e.g. *man, woman, male, female, brother, sister, etc.*). Use this set to compute the gender direction B in the vector space. Next, define the set N of words which need to be neutralized or debiased. Project the words in N onto the gender direction B, and normalize their length. Finally, define a set of equal pairs E, containing pairs like $(man, woman)$, which are also centered around the origin (to prevent vectors of one of the genders to have a greater length than the other).

After debiasing, for any neutralized word $w \in N$ and any equal pair $(e_1, e_2) \in E$, it should hold that $\vec{w} \cdot \vec{e_1} = \vec{w} \cdot \vec{e_2}$ and $||\vec{w} - \vec{e_1}|| = ||\vec{w} - \vec{e_2}||$. I.e., words that should be gender neutral have equal distance to the previously defined male and female words.

The authors of [1] have shared debiased pre-trained Google News embeddings, that we use in the empirical part of this work.

3.2 Retrieval Model and Experimental Setup

Having the debiased embeddings, we now explain how we use these in a retrieval experiment. We select two different sets of pre-trained word embeddings, the standard pre-trained Word2Vec embeddings on Google News as shared by [7] and the debiased version of these embeddings (as explained in the section above). For the dataset to test our model, we selected the TREC Robust 04 test collection consisting of news articles, matching the domain of our embeddings. This test collection consists of 250 queries (usually called topics in IR), with a total of 311410 relevance judgments.

We removed stopwords from these queries using the NLTK stopword list, and we cast query terms to all lower case. We expand each of these queries with $k = 5$ terms, by computing the five closest terms to the query embedding in the embedding space with each method regarding the cosine similarity. To compute these terms, we use the GENSIM most_similar function, where the input is the stopped lowercase query terms, and the output is the top-k closest words which are not in the input words. After this, we substitute the words of the query with the expanded terms and used these for retrieval. The score is based on the method used in [2], but not identical as we use cosine instead of the dot product, and we only expand with words that de not occur in the original query.

To run our experiment, we used Anserini [9]. We ranked the documents using RM3 and BM25. This gives us three ranking files, the one with the regular queries (*Standard*), with the biased expansions (*Biased*) and with the debiased expansions (*Debiased*).

To combine the biased or debiased word embeddings based score with the standard retrieval score, we used `Coordinate Ascent` from the `RankLib` package.

$$score_{total} = \lambda score_{standard} + (1 - \lambda)score_{(de)biased} \qquad \lambda \in [0, 1] \quad (2)$$

We used cross fold validation, where we trained with 5 folds, and we optimized regarding to the metrics of NDCG@10 and ERROR@10. This gave us, for all folds with both methods, the average λ score of 0.90 ($\sigma = 0.04$).

4   Results

As we can see in Table 1, there is no significant difference in score between biased and debiased query expansion. We also see no significant difference regarding the Expanded versus the Regular version. Table 1 has two columns, one where we evaluate with respect to the full Robust 04 qrels file, and one where we compare to only the 48 queries which got different expansions. The expansions only differ in about 20% of the queries, so differences are more clear if we confine ourselves to this subset. The two query sets are denoted as **Robust Full** and **Robust Changed**, respectively.

Table 1. Results of the retrieval documents. Both expansions did not lead to any significant improvement in P30 of MAP.

Model	Robust full		Robust changed	
Score	MAP	P30	MAP	P30
Expansion biased	0.106	0.135	0.126	0.156
Expansion debiased	0.105	0.135	0.117	0.158
Regular	0.290	0.337	0.303	0.372
Regular + Expansion biased	0.290	0.339	0.306	0.377
Regular + Expansion debiased	0.290	0.338	0.305	0.375

Of the 250 analyzed queries in TREC, 48 gain a different expansion. Of those 48, 16 have a substantial difference in MAP and 18 have a substantial difference in P_30. We denote a difference in score of 0.01 as substantial (an arbitrary number defined by the Anserini script to compare runs).

We show the queries with a substantial difference in Table 2, together with the difference in expanded terms with both methods. A positive number means that the biased method performs better, while a negative number means that the debiased version performed better. In some of these queries, the change in

Table 2. Difference between biased and debiased query expansion. The first term (in italics) is the query terms, the second term is the biased expansion and the third term is the debiased expansion. Only queries with a substantial change in either MAP or P30 are listed. Words of the original query might be repeated in expansion with different capitalization. Note that words often contain spelling errors ('anti_biotics' or 'prostrate').

P30	MAP	Query: query expansion difference
−0.067	−0.046	*international organized crime*: Organized → human_trafficking
'0.1	0.080	*hubble telescope achievements*: astronomical_telescope → inch_refractor_telescope
−0.267	−0.061	*women in parliaments*: gender_equality → females
0.067	0.068	*adoptive biological parents*: mother → birthmother
−0.067	−0.018	*territorial waters dispute*: Diaoyutais → Spratleys
−0.033	0.008	*anorexia nervosa bulimia*: bulimic → binge_eating
−0.033	−0.013	*health insurance holistic*: healthcare → preventative_medicine
−0.033	−0.003	*mental illness drugs*: mental_disorders → alzheimer_disease
0.033	0.006	*teaching disabled children*: cognitively_disabled → nondisabled_peers
0.367	0.119	*sick building syndrome*: headaches_nausea_diarrhea → persistent_sexual_arousal
−0.1	−0.059	*behavioral genetics*: neurobiological → neurogenetics
−0.013	0.0	*osteoporosis*: rheumatoid_arthritis → osteoarthritis
−0.033	−0.043	*heroic acts*: heroic_feats → bravery
−0.033	0.010	*women clergy*: clergywomen → bishops
−0.067	0.029	*antibiotics ineffectiveness*: anti_biotics → antibiotic_overuse antibiotic_therapy → antifungal_medications
0.0	0.084	*human genetic code*: epigenetic_reprogramming → primate_genomes
0.033	0.020	*women ordained church of england*: clergy → priests
0.033	0.018	*doctor assisted suicides*: psychiatrist → prescribed_anti_depressants
0.1	0.054	*maternity leave policies*: Maternity_Matters → Policies
−0.1	−0.069	*prostate cancer detection treatment*: differentiated_thyroid → prostrate_cancer

the expansion is as expected of a version without gender bias. For example, in the query 'women clergy', the expanded terms get changed from 'clergywomen' to 'bishops', which is a logical gender-neutral change of this word. We also see that the score here changes positively with the debiased terms.

However, in other cases, the changes in terms with the debiased version do not make much sense. For example, in the query 'sick building syndrome', query expansion 'headaches_nausea_diarrhea' changes into 'persistent_sexual_arrousal' (note the spelling mistake). Naturally, the biased version performs much better than the debiased version.

As for a possible explanation of why this might happen: If only one of the word vectors in either of the query terms changes, the aggregated query changes along, as do the 5 expanded query terms. Even if the input query changes ever so slightly, due to the sparsity of the embedding space, completely different terms can become the closest ones.

It is interesting to see some queries are expanded with words with spelling mistakes (e.g. 'prost*rate*'). A possible explanation is that these words are so uncommon in the corpus, that they are not seen enough during training. This may result in words which are not properly embedded, leading to nonsensical expansions.

While gender bias is removed, some other versions of bias remain in both versions of embeddings. For example, for query number 316 'polygamy polyandry polygyny' gets expanded in both cases with 'incestuous_marriages', which can be considered a lifestyle bias. Removing all potential biases from embedding space seems infeasible with the proposed approach, because one would need to specify actual examples of every single bias that may be encoded in the data.

5   Conclusion

We carried out a comparative study on the effect of biased and debiased word embeddings on information retrieval. In about 20% of the queries, query expansions differed; where 38% of those queries that changed led to a substantial difference in documents retrieved. This corresponds to only 7% of the total number of queries. Retrieval results for debiased word embeddings may change for the better or for the worse. Taking only these experimental outcomes into account, we may conclude that the effect of debiasing word embeddings on retrieved results is not dramatic.

However, when looking at the expanded terms of a query, these terms can still be biased. Debiasing for gender will not remove other types of bias that may occur in the data from which the word embeddings have been derived. Sometimes, biases can be present of which the user is not even aware they exist. Based on our experience, we conclude that the more general problem of unfairness in document ranking cannot be addressed by the debiasing approaches found in the literature.

For further research, literature has proven that locally trained embeddings work better than globally trained embeddings for query expansion. It would be interesting to see if when training the embeddings ourselves, and debiasing the embeddings ourselves, if results will change.

References

1. Bolukbasi, T., Chang, K.W., Zou, J.Y., Saligrama, V., Kalai, A.T.: Man is to computer programmer as woman is to homemaker? Debiasing word embeddings. In: Advances in Neural Information Processing Systems 29, pp. 4349–4357 (2016)
2. Diaz, F., Mitra, B., Craswell, N.: Query expansion with locally-trained word embeddings. In: Proceedings of the 54th Annual Meeting of the Association for Computational Linguistics, pp. 367–377 (2016)

3. Gerritse, E.: Impact of debiasing word embeddings on information retrieval. In: Proceedings of the 9th PhD Symposium on Future Directions in Information Access, CEUR Workshop Proceedings, pp. 54–59 (2019)
4. Gonen, H., Goldberg, Y.: Lipstick on a Pig: debiasing methods cover up systematic gender biases in word embeddings but do not remove them. In: Proceedings of the 2019 Conference of the North American Chapter of the Association for Computational Linguistics: Human Language Technologies, Volume 1 (Long and Short Papers), pp. 609–614 (2019)
5. Kim, Y.: Convolutional neural networks for sentence classification. In: Proceedings of the 2014 Conference on Empirical Methods in Natural Language Processing, pp. 1746–1751. ACL (2014)
6. Mikolov, T., Chen, K., Corrado, G., Dean, J.: Efficient estimation of word representations in vector space. In: 1st International Conference on Learning Representations, pp. 1–12 (2013)
7. Mikolov, T., Sutskever, I., Chen, K., Corrado, G.S., Dean, J.: Distributed representations of words and phrases and their compositionality. In: Advances in Neural Information Processing Systems, pp. 3111–3119 (2013)
8. Nissim, M., van Noord, R., van der Goot, R.: Fair is better than sensational: man is to doctor as woman is to doctor. arXiv preprint arXiv:1905.09866 (2019)
9. Yang, P., Fang, H., Lin, J.: Anserini: enabling the use of Lucene for information retrieval research. In: Proceedings of the 40th International ACM SIGIR Conference on Research and Development in Information Retrieval, pp. 1253–1256 (2017)
10. Zhang, X., Zhao, J., LeCun, Y.: Character-level convolutional networks for text classification. In: Advances in Neural Information Processing Systems 28, pp. 649–657. Curran Associates, Inc. (2015)

Matchmaking Under Fairness Constraints: A Speed Dating Case Study

Dimitris Paraschakis[(⊠)] and Bengt J. Nilsson

Malmö University, Nordenskiöldsgatan 1, 211 19 Malmö, Sweden
{dimitris.paraschakis,bengt.nilsson.TS}@mau.se

Abstract. Reported evidence of biased matchmaking calls into question the ethicality of recommendations generated by a machine learning algorithm. In the context of dating services, the failure of an automated matchmaker to respect the user's expressed sensitive preferences (racial, religious, etc.) may lead to biased decisions perceived by users as unfair. To address the issue, we introduce the notion of *preferential fairness*, and propose two algorithmic approaches for re-ranking the recommendations under preferential fairness constraints. Our experimental results demonstrate that the state of fairness can be reached with minimal accuracy compromises for both binary and non-binary attributes.

Keywords: Preferential fairness · Matchmaking · Speed dating

1 Introduction

In 2016, a number of incidents were reported by users of the dating app CoffeeMeetsBagel[1], who complained that the service had consistently been matching them against partners of their own ethnicity, despite the user's explicitly communicated ethnic neutrality [20]. Arguably, the observed bias of algorithmic matchmaking originates from two common assumptions: first, that an algorithm must strive to reproduce the preferences of existing users; and second, that these *inferred* preferences should inform matching decisions, overriding the user's *expressed* desires [11]. Another motivating example [26] shows that a classifier trained on speed dating data can learn to discriminate on the basis of protected characteristics of users, unless special preventive measures are taken. One such measure is re-ranking the recommendation output in a post-processing step, which can be applied to traditional recommender systems trained in pointwise or pairwise manner [25]. The idea of *preferentially fair* matchmaking therefore boils down to formulating and solving a recommendation problem under expressed preference constraints. In line with the above examples, we investigate the fairness of a matchmaking mechanism for speed dating, based on a publicly available dataset [7].

---

[1] https://coffeemeetsbagel.com/.

© Springer Nature Switzerland AG 2020
L. Boratto et al. (Eds.): BIAS 2020, CCIS 1245, pp. 43–57, 2020.
https://doi.org/10.1007/978-3-030-52485-2_5

2   Case Study

We begin our study by analysing how consistent people are in following their intimate preferences. The aforementioned dataset contains 4189 speed dates collected over a series of 21 meetups (a.k.a. 'waves') between 2002 and 2004. The participants were Columbia University students who all had a 4-minute date with each person of the opposite sex. At the end of each date, both parties had to make (or not make) their pick. In case of reciprocal liking, a 'match' was registered and the contact details were exchanged. Before attending, they filled in a pre-registration questionnaire to state their demographics, self-perceived traits, and preferences. In particular, attendees could express how important it was for them to date people of their own race or religion.

In Fig. 1, we compare the distributions of own-race and other-race partners in the candidate pool with the corresponding distributions of eventually liked partners (referred to as 'picks' in Fig. 1). We observe that for low values of own-race importance (namely, 1–4), the racial distribution of picked partners closely follows that of the candidate pool. The pattern starts changing after the value of 7 onwards, where we notice discrepancies between the racial distribution of candidate partners and the picked ones; namely, showing far less interest in other-race partners. This proves that people generally tend to follow their racial preferences, which therefore should be respected by a matchmaker.

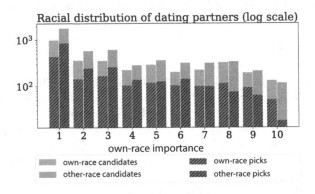

Fig. 1. Consistency patterns in racial preferences

2.1   Matchmaking

A matchmaker designed for speed dating offers assistance in mate selection and helps participants find their matches quicker. It works by comparing the content-based profile of a target user with the corresponding profiles of all other attendees of the opposite sex within the same wave, in attempt to predict a pick (individual positive decision) or a match (reciprocal positive decision). It is trained on historical data from the remaining waves containing the outcomes of all their dates. This describes a hybrid recommendation model known as *collaboration via content* [21], which practically boils down to a binary classification task. The percentage of picks and matches in the dataset are 42% and 16%, respectively. To tackle class imbalance, we employ cost-sensitive learning and classification threshold tuning established through cross-validation on training data.

The dataset structure offers a natural way of performing a 21-fold cross-validation, where each wave is used once as a test set, while the remaining waves are used for training. We use the aggregated *F1 score* as our accuracy metric:

$$F1 = \frac{2 \cdot Precision \cdot Recall}{Precision + Recall} \tag{1}$$

The number of participants in a wave varies from 9 to 44. Since each target user appears only in his/her wave, the matchmaker cannot rely on the their prior dating history and hence operates in the conditions of continuous cold-start.

Due to small candidate pools, the purpose of a matchmaker in speed dating is to suggest *all* good candidates to a user (as opposed to the classical top-k recommendation). In other words, it must decide not only *who* to recommend, but also *how many* of them. The cut-off k is thus dynamically determined by the classification threshold. This 'variable-k' recommendation setting can be generalized to other domains beyond speed dating that operate on short candidate lists (e.g. suggesting restaurants in the immediate neighborhood of a user).

3   Related Work

Speed dating is a relatively new format, which has become the topic of several studies [7,8,12,26,33] aiming to establish the key influential factors of 'rapid' matchmaking. First insights were provided by Fisman et al. [7,8], who showed that women tend to put much emphasis on the partner's race and ethnicity. Van der Zon [26] builds a classifier for speed dating to predict the partner's positive decision, and shows that it can produce racially discriminatory rules. Issues of bias and discrimination on intimate platforms have been studied by Hutson et al. [11], who advocate the design of matchmaking services able to intervene in discrimination without overriding the user's preferential autonomy. All the above insights motivate our study as they stress the need for the careful consideration of sensitive attributes in a non-invasive way when making mate suggestions.

A reciprocal recommender for speed dating was recently proposed by Zheng et al. [33]. The authors focus on the multi-stakeholder notion of fairness, which in their case does not involve any protected attributes and hence is less ethically charged than the interpretation of fairness that we put forward in this paper. Joel et al. [12] investigate whether the mutual attraction in speed dating can be predicted from the users' traits and preferences reported before the dating event. This is identical to the experimental setup of our work. Despite the use of cutting-edge machine learning algorithms, predicting a match above chance has proved to be extremely challenging [12]. Although the predictive accuracy is not the focal point of our study, our experience with predicting matches has been similar. Sapiezynski et al. [23] propose a new fairness metric for ranked outputs, in which fairness depends not only on the ranking algorithm itself, but also on the model of user attention. This way, the same ranking can appear biased both in favor and against the protected group depending on how the user attention is distributed over items. This metric is used to reveal societal biases in online dating, which can be corrected by reshuffling the system's outputs. Although different in approach, the general idea of their work is similar to ours.

The role of fairness-aware algorithms in promoting non-discrimination, neutrality, and fair treatment in recommender systems has gained wide recognition [3,14,15,17,28,31,34]. Fairness is a multifaceted notion allowing a range of definitions, e.g. see [9,27]. It is also a multisided concept [3] as it concerns both parties: those receiving recommendations, and those being recommended. This obviously holds true in dating contexts. Steck [25] expresses fairness in terms of preserving the proportionality of user interests in recommendations (a.k.a. 'calibration'). Conversely, Kamishima et al. [14] define fairness as staying neutral to user's viewpoints to enforce diversity in recommendations and avoid filter bubbles. In general, diversity and fairness are closely related concepts [15–17].

Our work is along the lines of recent studies focusing on how to achieve fairness via re-ranking [2,15,17,30,32], and how to quantify the fairness of existing rankings [30,31]. Adopting this approach typically incurs tolerable compromises in prediction accuracy [17,25]. We empirically validate this hypothesis in Sect. 6.

4   Preferential Fairness

4.1   Background

Presently, at least 20 different definitions of fairness are known in the machine learning community [9,27]. In a broad sense, preferential fairness falls under the category of *individual fairness*, which requires that 'similar individuals are treated similarly' [6]. To relate it to our case, two individuals can be considered similar if they have expressed similar racial preferences. All other things being equal, the 'treated similarly' part implies that they both receive partner recommendations with similar racial distributions.

Two edge cases are possible. When the strongest preference is expressed, the matchmaker is restricted to recommendations of own-race partners to satisfy the user's request. From the ethical viewpoint, acting differently would mean a violation of the freedom of choice (i.e. depriving the user of the ability to form a relationship with a partner of the desired race). Conversely, the weakest preference implies that the user is equally interested in all the races. Ignoring this preference could lead to unjustified racial biases akin to filter bubbles [14]; see CoffeeMeetsBagel example above [20].

In most cases, the distribution of races (or any other sensitive attribute) is not uniform in the candidate pool, which raises the question of how to sample the candidates. Should all the races have equal representation in recommendations, or should this representation be proportional to the racial distribution of the candidate pool? A recent user study investigating public attitudes towards fairness [24] shows that the latter option is generally perceived as the fairer choice in such scenarios[2]. Selecting individuals in proportion to their merit is known as *calibrated fairness*, whose several interpretations exist [18,25]. Its general idea is rooted in the theory of *proportional equality* conceived by the ancient philosopher Aristotle, and serving as a basis for distributive justice [10]. Therefore, preferential fairness is a special case of calibrated fairness, where the calibration is done on the basis of expressed user preferences. We argue that this meritocratic formulation also satisfies the conditions for *multi-sided fairness* [3], where the ethical treatment of both parties (i.e. users and candidates) is taken into account. As follows from Fig. 1, it is in the interest of both sides that candidates are selected in proportion to the target user's expressed preference for race because it increases the chance of a positive outcome. In practice, the merit for picking a candidate for recommendation is the combination of his/her level of compliance with the target user's sensitive preferences, and the estimated probability of their match. In the meritocratic sense, this serves as a 'minimal guarantee of fairness' [13]: any candidate who is presently more qualified than another candidate should have a better (or at least equal) chance of exposure as the less qualified candidate. Thus, the task of a preferentially fair matchmaker is to calibrate its recommendations by mapping the user's preference to the distribution of a sensitive attribute in the candidate pool.

4.2   Model

To make calibration possible, we need to find the optimal mean μ_u^* for the race attribute of the generated k-sized recommendation list for user u. The mean μ_u^* should reflect the distribution of this attribute in the candidate pool in proportion to the user's expressed preference for race. For our running example, let us consider a binary sensitive attribute $a \in \{0, 1\}$, and the user's associated degree of preference for this attribute, $p_u \in [0, 1]$. Let $A_C = (a_1, a_2, \cdots, a_n)$ denote the attribute distribution of the complete candidate pool C, and define the two values μ_{max} and μ_{A_c} to be the mean of the k largest attribute values in A_C and the mean of all the n attribute values in A_C, respectively. According to the previously defined idea of fairness, we can define the optimal mean as:

$$\mu_u^* = (1 - p_u) \cdot \mu_{A_C} + p_u \cdot \mu_{max} \tag{2}$$

Further, let $A_u = (a_1, a_2, \cdots, a_k), k < n$ be the attribute distribution of the recommendation list for user u. By analogy, μ_{A_u} is the mean of the attribute values in A_u.

If we encode the race attribute for user u such that the value of 0 denotes 'other race' and the value of 1 denotes 'own race', it is easy to see that the above equation satisfies both edge cases presented earlier. For $p_u = 1$ (strong preference), the optimal mean enforces the maximal skewness of recommendations

---

[2] The assumption of proportionality may not hold for all individuals. More user studies are needed to better understand what users actually mean by 'no racial preference'.

towards own-race partners, whereas for $p_u = 0$ (weak preference), the optimal mean reduces to the mean of the candidate pool.

Therefore, the calibrated fairness of a recommendation list can be expressed by its closeness to the optimal mean. To be able to quantify this fairness on a $[0, 1]$ scale, we first compute its offset from the optimal mean, $\delta_u = |\mu_u^* - \mu_{A_u}|$. We then find the minimum and the maximum offsets $\delta_{min} = \min_\mu |\mu_u^* - \mu|$ and $\delta_{max} = \max_\mu |\mu_u^* - \mu|$, where the means μ are taken over all possible item combinations of size k from the candidate pool, C. This allows us to formally define the *preferential fairness* ϕ_u of a given user's recommendation list as follows:

$$\phi_u \stackrel{\text{def}}{=} 1 - \frac{\delta_u - \delta_{min}}{\delta_{max} - \delta_{min}}, \tag{3}$$

where the term $(\delta_u - \delta_{min})/(\delta_{max} - \delta_{min})$ represents the *unfairness penalty* henceforth denoted by ε_u.

In the extreme case when all candidates share the same attribute value (e.g. they are all of the same race), we simply set $\phi_u = 1$ to avoid division by zero. ϕ_u takes values from 0 to 1, where higher values suggest greater fairness and we can also express it as a percentage score.

5   Re-ranking Methods

The above measure allows us to quantify the fairness of recommendations with respect to the user's sensitive preferences. Further, it can be used to constrain a potentially biased recommender system in order to make it fair(er). As mentioned earlier, the recommender system is essentially a binary classifier which outputs a vector of matching scores for all the candidates, and recommends the ones above some threshold value, θ. The generated predictions can be optimized for fairness using re-ranking methods, with the possibility to control the accuracy-fairness trade-off via a tolerance constant $\alpha \in [0, 1]$. We refer to the resulting solutions as α-fair recommendations, whose fairness is bounded by the condition $\varepsilon_u \leq \alpha$.

5.1   Knapsack

One way of modelling the accuracy-fairness trade-off is by viewing it as a variant of a *0–1 Knapsack problem* (KP). In its classical formulation, we are given a set of items $\{x_i\}_{i=1}^n$ each with a weight $w_i > 0$ and a value $v_i > 0$, and are tasked with filling the knapsack with items that would maximize its total value without exceeding its upper bound on the weight capacity W:

$$\max \sum_{i=1}^n v_i x_i$$

$$\text{subject to} \sum_{i=1}^n w_i x_i \leq W, \text{and } x_i \in \{0, 1\} \tag{4}$$

The Knapsack problem is NP-complete, and can be solved to optimality using dynamic programming (DP) in pseudo-polynomial time [19].

Equation 4 clearly resembles our task of maximizing the overall accuracy of recommendations (i.e. the sum of prediction scores) without exceeding the unfairness score ε_u bounded by α. Let A_C and S_C denote the attribute vector and the prediction score vector of the candidate itemset, respectively. Knapsack weights and values can then be represented as $w_i = A_C[i]$ and $v_i = S_C[i]$, for $1 \leq i \leq n$, where $n = |C|$ is the total number of candidates. Because the resulting capacity of our knapsack (i.e. the sum of attribute values) must be evaluated in terms of its (un)fairness, two important adaptations are needed.

Adaptation 1: Lower Bound on Capacity. The tolerance constant α basically defines the allowed range of means for the attribute vector of a candidate solution. Hence, there is a need to satisfy not only the upper bound (as in the classical KP), but also the *lower bound* on the knapsack capacity in the DP algorithm, i.e. $\sum_{i=1}^{n} w_i x_i \geq W_L$. This variant of the Knapsack problem has rarely been addressed in the literature (we are only aware of two works, namely [4,29]).

To compute the bounds satisfying the given tolerance α, we first find the corresponding δ_α offset:

$$\delta_\alpha = (1 - \alpha) \cdot \delta_{min} + \alpha \cdot \delta_{max} \tag{5}$$

Let $\mu_L = \max(\mu_u^* - \delta_\alpha, \mu_{min})$ and $\mu_U = \min(\mu_u^* + \delta_\alpha, \mu_{max})$. Then any α-fair solution R^α must have its attribute mean in the interval $\mu_L \leq \mu_{A_{R^\alpha}} \leq \mu_U$.

Considering that $\mu_{A_{R^\alpha}} = \frac{\sum_{w \in A_{R^\alpha}} w}{|R^\alpha|}$, we get:

$$W_L \stackrel{\text{def}}{=} |R^\alpha| \cdot \mu_L \leq \sum_{w \in A_{R^\alpha}} w \leq |R^\alpha| \cdot \mu_U \stackrel{\text{def}}{=} W_U \tag{6}$$

The above equation defines the bounds on the knapsack capacity guaranteeing α-fairness at size $k = |R^\alpha|$.

Adaptation 2: Exact-k Solution. The original KP formulation does not restrict the size of a solution. Since the computation of fairness is done for some specific list size k, we introduce a new constraint: $\sum_{i=1}^{n} x_i = k$. This variant is known as the *exact k-item Knapsack problem* (E-kKP) [5], and can be solved by adding a 3rd dimension to the DP algorithm to keep track of the knapsack size.

Since our end goal is to find the most accurate ranking of arbitrary size such that it satisfies the fairness constraint, we run a separate instance of E-kKP for each $k = 1, \ldots, n-1$ to obtain a set of α-fair solutions $\mathcal{F} = \{R_k^\alpha\}_{k=1}^{n-1}$, where R_k^α is a proper subset of C. Note that the DP algorithm simply optimizes the sum of item values without distinguishing between positive ($v_i \geq \theta$) and negative ($v_i < \theta$) predictions. Since KP does not support negative values, we introduce a *relevance criterion* that allows us to pick the optimal solution R^* as follows:

$$R^* = \underset{R^\alpha \in \mathcal{F}}{\arg\max} \ \frac{\min(|R|, |R^\alpha|)}{\max(|R|, |R^\alpha|)} \cdot \left(\sum_{v \in S_{R^\alpha}} v - \theta \right) \tag{7}$$

where R is the original (presumably unfair) recommendation list, and S_{R^α} is the prediction score vector of an α-fair solution, R^α.

The first factor in Eq. 7 optimizes the F1 score by penalizing solutions whose sizes diverge from the original recommendation list (causing losses in precision or recall), whereas the second one penalizes solutions containing negative predictions. The criterion is generalizable to any re-ranking method, and can potentially be adjusted to optimize other measures of interest.

Adapted KP. The above adaptations are unified in a KP variant with cardinality and dual capacity constraints:

$$\max \sum_{i=1}^{n} v_i x_i$$

$$\text{subject to } W_L \leq \sum_{i=1}^{n} w_i x_i \leq W_U, \sum_{i=1}^{n} x_i = k, x_i \in \{0,1\} \tag{8}$$

A DP solution can be constructed based on the following recurrence relation:

$$T[i,k,l,u] = \max \begin{cases} T[i-1,k,l,u], \\ \text{if} \sum_{w \in \{k \text{ largest of } \{w_j\}_{j=i}^{n}\}} w \geq l \\ \\ T[i-1,k-1,l-w_i,u-w_i] + v_i, \\ \text{if} \sum_{w \in \{k-1 \text{ largest of } \{w_j\}_{j=i}^{n}\}} w \geq l - w_i, w_i \leq u \end{cases} \tag{9}$$

where indices i, k, l, u correspond, respectively, to item index, solution size, capacity lower bound, capacity upper bound.

Since for binary attributes the upper bound is at most n, the overall time complexity of the KP re-ranking algorithm is $\mathcal{O}(n^4)$, yielding an optimal solution that would otherwise require $\mathcal{O}(n \cdot 2^n)$ time to compute the score in Eq. 7 in the case of an exhaustive search.

It turns out that a special case of KP can also be used to speed up the computation of the fairness measure. Recall that it relies on quantities δ_{min} and δ_{max}, where the former is expensive to compute as it requires enumerating all combinations. An alternative solution is to formulate it as a *subset sum* problem [1], which is a variant of KP with item values being equal to their weights. The goal is to determine if some subset of items sums up to a predefined number t. In our case, $t = k\mu^*$. But instead of searching for exact matches, we seek a subset whose sum of values is *the closest* to t. Again, we use DP to fill in the memoization array $T[n,k,W_u]$, from which it is easy to compute δ_{min}:

$$\delta_{min} = \underset{j=1,\dots,W_U}{\arg\min} \frac{|t - T[n,k,j]|}{k} \tag{10}$$

Continuous Attributes. To use KP with continuous attributes, we simply multiply the fractional weights by a scaling factor and take the integer part. Clearly, the choice of a scaling factor will affect the precision of the solution and the running time. This would allow us to work with attributes that contain, for instance, probabilities of candidates being of the same religion as the target user.

5.2 Tabu Search

Another re-ranking method we develop is a hill climbing heuristic based on *Tabu search*. It starts with an initial solution and gradually improves it according to some optimization criterion until the stopping condition is met. Unlike Knapsack, Tabu search does not guarantee an optimal solution, but has the advantage of finding a good approximation fast[3].

Here, the initial solution is the original (presumably unfair) recommendation list R. In each iteration, the algorithm chooses between two types of operations:

1. Adding the highest-scored item from $C \setminus R$ to R, yielding the solution R^+
2. Removing the lowest-scored item from R, yielding the solution R^-

To drive these choices, the algorithm evaluates both possibilities using the criterion given in Eq. 7 with $\mathcal{F} = \{R^+, R^-\}$, and selects the maximum one. The 'tabu' part restricts the neighborhood of candidates to those that:

1. Will move the resulting mean in the direction of μ_u^*
2. Have not been used in the previous iteration(s)

This is implemented by maintaining a dynamic tabu list containing currently prohibited items. The algorithm terminates as soon as the unfairness penalty ε_u of the solution becomes lower or equal to the chosen tolerance α.

Continuous Attributes. Escaping from local minima can be challenging for Tabu search in case of continuous attributes. We solve this by employing a restarting mechanism that is triggered when a limit of iterations has been reached. With each algorithm restart, the size of the tabu list is incremented by 1.

6 Experimental Results

We implement a matchmaker for speed dating[4] as described in Sect. 2.1, using four different classifiers: Logistic Regression, Random Forest, XGBoost, and Gaussian Naive Bayes. The target label is 'match' (i.e. reciprocal liking). Our implementation follows the standard pipeline involving missing data imputation, feature selection/encoding, and hyperparameter tuning. After the pre-processing step, there are 39 total attributes describing each pair of potential dating partners. We measure the F1 score and the fairness (in %) of generated recommendations before and after re-ranking. We set $\alpha = 0$ to enforce 100% fair solutions.

---

[3] Due to the termination criterion, the precise running time of Tabu search is unknown.
[4] Source code: https://git.io/preferential_fairness.

6.1   Racial Bias

We first resolve the *racial* bias of recommendations on the basis of two attributes: (a) the 'same-race importance' attribute expressed by the user on an ordinal scale from 1 to 10, and (b) the binary 'same race' attribute indicating whether the given pair belongs to the same race (in essence, this attribute is a result of collapsing a complex multivalued 'race' variable into a single binary one)[5]. For re-ranking, we employ the two methods introduced in the previous section. The results are summarized in Table 1.

6.2   Religious Bias

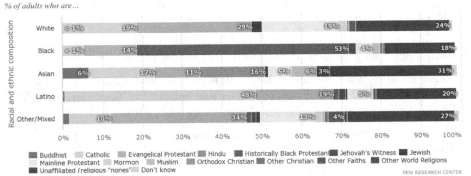

Fig. 2. Religious tradition by race/ethnicity [22]

Resolving the *religious* bias requires a slightly more involved procedure. For reasons beyond our knowledge, the speed dating dataset only provides the 'importance of the same religion' preferential attribute, without the corresponding 'same religion' attribute on which re-ranking methods could rely. One way to address the problem is to estimate the missing attribute probabilistically from external data sources. Although possibly lacking in precision, such estimates are commonly acceptable for illustration purposes (e.g. inferring race from profile pictures, as done in [23]). We make our estimation of religion on the basis of the U.S. religious landscape study [22]. It contains statistics about the racial and ethnic composition by religious group, covering all 50 U.S. states[6]; see Fig. 2. Let $X = \{x_1, x_2, \cdots, x_n\}$ be the set of n religions and $Y = \{y_1, y_2, \cdots, y_m\}$ be the set of m races. Given the knowledge about the races of users, the probability of two users u_1 and u_2 being of the same religion can be estimated as follows: $\mathbb{P}(x_{u_1} = x_{u_2}|y_{u_1}, y_{u_2}) = \sum_{x \in X} \mathbb{P}(x|y_{u_1}) \cdot \mathbb{P}(x|y_{u_2})$.

---

[5] A limitation of this approach is that it cannot properly match participants having biracial or multiracial identity.

[6] Although the speed dating study also took place in the U.S., we allow some margin of error due to state-to-state variability of racial/religious composition.

Table 1. Re-ranking under *racial* fairness constraints

Measure	Original	Fair (Knapsack)	Fair (Tabu)
Logistic Regression			
F1 score	0.2647	0.2566	0.2530
Fairness	54.71%	100%	100%
Random Forest			
F1 score	0.2524	0.2466	0.2467
Fairness	53.28%	100%	100%
XGBoost			
F1 score	0.2625	0.2526	0.2592
Fairness	51.99%	100%	100%
Gaussian Naive Bayes			
F1 score	0.2357	0.2379	0.2334
Fairness	52.63%	100%	100%

Table 2. Re-ranking under *religious* fairness constraints

Measure	Original	Fair (Knapsack)	Fair (Tabu)
Logistic Regression			
F1 score	0.2647	0.2473	0.2390
Fairness	56.31%	100%	100%
Random Forest			
F1 score	0.2524	0.2368	0.2378
Fairness	52.31%	100%	100%
XGBoost			
F1 score	0.2625	0.2479	0.2559
Fairness	49.69%	100%	100%
Gaussian Naive Bayes			
F1 score	0.2357	0.2339	0.2298
Fairness	58.63%	100%	100%

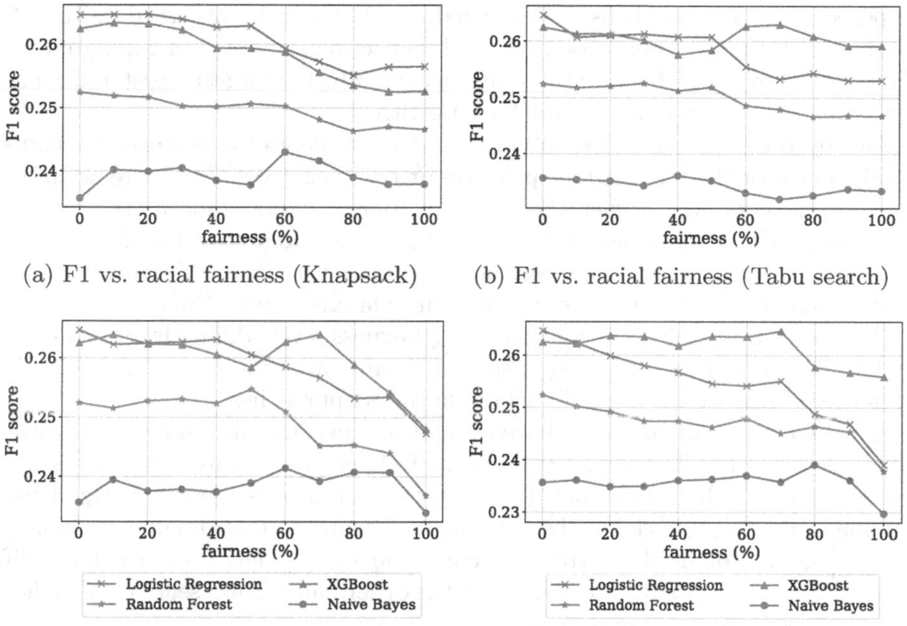

(a) F1 vs. racial fairness (Knapsack)   (b) F1 vs. racial fairness (Tabu search)

(c) F1 vs. religious fairness (Knapsack)   (d) F1 vs. religious fairness (Tabu search)

Fig. 3. F1 score vs. fairness

After the analysis, the lowest and the highest estimates correspond, respectively, to combinations $\langle Black, Asian \rangle$ with $\mathbb{P} = 0.09$, and $\langle Black, Black \rangle$ with $\mathbb{P} = 0.34$.

To use re-ranking methods with probabilistic attributes, we apply the methodologies described in the previous section. For Knapsack, we multiply all weights by a scaling factor of 10^3 to keep good balance between running time and precision of a DP algorithm. For Tabu search, we employ a restarting mechanism to escape from local optima. We set the initial tabu list size to 2, and the limit of iterations to 100. According to our observations, it can take up to 5 algorithm restarts to obtain a solution. However, occasions like these have been very rare. The results of re-ranking with religious preferences are summarized in Table 2. To better see the impact of re-ranking on accuracy at various fairness levels, we compare their trade-off for racial and religious preferences in Fig. 3.

6.3 Discussion

It appears that the preferential fairness of off-the-shelf classifiers before re-ranking does not exceed 55% for race, and 59% for religion (column 'Original' in Tables 1 and 2). Nevertheless, maximizing fairness from the state of being nearly 'half fair' in the beginning is possible with minimal accuracy losses thanks to the proposed re-ranking methods. As expected, the losses in F1 observed in Table 2 are more substantial than those in Table 1, reflecting a more demanding nature of re-ranking over non-binary attributes. Specifically, the largest registered accuracy drop is 9.7% for religion, and 4.4% for race.

During the experiments, we observe that re-ranking of a non-oracle recommender occasionally triggers true positives or true negatives. The more accurate the recommender, the higher the loss due to re-ranking. Indeed, the largest decrease in F1 score is associated with our most accurate classifier, Logistic Regression. Conversely, our least accurate classifier—Naive Bayes—actually enjoys a small increase in F1 after re-ranking via Knapsack (Table 1).

The trajectory of F1 loss for increasing fairness levels differs from model to model (Fig. 3). In general, we see a steeper decline in accuracy for probabilistic attributes (Figs. 3c, d), especially as the fairness approaches 100%.

The two re-ranking methods have comparable performance in practice, without a clear winner. The choice of a method should be dictated by the nature of a sensitive attribute (whether it is binary or continuous), and the size of the candidate pool. Knapsack has the advantage of guaranteed optimality for binary attributes, and potentially better runtime efficiency for continuous attributes (if a reasonable scaling factor is chosen). On the other hand, Tabu search has higher efficiency for larger candidate pools.

In view of the modest accuracy compromises, and of the legal and ethical ramifications of racially and religiously biased predictions, the use of re-ranking is easily justifiable.

7   Conclusion

In response to the provided evidence for algorithmically biased matchmaking, we introduce the notion of *preferential fairness* – a special case of calibrated fairness, where the user's preference for the sensitive attribute and its distribution in the candidate pool set the merit for choosing the right candidates for recommendation. Using the proposed fairness measure and re-ranking algorithms, we show how to quantify and eliminate racial and religious bias in the outputs of matchmaking classifiers for speed dating. This measure can be useful in other domains where the preferential aspect of fairness is the key factor for establishing the ethicality of recommendations.

As a theoretical contribution, we have formulated and solved the Knapsack problem with cardinality and dual capacity constraints, which guarantees optimality in re-ranking. We also present a variation of Tabu search, offering potentially better scalability and comparable re-ranking performance. Both methods are driven by the proposed relevance criterion, which maximizes the accuracy of fair recommendations to a user. Contrary to the established 'top-k' standard, we address a harder problem of generating recommendations with a dynamic cut-off. Our methodology can be generalized to other scenarios where multi-objective, variable-size recommendations are meaningful. Re-ranking under multiple fairness constraints would be an interesting avenue for future work.

To conclude, we agree with the vision that future designs and policies of matchmaking services should strive to discourage users from expressing socially sensitive preferences to protect the dignity and self-esteem of the concerned minority groups [11]. We show that when such preferences do exist, the proposed methodology can aid in assessing and de-biasing the output of a recommender system for the affected user.

References

1. Alfonsín, R.J.: On variations of the subset sum problem. Discrete Appl. Math. **81**(1–3), 1–7 (1998)
2. Biega, A.J., Gummadi, K.P., Weikum, G.: Equity of attention: amortizing individual fairness in rankings. In: The 41st International ACM SIGIR Conference on Research & Development in Information Retrieval, SIGIR 2018, pp. 405–414. ACM (2018)
3. Burke, R.: Multisided fairness for recommendation. CoRR abs/1707.00093 (2017). http://arxiv.org/abs/1707.00093
4. Cappanera, P., Trubian, M.: A local-search-based heuristic for the demand-constrained multidimensional knapsack problem. INFORMS J. Comput. **17**(1), 82–98 (2005)
5. Caprara, A., Kellerer, H., Pferschy, U., Pisinger, D.: Approximation algorithms for knapsack problems with cardinality constraints. Eur. J. Oper. Res. **123**(2), 333–345 (2000)
6. Dwork, C., Hardt, M., Pitassi, T., Reingold, O., Zemel, R.: Fairness through awareness. In: Proceedings of the 3rd Innovations in Theoretical Computer Science Conference, pp. 214–226. ACM (2012)
7. Fisman, R., Iyengar, S.S., Kamenica, E., Simonson, I.: Gender differences in mate selection: evidence from a speed dating experiment. Q. J. Econ. **121**(2), 673–697 (2006)
8. Fisman, R., Iyengar, S.S., Kamenica, E., Simonson, I.: Racial preferences in dating. Rev. Econ. Stud. **75**(1), 117–132 (2008)

9. Gajane, P., Pechenizkiy, M.: On formalizing fairness in prediction with machine learning. CoRR abs/1710.03184 (2017). http://arxiv.org/abs/1710.03184

10. Gosepath, S.: Equality. In: Zalta, E.N. (ed.) The Stanford Encyclopedia of Philosophy, 2011 edn. Metaphysics Research Lab, Stanford University, Spring (2011)

11. Hutson, J.A., Taft, J.G., Barocas, S., Levy, K.: Debiasing desire: addressing bias & discrimination on intimate platforms. Proc. ACM Hum.-Comput. Interact. 2(CSCW), 73:1–73:18 (2018)

12. Joel, S., Eastwick, P.W., Finkel, E.J.: Is romantic desire predictable? Machine learning applied to initial romantic attraction. Psychol. Sci. 28(10), 1478–1489 (2017)

13. Joseph, M., Kearns, M., Morgenstern, J., Neel, S., Roth, A.: Meritocratic fairness for infinite and contextual bandits. In: Proceedings of the 2018 AAAI/ACM Conference on AI, Ethics, and Society, AIES 2018, pp. 158–163. ACM (2018)

14. Kamishima, T., Akaho, S., Asoh, H.: Enhancement of the neutrality in recommendation. In: Proceedings of the 2nd Workshop on Human Decision Making in Recommender Systems, pp. 8–14 (2012)

15. Karako, C., Manggala, P.: Using image fairness representations in diversity-based re-ranking for recommendations. In: Adjunct Publication of the 26th Conference on User Modeling, Adaptation and Personalization, UMAP 2018, pp. 23–28. ACM (2018)

16. Kyriakidi, M., Stefanidis, K., Ioannidis, Y.: On achieving diversity in recommender systems. In: Proceedings of the ExploreDB 2017, pp. 4:1–4:6. ACM (2017)

17. Liu, W., Burke, R.: Personalizing fairness-aware re-ranking. CoRR abs/1809.02921 (2018). http://arxiv.org/abs/1809.02921

18. Liu, Y., Radanovic, G., Dimitrakakis, C., Mandal, D., Parkes, D.C.: Calibrated fairness in bandits. In: Proceedings of the 4th Workshop on Fairness, Accountability, and Transparency in Machine Learning (Fat/ML 2017) (2017). https://arxiv.org/abs/1707.01875

19. Martello, S., Toth, P.: Algorithms for knapsack problems. North-Holland Math. Stud. 132, 213–257 (1987)

20. Notopoulos, K.: The dating app that knows you secretly aren't into guys from other races, January 2016. https://www.buzzfeednews.com/article/katienotopoulos/coffee-meets-bagel-racial-preferences. Accessed 26 June 2019

21. Pazzani, M.J.: A framework for collaborative, content-based and demographic filtering. Artif. Intell. Rev. 13(5–6), 393–408 (1999)

22. Pew Research Center: Racial and ethnic composition by religious group (2014). https://www.pewforum.org/religious-landscape-study/racial-and-ethnic-composition/. Accessed 09 July 2019

23. Sapiezynski, P., Zeng, W., Robertson, R.E., Mislove, A., Wilson, C.: Quantifying the impact of user attention on fair group representation in ranked lists. In: Companion Proceedings of the 2019 World Wide Web Conference, WWW 2019, pp. 553–562. ACM (2019)

24. Saxena, N.A., Huang, K., DeFilippis, E., Radanovic, G., Parkes, D.C., Liu, Y.: How do fairness definitions fare?: examining public attitudes towards algorithmic definitions of fairness. In: Proceedings of the 2019 AAAI/ACM Conference on AI, Ethics, and Society, AIES 2019, pp. 99–106. ACM (2019)

25. Steck, H.: Calibrated recommendations. In: Proceedings of the 12th ACM Conference on Recommender Systems, pp. 154–162. ACM (2018)

26. Van Der Zon, S.B.: Predictive performance and discrimination in unbalanced classification. Master's thesis, TU Eindhoven (2016)

27. Verma, S., Rubin, J.: Fairness definitions explained. In: Proceedings of the International Workshop on Software Fairness, FairWare 2018, pp. 1–7. ACM (2018)
28. Xiao, L., Min, Z., Yongfeng, Z., Zhaoquan, G., Yiqun, L., Shaoping, M.: Fairness-aware group recommendation with pareto-efficiency. In: Proceedings of the Eleventh ACM Conference on Recommender Systems, RecSys 2017, pp. 107–115. ACM (2017)
29. Xu, Z.: The knapsack problem with a minimum filling constraint. Naval Res. Logist. **60**(1), 56–63 (2013)
30. Yang, K., Stoyanovich, J.: Measuring fairness in ranked outputs. In: Proceedings of the 29th International Conference on Scientific and Statistical Database Management, pp. 22:1–22:6. ACM (2017)
31. Yao, S., Huang, B.: New fairness metrics for recommendation that embrace differences. CoRR abs/1706.09838 (2017). http://arxiv.org/abs/1706.09838
32. Zehlike, M., Bonchi, F., Castillo, C., Hajian, S., Megahed, M., Baeza-Yates, R.: FA*IR: a fair top-k ranking algorithm. In: Proceedings of the 2017 ACM on Conference on Information and Knowledge Management, CIKM 2017, pp. 1569–1578. ACM (2017)
33. Zheng, Y., Dave, T., Mishra, N., Kumar, H.: Fairness in reciprocal recommendations: a speed-dating study. In: Adjunct Publication of the 26th Conference on User Modeling, Adaptation and Personalization, UMAP 2018, pp. 29–34. ACM (2018)
34. Zhu, Z., Hu, X., Caverlee, J.: Fairness-aware tensor-based recommendation. In: Proceedings of the 27th ACM International Conference on Information and Knowledge Management, CIKM 2018, pp. 1153–1162. ACM (2018)

Recommendation Filtering à la carte for Intelligent Tutoring Systems

Wesley Silva[1]([✉])[iD], Marcos Spalenza[1][iD], Jean-Rémi Bourguet[2][iD], and Elias de Oliveira[1][iD]

[1] Federal University of Espírito Santo,
Av. Fernando Ferrari, 514 - Goiabeiras, Vitória, ES 29075-910, Brazil
{wpsilva,mspalenza,elias}@lcad.inf.ufes.br
[2] Vila Velha University, Av. Comissário José Dantas de Melo, 21,
Vila Velha, ES 29102-920, Brazil
jean-remi.bourguet@uvv.br

Abstract. In computerized adaptive testing, the activities have to be well adjusted to the latent knowledge of the students. Collaborative and content-based filters are usually considered as two solutions of data-centric approach using the evaluation data to uncover the student abilities. Nevertheless, past lecturer recommendations can induced possible bias by using a single and immutable training set. We try to reduce this issue by releasing a hybrid recommendation filtering. Our approach is supported by the Item Response Theory and techniques of clustering to output purely objective recommendation filters selecting activities and building an evaluation path based on historical evolutions of past students. In this paper, we particularly highlight the crucial clustering task by offering plots and metrics to adjust the decisions of the practitioners.

Keywords: Item response theory · Clustering · Recommendation-based system · Collaborative filtering · Content-based filtering

1 Introduction

Among the innumerous services acting as recommendation-based systems, applications that support users to order their meals (e.g. Ifood, Uber Eats) recently stand out from the others. They are now focused on better understanding eaters intentions and particularly when eaters do not know really what they want to eat. Such recommendation systems, if based on history and comparisons with other eaters, would recommend items that were already chosen by eaters with similar behaviors. This kind of recommendations is based on a collaborative filtering approach (see [4]). With this a priori knowledge, it can be generated a group of similar users in terms of interest and performed a set of recommendations based on singular characteristics analysis in the group. On the other hand, if the eater reports a preference for a specific types of cuisine, the recommendation system would check, in terms of contents, which items would have a

L. Boratto et al. (Eds.): BIAS 2020, CCIS 1245, pp. 58–65, 2020.
https://doi.org/10.1007/978-3-030-52485-2_6

high similarity based on the elicited preferences. This kind of recommendations is called content-based filtering (see [7]). Finally, the hybrid recommendation filtering combines two or more techniques (i.e. collaborative and content-based), in order to reduce the limitations of a single technique (see [11]).

Similar cases exist with computerized adaptive testing, especially when teachers have to select assessment items *à la carte* according to some expected performances from their students. Considering ongoing grades in a discipline, it is possible to cluster current and past students by the similarity of their performances in different levels of the teaching-learning process. In seminal works presented in [5], collaborative filters select assessment items that are expected to be the most compatible by mimicking past lecturer recommendations.

We propose to reduce the possible immutable bias induced by lecturers by releasing different kinds of purely objective recommendation filters. By grouping students based on their similar past performances our filters build an evaluation path that may maximize the students' future performances. The characterization of the assessment items is supported by the Item Response Theory (IRT) that generates descriptors based on probabilities of success in function of presupposed student latent traits. IRT allows both qualitative and quantitative items analysis to support the construction of an evaluation path [6]. Therefore, our hybrid recommendation filtering deals with both the students characteristics and the probabilities of success or fail. With our data processing, we can select a neat sequence of items to build a tailored evaluation path *à la carte* for each student. If a student has a certain ongoing latent trait, our recommendation filters can progressively route this student through a steady and coherent evaluation path. By identifying their weaknesses and strengths, such filters recommend the most suitable activities to improve students performances. Therefore, our approach tries to soften the exams recommending questions guided by the detections of students learning gaps as promoted in [8]. In this paper, we particularly highlight the crucial clustering task by offering plots and metrics to adjust the decisions of the practitioners.

The organization of this paper is structured as follows. In Sect. 2, we introduce the theories and techniques that support our methodology. The description of our filtering-based approach and particularly the clustering phase is presented in Sect. 3. Finally, we conclude the paper with some remarks and perspectives in Sect. 4.

2   Background

As evoked in the previous section, seminal works have proposed to employ clustering and classification-based techniques to bridge learning gaps through text processing [5]. In this paper, we extend this approach by using IRT. The remainder of this section will present the aforementioned techniques and theories.

2.1   Clustering

The clustering process aims to identify students who are similar to others according to their performances. Clustering by the *k-means* technique establishes centroids according to a specified number *k*. In our case, we assume three groups of performances in a classroom: a high, medium and low performing group. Similarity by cosine distance was used to classify students in the clusters. The evaluation of the clusters was performed by checking the distribution density of the grades in each cluster.

2.2   Item Response Theory

IRT [1] has been considered by many experts as a milestone for the modern Psychometrics and an extension of the Classical Test Theory (CTT). While CTT is founded on the proposition that measurement error, a random latent variable, is a component of the evaluation score [12], IRT considers the probability of getting particular items right or wrong given the ability of the examinees. Each examinee possesses some amount of the underlying ability (also called latent trait) materialized as an ability score (i.e. a numerical value denoted θ) on a rating scale. IRT advocates that depending of a certain ability level, there will naturally be a probability denoted $P(\theta)$ with which an examinee will answer correctly to the item. This probability depends on three parameters: i-th difficulty of an item i denoted $\delta(i)$ is the ability score which corresponds to a probability of success; the discrimination of an item i denoted $\alpha(i)$ is its discriminative power, i.e. its capacity to differentiate examinees (i.e. distinguish those who succeed from those who fail the item) in relation to their underlying ability score; the pseudo-guessing of an item i denoted $\gamma(i)$ is the probability of success in the item corresponding to the minimal underlying ability score. Equation 1 presents the probability with the three aforementioned parameters.

Let an item i and $\delta(i)$ (resp. $\alpha(i)$, $\gamma(i)$) its difficulty (resp. discrimination, pseudo-guessing), the probability of success in the item i for an examinee with an ability score of θ is defined as follow:

$$P(\theta) = \gamma(i) + \frac{1 - \gamma(i)}{1 + e^{-1.7\alpha(i)(\theta - \delta(i))}} \tag{1}$$

In the next section, we will describe our methodology to perform recommendation filtering *à la carte* and illustrate our approach through a simulation.

3   Methodology

We propose to compute models of performances by clustering similar students and recommending activities. Then, we intend to select items with a controlled probability of success that match with the estimated capacity of a given student.

We presuppose that a pool of activities P is stratified and sequentially organized such that $P = A^1 \cup \cdots \cup A^n = 0$ with A^i a set of activity corresponding to the i-th scope of a given discipline. The evaluation path of a student is a function returning the sequence of activities for each student $s_i \in S$ such that $E(s_i) = (A_i^0, \ldots, A_i^n)$ and $\forall j \in [\![1, n]\!]$ we have $A_i^j \subseteq A^j$, $|A_i^j| = N$ and $|A^j| = M$. Note that $a(k, A_i^t)$ returns the k-th activity from the set of the activities realized by the student s_i in the level t. Finally, the function $g : S, P \rightarrow [0, 1]$ will return the grade of a given student performing a given activity.

To compute our recommendation filtering-based approach, we used the clustering technique, in order to group similar students grades vectors. By considering each student's list of grades as a vector, a clustering algorithm is able to group the most similar vectors related to a centroid. On the other hand, to discriminate the evaluation items, our system can generate for each item the values of the so-called IRT parameter of difficulty, discrimination and pseudo-guessing. Figure 1 represents our iterative workflow of our approach.

Students   Clusters   Recommendation

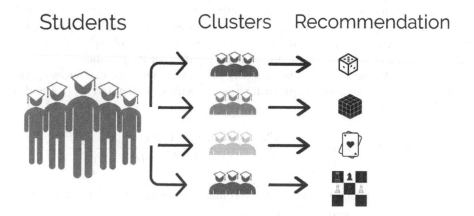

Fig. 1. Recommendation-based system workflow.

The first column represents all the students from a given class (each student can be represented through its current evaluation path). The second column represents a clustering performed in order to characterize groups of similar students with regard to their proper evaluation paths. Once such a task is performed, a recommendation is realized by applying different filters. The third column represent a filtering recommendation based on the predicted maximization of the students' future performances. Thus, by combining the information generated by IRT and clustering, our approach composes a personalized assessment path for each student through a recommendation filtering process as explained thereafter.

3.1   Recommendation Process

When a student will perform a new activity at a certain level t $(1 \leqslant t \leqslant n)$, the system considers that his latent trait is actually the pondered (by item difficulty δ) mean of all the grades obtained until to be confronted with the new activity as described in Eq. 2.

$$\theta_t(s_i) = \frac{1}{t} \sum_{j=1}^{t} \frac{\sum_{k=1}^{N} \delta(a(k, A_i^j)) \cdot g(s_i, a(k, A_i^j))}{\sum_{k=1}^{N} \delta(a(k, A_i^j))} \tag{2}$$

The set of past activities of a student at a given level t is outputted through the function $A^p : S \to P$. Each time a student performed a given set of activities, the vector of his past activities is upgraded by adding a new position at the end of the vector with the aforementioned activities. The function $g^p : S \to [0,1]^{t \times N}$ will associate a student with his current vector of grades.

Recommendation Filtering Guided by Difficulty
The first filter guides the recommendation by using the parameter of difficulty. After having upgraded the vector of past activities, we select the set of students $S(s_i)$ who performed the same past activities as those of the student s_i such that $S(s_i) = \{s_j | A^p(s_j) = A^p(s_i)\}$. Thus, we proceed to a clustering using the vector $g^p(s_i)$ together with the vectors of the set $\bigcup_{s_j \in S(s_i)} g^p(s_j)$. Note that a cluster is built in relation to the internal similarity ρ of its members.

Let $C_\rho(s_i)$ the set of students currently present in the same cluster as s_i, the set of the κ activities recommended for the student s_i is denoted $R_1^\kappa(s_i)$ and is described in the Eq. 3.

$$R_1^\kappa(s_i) = \underset{\substack{a \in A_j^{t+1} \\ s.t. \ s_j \in C_\rho(s_i)}}{\kappa \text{argmax}} \sum_{l=t+1}^{n} \frac{\sum_{k=1}^{N} \delta(a(k, A_j^l)) \ g(s_i, a(k, A_j^l))}{(n-t) \sum_{k=1}^{N} \delta(a(k, A_j^l))} \tag{3}$$

Note that κargmax will select the arguments from the κ maximum scores.

Recommendation Filtering Guided by Discrimination
The second filter guides the recommendation by using the parameter of discrimination. As explained in Sect. 2, the discrimination is the capacity to differentiate examinees (i.e. distinguish those who succeed from those who fail the item) in relation to their underlying ability score. The higher the value of the parameter α, the more the item is considered discriminating. To guide the interpretation of the parameter α, an evaluation grid is presented in [2]: null if $\alpha = 0$, very weak if $\alpha \in [0,01; 0,34]$, weak if $\alpha \in [0,35; 0,64]$, moderate if $\alpha \in [0,65; 1,34]$, strong if $\alpha \in [1,35; 1,69]$, very strong if $\alpha > 1,70$ and perfect if α tends to $+\infty$. In the case of our recommendation filtering, the student will be challenged by recommending an evaluation in a certain level of knowledge that corresponds to the student's latent trait. Instead of directly using the κargmax operator as previously, the system selects a set of items that correspond to the level of the student by applying a threshold parameter. Once selected, these items are ranked using their own parameters of discrimination. Let a student s_i at a level t, and his latent trait $\theta_t(s_i)$ as described in Eq. 2, the system builds a preorder $\leq$ on the set activities such that $\forall (a_j, a_k) \in A^{t+1}$ we have:

$$(a_j, a_k) \in \leq \Leftrightarrow |\theta_t(s_i) - \delta(a_j)| \leqslant |\theta_t(s_i) - \delta(a_k)| \tag{4}$$

Let d a threshold s.t. $d \in [\![N, M]\!]$, this filter selects the d-th closest difficulties in relation to the latent trait of the student by applying a function $D : S, A^k, N \rightarrow A^k$. After what, as described in Eq. 5, a κargmax operator is applied in order to select the κ items that will challenge the most the student.

$$R_2^\kappa(s_i) = \underset{a \in D(s_i, A^{t+1}, d)}{\kappa \text{argmax}} \alpha(a) \tag{5}$$

Recommendation Filtering Guided by Pseudo-Guessing
Note that the two last filters can be used together. Nevertheless, a third filter considers the pseudo-guessing parameter. With this filter, the chance can be minimized by selecting the activities with minimal pseudo-guessing as described in Eq. 6.

$$R_3^\kappa(s_i) = \underset{a \in D(s_i, A^{t+1}, d)}{\kappa \text{argmin}} \gamma(a) \tag{6}$$

Applying all the filters together, the system can allocate weights by setting different values for the parameters κ.

Let κ_1, κ_2, κ_3 the weights for the different recommendation filters $R_1^{\kappa_1}$, $R_2^{\kappa_2}$ and $R_3^{\kappa_3}$, a recommended set of activities for a given student is described in Eq. 7.

$$W(s_i) = \bigcap_{j \in [\![1,3]\!]} R_j^{\kappa_j}(s_i) \tag{7}$$

3.2   Clustering Phase

In our simulation, we used a dataset with 1000 students confronted with 10 activities from the example presented in [2]. Three clusters were generated[1] in order to support recommendations guided by difficulties as described in Sect. 3. Figure 2 shows the characteristics of the clustering task at the last level. The first plot shows the repartition of the grades means in each cluster for each activity. We can observe significant differences between the cluster 0, the cluster 1 and the cluster 2. In the second plot, we present the density of the Euclidean distances, demonstrating the differences of the grades vectors in each cluster. In this example, the cluster 2 appears much more homogeneous than the others. In the third plot, we present the cosine similarities in the clusters. In the fourth plot, the different p-values between pairs of clusters are observable.

This part of our approach supports an essential phase of our recommendation filter based on difficulty. By providing a set of metrics and plots to evaluate the efficiency of a given clustering task, the practitioners can adjust crucial hyperparameters like the number of clusters or the measure used to assess the distance.

---

[1] Our data processing is available at https://gitlab.com/rii_lcad/bias2020.

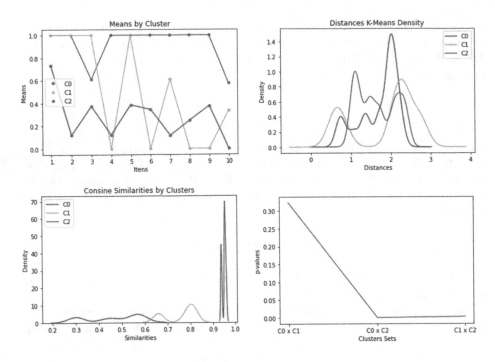

Fig. 2. Analysis of the clusters

4   Conclusion

Helping students to develop their skills usually requires changes in the assessment culture and the assessment practice [9]. The data gathered along the history of a discipline can be used to develop the effectiveness of the teaching-learning process. In [5], a prototype was released to recommend activities indicated for similar profiles by mimicking past lecturer recommendations. Such approach can induce possible bias by basing the whole recommendation system on a single training set. Thus, we try to reduce this aspect by using IRT and techniques of clustering to constantly output fresh recommendations based on items features. We use assessments of previous students to design an evaluation path *à la carte* in which the levels of knowledge of each student are frequently refreshed and contextualized across the set of available items. In this paper, we particularly focus our work on the crucial phase of clustering by offering a set of metrics and plots in order to adjust the decisions of the practitioners.

We argue that successful past actions may be applied to similar students in order to stimulate their developments through a tailored evaluation path. As future proposals, we intend to optimize the clustering techniques like those developed by [10]. We also plan to increase the statistical treatment of recommendations, as proposed by [3], with more adjusted models of IRT.

References

1. Baker, F.B.: The basics of item response theory. Education Resources Information Center (2001)
2. Baker, F.B., Kim, S.H.: The Basics of Item Response Theory Using R, 1st edn. Springer, Cham (2017). https://doi.org/10.1007/978-3-319-54205-8
3. Cúri, M., Silva, V.: Academic English proficiency assessment using a computerized adaptive test. Tendências em Matemática Aplicada e Computacional (São Carlos) **20**(2), 381–401 (2019)
4. Herlocker, J.L., Konstan, J.A., Terveen, L.G., Riedl, J.T.: Evaluating collaborative filtering recommender systems. ACM Trans. Inf. Syst. (TOIS) **22**(1), 5–53 (2004)
5. Oliveira, M.G., Marques Ciarelli, P., Oliveira, E.: Recommendation of programming activities by multi-label classification for a formative assessment of students. Expert Syst. Appl. **40**(16), 6641–6651 (2013)
6. Pasquali, L.: Psicometria - Teoria dos Testes na Psicologia e na Educação. Editora Vozes, Petrópolis (2004)
7. Pazzani, M.J., Billsus, D.: Content-based recommendation systems. In: Brusilovsky, P., Kobsa, A., Nejdl, W. (eds.) The Adaptive Web. LNCS, vol. 4321, pp. 325–341. Springer, Heidelberg (2007). https://doi.org/10.1007/978-3-540-72079-9_10
8. Perrenoud, P.: L'évaluation des élèves. De la fabrication de l'excellence à la régulation des apprentissages. De Boeck, Bruxelles (1998)
9. Segers, M., Dochy, F., Cascallar, E.: Optimising New Modes of Assessment: In Search of Qualities and Standards, vol. 1. Springer, Dordrecht (2006)
10. Spalenza, M.A., Pirovani, J.P.C., de Oliveira, E.: Structures discovering for optimizing external clustering validation metrics. In: 19th International Conference on Intelligent Systems Design and Applications (2019)
11. Thorat, P.B., Goudar, R., Barve, S.: Survey on collaborative filtering, content-based filtering and hybrid recommendation system. Int. J. Comput. Appl. **110**(4), 31–36 (2015)
12. Traub, R.E.: Classical test theory in historical perspective. Educ. Meas. **16**, 8–13 (1997)

bias goggles: Exploring the Bias of Web Domains Through the Eyes of Users

Giannis Konstantakis[1], Gianins Promponas[1], Manthos Dretakis[1], and Panagiotis Papadakos[1,2(✉)] (iD)

[1] Computer Science Department, University of Crete, Crete, Greece
{jkonstan,csd3522,csd3357}@csd.uoc.gr
[2] Institute of Computer Science, FORTH-ICS, Heraklion, Greece
papadako@ics.forth.gr

Abstract. Ethical issues, along with transparency, disinformation and bias are in the focus of our information society. In this demo, we will present the *bias goggles* system, that based on the web graph computes the bias characteristics of web domains to user-defined concepts. Our approach uses adaptations of propagation models and a variation of the pagerank algorithm named Biased-PR, that models various behaviours of biased surfers. Currently, the system runs over a subset of the greek web graph. We have developed cross-browser plugins that let users explore the bias characteristics of domains, define their own biased concepts and monitor the consumption of biased information through some analytics.

Keywords: Bias · Web graph · Propagations models · Biased pagerank · Browser plugins

1 Introduction

There is an increasing concern about the potential risks in the consumption of the abundant biased information in online platforms like Web Search Engines (WSEs) and social networks. Terms like echo chambers and filter-bubbles [2] depict the isolation of groups of people and its aftereffects that result from the selective and restricted exposure to information. This restriction can be the result of helpful personalized algorithms that suggest user connections or rank high information relevant to the users' profile. Yet, this isolation might inhibit the growth of informed and responsible humans/citizens/consumers, and can also be the result of malicious algorithms that promote and resurrect social, religious, ethnic, and other kinds of discriminations and stereotypes.

Currently, the community focus is towards the transparency, fairness and accountability of mostly machine learning algorithms for decision making, classification, and recommendation in social platforms like twitter. However, social

---

The original version of this chapter was revised: The title of the paper has been corrected as "bias goggles: Exploring the Bias of Web Domains Through the Eyes of Users". The correction to this chapter is available at https://doi.org/10.1007/978-3-030-52485-2_18

© Springer Nature Switzerland AG 2020, corrected publication 2020
L. Boratto et al. (Eds.): BIAS 2020, CCIS 1245, pp. 66–71, 2020.
https://doi.org/10.1007/978-3-030-52485-2_7

platforms and WSEs mainly act as gateways to information published on the web as common web pages (e.g., blogs and news). But, users are unaware of the bias characteristics of these pages, except from obvious facts like that a page in a political party's web site will be biased towards this party.

bias goggles is a system that allows users to explore the bias characteristics of web domains for a specific concept (i.e., a bias goggle). Since there is no objective definition about what bias and biased concepts are [3], we let users define them. For these concepts, the system computes the *support* and the *bias score* of the domains, using the *support* of this domain for each aspect of the biased concept. These *support* scores are calculated by graph-based algorithms that exploit the structure of the web graph and a set of user-defined seeds for each aspect of bias. As an example consider the bias goggle of "politics in Greece", which is defined using as aspects the 9 most popular greek political parties, and their homepages as seeds. More information about the model, its assumptions, the computation of *support* and *bias* scores, the propagation and `Biased-PR` algorithms, and an experimental evaluation, is provided in [1].

In this demo we showcase two front-ends that allow users to search the bias characteristics of web domains. The first one is a simple web-page that can be used for searching web domains over predefined biased concepts. The second one is a cross-browser plugin that allows users to define or search the available biased concepts and aspects of bias, explore and compare the bias characteristics of the web domains as they visit or show interest for specific web pages, and finally to monitor their behavior regarding the bias characteristics of the sites and the information they consume.

2 Implementation Discussion

2.1 Back-End

The developed prototype of the *bias goggles* system allows the exploration of biased concepts over a set of mainly greek domains. For gathering pages from the web, we have developed a crawler based on the open-source Java crawler4j[1] project, which is a multi-threaded but unfortunately non-distributed crawler. The rest of the system is also implemented in Java. Specifically, we have developed two propagation models and the `Biased-PR` algorithm, which is a variation of the PageRank algorithm that models a biased surfer. These algorithms exploit the structure of the web graph to compute the bias scores of the domains and can be used on demand. Further, we have developed highly efficient inverted-file indexes, that provide fast access to the bias scores of the crawled domains, and to any information related to the available biased concepts and aspects of bias. Such functionality includes searching specific biased concepts or aspects of bias, either over their descriptions or the names of the domains over which they are defined. On top of all this functionality we have implemented a REST-API based

---

[1] https://github.com/yasserg/crawler4j.

on the spark-java micro-services library[2], which is available at http://pangaia. ics.forth.gr:4567/bias-goggles-api/, that allows users to query and insert relevant information.

2.2 Front-Ends

Currently, we offer two different front-ends that provide access to the underlying information. The first one is a simple web-page that allows users to search the bias characteristics of web domains for two biased concepts: the "greek political parties" and the "greek football teams". Also, this page helps users to explore the currently crawled domains in descending order according to their bias scores for the two previously mentioned biased concepts. A screenshot of our web front-end that depicts the top-k biased results for the "greek political parties" goggle is given in Fig. 1. The web site is publicly accesible at http://pangaia.ics.forth. gr/bias-goggles.

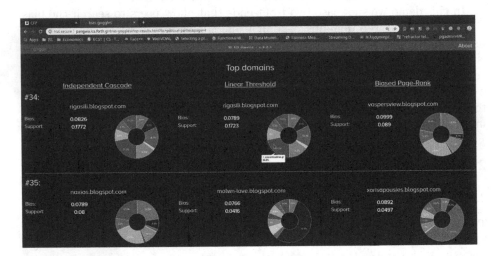

Fig. 1. A screenshot of the web interface, listing the top-biased domains for the Independent Cascade and Linear Threshold propagation models along with the `Biased-PR` algorithm.

We have also implemented cross-browser plugins[3] based on the WebExtensions API[4], along with a user friendlier sidebar extension[5] for Firefox. These plugins allow users to define their own bias goggles, retrieve the bias characteristics of the currently visited page and its linked pages, and compare the bias

---

[2] http://sparkjava.com/.
[3] The plugins have been tested only on the Firefox and Chrome/Chromium browsers.
[4] https://developer.mozilla.org/en-US/docs/Mozilla/Add-ons/WebExtensions.
[5] https://developer.mozilla.org/en-US/docs/Mozilla/Add-ons/WebExtensions/ user_interface/Sidebars.

scores of domains. Finally, they offer various analytics and graphs about the bias scores of the sites that a user has visited over a period of time for specific bias-goggles (e.g., average bias score, average support score, top-biased domains, etc.). Figure 2 depicts how the bias scores are shown for a specific web site, along with a comparison of the scores of 3 different domains in the Firefox sidebar plugin. Finally, Fig. 3 shows the UIs for searching and creating bias goggles, along with the analytics information in the Chrome plugin. The plugins will be made available in the prototype's web site in the near future.

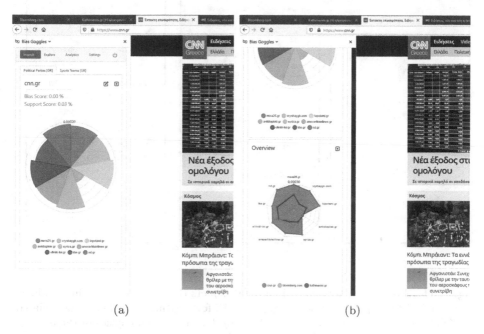

(a)   (b)

Fig. 2. The Firefox browser plugin. Figure (a) depicts the CNN.gr bias characteristics for the greek politics bias goggle, while Fig. (b) compares CNN.gr to bloomberg.com and the greek news paper kathimerini.gr.

3   Crawled Data

We have crawled a subset of the greek web by running four instances of the crawler: one with 383 sites related to the greek political life, one with 89 sport related greek sites, one with the top-300 popular greek sites according to Alexa, and a final one containing 127 seeds related to big greek industries. We blacklisted popular sites like facebook and twitter to control the size of our data and avoid crawling non-greek domains. The crawlers were restricted to depth seven for each domain, and free to follow any link to external domains. In total we downloaded 893,095 pages including 531,296,739 links, which lead to the non-connected **Support Flow Graph** (SFG)[6] of 90,419 domains, 288,740 links (on average 3.1 links per domain) and with a diameter $k = 7,944$. More information about the crawled pages, the hand-crafted gold standard that we used in our evaluation in [1], the SFG graph and the graph itself are available in the prototype's web site.

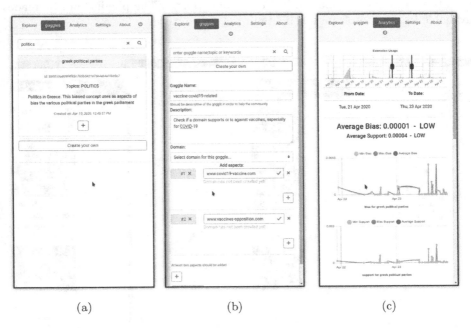

(a)   (b)   (c)

Fig. 3. The chrome browser plugin. Figure (a) depicts the results of searching available bias goggles for the query 'politics', Fig. (b) the UI for creating a new bias goggle related to COVID-19 and vaccines, and finally Fig. (c) depicts some analytics of the average bias and support scores over the consumed information for a specific period of time.

4   Performance Discussion

The most expensive part of our approach is the computation of the *support* scores of the domains for a specific bias goggle, due to the huge scale of the web graph. What is encouraging though is that the algorithms are applied to the much more compact SFG graph, that contains only the Second and Third Level Domains (SLDs & TLDs)[7] of the urls of the pages and their corresponding links, instead of the original web graph. In our experiments (reported in [1]), we have shown that one propagation model can be used in real-time to compute the *support*

---

[6] The SFG graph is the crawled graph, where the nodes are the crawled domains and the links are the corresponding inverse links.

[7] We follow the standard URL normalization method (see https://en.wikipedia.org/wiki/URL_normalization) and get the SLD/TLD of an url.

scores. On the other hand the whole process of computing the *support* scores of the domains for a specific bias goggle, can be considered an offline process. The user can submit his/her own bias concepts to the system and then query the results after being notified that the system has computed the required *support* scores. However, what is crucial, is the ability to let users explore in real-time the `bias` scores of the domains space for any precomputed and commonly used bias goggle. This can be easily supported by providing efficient ways to store and retrieve the computed *support* scores of domains, which we have implemented through appropriate indexes that allow the fast retrieval of offsets in files, where the *support* scores and the related metadata are stored. Given the above, the computation of the *bias score* of a domain for a bias goggle is rather fast.

5   Future Work

In the future, we plan to explore variations of the proposed approach where our assumptions do not hold. For example, currently we are trying to exploit the supportive, neutral or oppositive nature of the available links, as identified by sentiment analysis methods, along with the importance of the web pages they appear in. Content-based and hybrid approaches for computing the *support* scores of domains are also in our focus, as well as the exploitation of other available graphs, like the graph of friends, retweets, etc. In addition interesting aspects include how the *support* and *bias scores* of multiple biased concepts can be composed, providing interesting insights about possible correlations, as well as how the *bias* scores of domains change over time. Finally, our vision is to integrate the approach in a large scale WSE/social platform, in order to study how users define bias, create a globally accepted gold standard of biased concepts, and explore how such tools can affect the consumption of biased information. In this way, we will be able to evaluate and tune our approach to real-life scenarios, and mitigate any performance issues. Also, by conducting a large scale user study and releasing the plugins to the public, we will gather useful insights about how various users define bias and biased concepts. At the same time, based on the gathered user analytics we will be able to study how such tools affect online user behavior and the consumption of biased information.

References

1. Papadakos, P., Konstantakis, G.: bias goggles: graph-based computation of the bias of web domains through the eyes of users. In: Jose, J.M., et al. (eds.) ECIR 2020. LNCS, vol. 12035, pp. 790–804. Springer, Cham (2020). https://doi.org/10.1007/978-3-030-45439-5_52
2. Pariser, E.: The Filter Bubble: What the Internet is Hiding From You. Penguin, New York (2011)
3. Pitoura, E., et al.: On measuring bias in online information. ACM SIGMOD Rec. **46**(4), 16–21 (2018)

Data Pipelines for Personalized Exploration of Rated Datasets

Sihem Amer-Yahia[1]([✉]), Anh Tho Le[1,2], and Eric Simon[2]

[1] CNRS Univ. Grenoble Alpes, Grenoble, France
sihem.amer-yahia@univ-grenoble-alpes.fr
[2] SAP, Paris, France

Abstract. Rated datasets are characterized by a combination of user demographics such as age and occupation, and user actions such as rating a movie or reviewing a book. Their exploration can greatly benefit end-users in their daily life. As data consumers are being empowered, there is a need for a tool to express end-to-end data pipelines for the personalized exploration of rated datasets. Such a tool must be easy to use as several strategies need to be tested by end-users to find relevant information. In this work, we develop a framework based on mining labeled segments of interest to the data consumer. The difficulty is to find segments whose demographics and rating behaviour are both relevant to the data consumer. The variety of ways to express that task fully justifies the need for a productive and effective programming environment to express various data pipelines at a logical level. We examine how to do that and validate our findings with experiments on real rated datasets.

1 Introduction

We are interested in providing a tool for data consumers to explore rated datasets in a personalized fashion. Rated datasets are characterized by a combination of user demographics such as age and occupation, and user actions such as rating a movie or reviewing a book. We aim to provide data consumers with the ability to mine and explore labeled segments such as "young people who like German comedies from the 90's". The variety of ways such segments can be extracted justifies the need for a tool to express end-to-end data pipelines easily. Ease of use is of particular importance here as there is an infinite number of ways to express and find relevant segments. *In this paper, we lay the foundations for a framework to express data pipelines with a particular focus on improving the quality of extracted segments.*

Several frameworks to express pipelines have been proposed for large-scale data analytics. The approaches followed for data pipelines rely on the traditional separation between logical and physical operators. Logical operators capture fundamental operations required for data preparation and mining, whereas physical operators provide alternative implementations of the logical operators. The most

© Springer Nature Switzerland AG 2020
L. Boratto et al. (Eds.): BIAS 2020, CCIS 1245, pp. 72–78, 2020.
https://doi.org/10.1007/978-3-030-52485-2_8

prominent systems are SystemML[1] and KeystoneML [7][2] for the development of machine learning pipelines. For instance, in KeystoneML, logical operators are tailored to the training and application of models whereas optimization techniques perform both per-operator optimization and end-to-end pipeline optimization using a cost-based optimizer that accounts for both computation and communication costs. By contrast, our goal is quality of the data pipeline without compromising response time.

The focus on quality is particularly important in our context. A user wishing to select a restaurant, movie or hotel, will benefit from the opinion of different segments, e.g., those with similar demographics or those with a similar opinion on other items. Indeed, while common demographics matter when inquiring about movies, they matter less for hotels. In practice, a user would benefit from the opinion of a variety of segments. While it is not possible to examine the opinion of all relevant segments at once, providing the data consumer with the ability to *quickly prototype which segments to explore would be greatly useful*. A data pipeline would then take as input the profile of a data consumer and a rated dataset and return a set of segments whose quality is optimized for the data consumer, using some objective measures.

Several approaches could be used to extract labeled segments from rated datasets. Most of them are expressed as optimization problems that tackle one or multiple quality dimensions [1–5]. We design data pipelines that encapsulate those problems (Sect. 2). A pipeline could for instance look for the K most uniform segments, in terms of their ratings, and whose coverage of input data exceeds a threshold [2]. Alternatively, it could look for the K most diverse segments with the shortest labels [4]. Data consumers should be able to quickly prototype those pipelines by specifying which subset of the raters' population they want to hear from (e.g., people living in some part of the world, or people who like Indian restaurants) and letting our framework explore different physical implementations of their pipeline (Sect. 3). As a first step toward designing a full-fledged optimizer, our experiments assess the quality of segments generated by different pipelines for different data consumers (Sect. 4).

2   Data Model

2.1   Rated Datasets and Labeled Segments

A rated dataset $\mathcal{R}$ consists of a set of users with schema $S_{\mathcal{U}}$, items with schema $S_{\mathcal{I}}$ and rating records with schema $S_{\mathcal{R}}$. For example, $S_{\mathcal{U}} = \langle$uid, age, gender, state, city$\rangle$ and a user instance may be $\langle u1, young, male, NY, NYC \rangle$. Similarly, movies on IMDb[3] can be described with $S_{\mathcal{I}} = \langle$item_id, title, genre, director$\rangle$, and the movie *Titanic* as $\langle i2, Titanic, Romance, James\ Cameron \rangle$. The schema of rating records is $S_{\mathcal{R}} = \langle$uid, item_id, rating$\rangle$. The domain

---

[1] https://systemml.apache.org/.

[2] http://keystone-ml.org/.

[3] http://www.imdb.com/.

of `rating` depends on the dataset, e.g., $\{1, ..., 5\}$ in MovieLens,[4] $\{1, ..., 10\}$ in BookCrossing.[5] The record $\langle u1, i2, 5 \rangle$, represents *a young male from NYC assigned 5 to the movie Titanic, directed by James Cameron*.

Given a rated dataset $\mathcal{R}$, we could generate a set of labeled segments $\mathcal{S}$ that are *structurally describable* using a conjunction of predicates on user and item attributes, e.g., the label of a segment $s \in \mathcal{S}$ can be {`genre` = Romance, `gender` = male, `state` = NY}. We use $records(s, \mathcal{S}) = \{\langle u, i, r \rangle \in \mathcal{S} \mid u \in s \wedge i \in s\}$ to denote the set of rating records of users on items in s.

Rating Distributions. We define the rating distribution of a segment $s \in \mathcal{S}$ as a probability distribution, $dist(s, \mathcal{S}) = [w_1, ..., w_M]$ where the rating scale is $\{1, ..., M\}$ and $w_j = \frac{|\{\langle u,i,r \rangle \in records(s,\mathcal{S}) | r=j\}|}{|records(s,\mathcal{S})|}$ is the fraction of ratings with value j in $records(s, \mathcal{S})$.

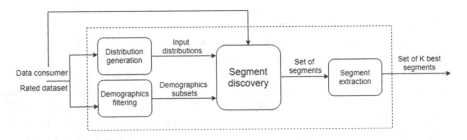

Fig. 1. Example data pipeline

2.2 Data Pipelines

A data pipeline $\mathcal{D}$ is formed by a set of logical operators. Each operator o admits a set of segments as input and returns another set of segments. When o operates in a single set of rating records, its input is a single segment containing all those records. Figure 1 shows a pipeline that takes a data consumer profile and a rated dataset and returns a set of K segments relevant to that data consumer. The pipeline has 4 operators. The distribution generation operator takes the rating records of the data consumer and builds a set of segments and their distributions that represent the data consumer. The demographics filtering operator splits an input segment, in this case the input dataset, into demographics subsets, one for each value of the attributes of a data consumer. It is defined as a filtering of the input segment over the attribute value of the data consumer. The segment discovery operator creates a set of segments that are relevant to the data consumer, and the segment extraction chooses the K best segments. Every logical operator must have at least one physical operator associated with it which implements its logic. The presence of multiple physical implementations for each operator make the data pipeline a candidate for optimization.

---

[4] https://grouplens.org/datasets/movielens/.
[5] http://www2.informatik.uni-freiburg.de/~cziegler/BX/.

The distinction from previous work is our focus on the quality of returned segments and the optimization of a logical data pipeline with respect to that quality goal. Quality is expressed as a function of several dimensions. For a set of segments, quality reflects their coverage of input records and their diversity, i.e., their ability to reflect the opinion of a variety of users. The quality of a single segment can be computed as the length of its description and the relevance of the segment to the data consumer, i.e., how close the demographics or the opinion of users in that segment are to the data consumer.

Algorithm 1. Physical algorithm for segment discovery (`Alg`)

1: Input: $(\mathcal{R}, \{\rho_1, \ldots, \rho_j, \ldots, \rho_p\}, \theta)$
2: *parent* $= \mathcal{R}$
3: *Array children*
4: **if** $min_{j \in [p]}$`EMD`$(parent, \rho_j) \leq \theta$ **then**
5:    Add *parent* to *Output*
6: **else**
7:    *Attribute* `Attr` $=$ findBestAttribute(*parent*)
8:    *children* $=$ split(*parent*, `Attr`)
9:    **for** $i = 1 \rightarrow$ *No. of children* **do**
10:      `Alg`(*children*[i], $\{\rho_1, \ldots, \rho_j, \ldots, \rho_p\}, \theta)$
11:    **end for**
12: **end if**

Algorithm 2. Physical algorithm for segment discovery (`Alg`)

1: Input: $(\mathcal{R}, \{\rho_1, \ldots, \rho_j, \ldots, \rho_p\}, \theta)$
2: *parent* $= \mathcal{R}$
3: *Array children*
4: **if** $min_{j \in [p]}$`EMD`$(parent, \rho_j) \leq \theta$ **then**
5:    Add *parent* to *Output*
6: **else if** $min_{j \in [p]}$`EMD`$(parent, \rho_j) > \theta$ **then**
7:    *Attribute* `Attr` $=$ findBestAttribute(*parent*)
8:    *children* $=$ split(*parent*, `Attr`)
9: **end if**
10: **for** $i = 1 \rightarrow$ *No. of children* **do**
11:    **if** $min_{j \in [p]}$`EMD`$(children[i], \rho_j) \leq \theta$ **then**
12:      Add *children*[i] to *Output*
13:    **else**
14:      `Alg`(*children*[i], $\{\rho_1, \ldots, \rho_j, \ldots, \rho_p\}, \theta)$
15:    **end if**
16: **end for**

---

3   Data Pipelines Implementation

Each logical operator of a data pipeline can be implemented with different physical algorithms. Algorithm 2 is an example of an implementation of the segment discovery operator. This algorithm was proposed in [1] and relies om generating a partition decision tree. It takes as input a rating dataset $\mathcal{R}$ and a set of distributions $\{\rho_1, \cdots, \rho_p\}$ that represent a data consumer. The algorithm uses Earth Mover's Distance (EMD) for segment comparison [6] and returns segments whose rating distribution is within a threshold θ of the distributions representing the data consumer. Whereas classic decision trees [8] are driven by gain functions like entropy[6] and gini-index,[7] Alg uses the *minimum average* EMD as its gain function. Suppose splitting a segment s using an attribute $\texttt{Attr}_i$ yields l children $y_1^i \ldots y_l^i$. The gain of $\texttt{Attr}_i$ is defined as the reciprocal of the average EMD of its children. More formally:

$$\texttt{Gain}(\texttt{Attr}_i) = \frac{l}{\sum_{j=1}^{l} min_{\rho \in \{\rho_1, \cdots, \rho_p\}} \texttt{EMD}(y_j^i, \rho)}$$

At each node, Alg checks if the current segment has EMD $\leq \theta$ to some input distribution (lines 4–5). If the segment's EMD distance to the closest input distribution is $> \theta$ (line 6), Alg uses our gain function to choose a splitting attribute (line 7), and the segment is split into child segments which are retained (line 8); Finally, retained segments are checked and are either added to the output (line 12) or recursively processed further (line 14). The algorithm finally returns a set of segments that are relevant to the data consumer, i.e., whose rating distributions are within θ of the data consumer's.

There exist other implementations for segment discovery [1–5]. Our goal is to optimize pipelines by comparing the quality of their returned segments.

4   Empirical Validation and Discussion

4.1   Validation

The purpose of validation is to examine the quality of returned segments for different data pipelines and users and make a case for an optimization framework. We sample the MovieLens dataset and choose rating records for "Drama" movies generated by the 137 random users (out of 6,040 users who rated those movies). Our dataset contains 2,000 rating records for 405 movies. We use the algorithm described in the previous section for segment discovery. For segment extraction, we chppse the top 10 largest segments in size. We run two data pipelines. The first one is an implementation of the pipeline in Fig. 1 with Algorithm 2 for segment discovery. The second pipeline splits on both user demographics and movie attributes; and allow a segment which contain at least one of 4 keys <age,

---

[6] http://en.wikipedia.org/wiki/Entropy.
[7] http://en.wikipedia.org/wiki/Gini_index.

occupation, gender, location>. The second implements a variant where no demographics filtering operator is provided and segment discovery splits input rating records on demographics. In the second pipeline, the obtained segments may correspond to users whose demographics are different from the data consumer's.

Table 1 reports our results for 3 kinds of consumers and their distributions: the neutral consumer, the polarized consumer, and a random consumer sampled from our dataset. We measure the quality of returned segments, i.e., their coverage of input records, their diversity, and the average description length. We also show some example segments. The higher the coverage and diversity, the better. The lower the description length, the better since data consumers prefer to read shorter segment descriptions. Our results show that there is a big difference in segment quality for different pipelines and users and that no pipeline wins on all fronts, thereby justifying to study the automatic optimization of data pipelines.

Table 1. Segment quality for different data consumers and pipelines

Data consumers	Pipeline 1	Pipeline 2
Neutral data consumer: *Young female executive from FL* [0.2, 0.2, 0.2, 0.2, 0.2]	Coverage: 0.581 Diversity: 0.007 Desc. Length: 1.8 e.g., *Females who rated movies from 2000*	Coverage: 0.533 Diversity: 1 Desc. Length: 2.8 e.g., *Young male artists living from MD*
Polarized data consumer: *Middle-aged male engineer from CA* [0.5, 0, 0, 0, 0.5] [1, 0, 0, 0, 0] [0, 0, 0, 0, 1]	Coverage: 0.230 Diversity: 0.014 Desc. Length: 1.9 e.g., *Males who rated movies written by Stephen King*	Coverage: 0.016 Diversity: 1 Desc. Length: 2.0 e.g., *Artists who rated movies written by Kenneth Branagh*
Random data consumer: *Young male scientist from WI* [0, 0.5, 0.17, 0.33, 0] [0.33, 0,33, 0.33, 0, 0] [0, 0.67, 0.33, 0, 0]	Coverage: 0.691 Diversity: 0.006 Desc. Length: 1.6 e.g., *Young people who rated Steven Soderbergh movies*	Coverage: 0.486 Diversity: 1 Desc. Length: 1.6 e.g., *Male academics from MA*

4.2 Discussion

Our work opens several directions. The immediate one we are working on is to design an optimizer that switches between different data pipelines to find the most desired combination of coverage, diversity, description length and relevance to the data consumer's rating distributions. We believe that a hybrid approach that switches between automatic decisions and a human-in-the-loop process, is necessary to converge. That is because the final target is a data consumer with an information need in mind. Moreover, similarly to KeystoneML, we would like to study how to automatically optimize execution at both the operator and whole-pipeline levels. Due to our focus on quality, this would translate into defining how to compose pipelines to enable feedback-based optimization. Feedback from a data consumer can translate into a new set of rating distributions and demographics to be used as input in the next iteration. We believe that the ability to integrate that feedback with the automatic computation of segment quality will enable exploratory tasks that go beyond single consumers and serve consumer groups. This opens new directions for multi-feedback optimization.

References

1. Amer-Yahia, S., Kleisarchaki, S., Kolloju, N.K., Lakshmanan, L.V.S., Zamar, R.H.: Exploring rated datasets with rating maps. In: Proceedings of the 26th International Conference on World Wide Web, WWW 2017, Perth, Australia, 3–7 April 2017, pp. 1411–1419 (2017)
2. Das, M., Amer-Yahia, S., Das, G., Yu, C.: MRI: meaningful interpretations of collaborative ratings. PVLDB 4(11), 1063–1074 (2011)
3. Das, M., Thirumuruganathan, S., Amer-Yahia, S., Das, G., Yu, C.: An expressive framework and efficient algorithms for the analysis of collaborative tagging. VLDB J. 23(2), 201–226 (2014)
4. Omidvar-Tehrani, B., Amer-Yahia, S., Dutot, P.-F., Trystram, D.: Multi-objective group discovery on the social web. In: Frasconi, P., Landwehr, N., Manco, G., Vreeken, J. (eds.) ECML PKDD 2016. LNCS (LNAI), vol. 9851, pp. 296–312. Springer, Cham (2016). https://doi.org/10.1007/978-3-319-46128-1_19
5. Omidvar-Tehrani, B., Amer-Yahia, S., Termier, A.: Interactive user group analysis. In: CIKM, pp. 403–412. ACM (2015)
6. Rubner, Y., Tomasi, C., Guibas, L.J.: The earth mover's distance as a metric for image retrieval. Int. J. Comput. Vis. 40(2), 99–121 (2000)
7. Sparks, E.R., Venkataraman, S., Kaftan, T., Franklin, M.J., Recht, B.: KeystoneML: optimizing pipelines for large-scale advanced analytics. In: 33rd IEEE International Conference on Data Engineering, ICDE 2017, San Diego, CA, USA, 19–22 April 2017, pp. 535–546 (2017)
8. Tan, P.-N., et al.: Introduction to Data Mining, 1st edn. W. W. Norton & Company, New York (2007)

Beyond Accuracy in Link Prediction

Javier Sanz-Cruzado$^{(\boxtimes)}$ (iD) and Pablo Castells (iD)

Universidad Autónoma de Madrid, Escuela Politécnica Superior, Madrid, Spain
{javier.sanz-cruzado,pablo.castells}@uam.es

Abstract. Link prediction has mainly been addressed as an accuracy-targeting problem in social network analysis. We discuss different perspectives on the problem considering other dimensions and effects that the link prediction methods may have on the network where they are applied. Specifically, we consider the structural effects the methods can have if the predicted links are added to the network. We consider further utility dimensions beyond prediction accuracy, namely novelty and diversity. We adapt specific metrics from social network analysis, recommender systems and information retrieval, and we empirically observe the effect of a set of link prediction algorithms over Twitter data.

Keywords: Link prediction · Social networks · Evaluation · Novelty · Diversity

1 Introduction

Link prediction can be considered today one of the classic areas in social network analysis research and development. The problem consists in finding links in a social network that have not been observed or formed yet, but may do so in the future, or may simply be useful to add. A paradigmatic application for the problem is recommending contacts in online social networks, a feature most social network applications, such as Facebook, Twitter or LinkedIn, nowadays provide.

A link prediction method can be evaluated in different ways, depending on the specific nuances in how the problem is stated. If seen as a classification task, the methods can be evaluated in terms of the predictive accuracy by usual metrics such as AUC, contingency tables, etc. [23]. If stated as a recommendation problem, information retrieval metrics can be used, such as precision, recall, etc. [15].

Yet as far as we are aware, most of the evaluation approaches to date, and therefore the solutions developed targeting them, seek to optimize a microscopic perspective of the network. In the classification perspective, a correctly classified link (true positive) adds as much to the accuracy metric as any other correct link, regardless where the people involved in the predicted edge are placed in the network, or what their social involvement may appear to be. Likewise, in the recommendation task, the metrics assess the accuracy or the benefit the recommendation brings to each target user in isolation, and then this microscopic benefit is simply aggregated into a "macro" average over all users.

Social networks are however not precisely about isolated users. It is well understood that a microscopic change (the formation of one link) has immediate direct and indirect

L. Boratto et al. (Eds.): BIAS 2020, CCIS 1245, pp. 79–94, 2020.
https://doi.org/10.1007/978-3-030-52485-2_9

effects in its surroundings; that small nearby changes combined produce something more than the sum of their effects; and that a few small changes spread across the network may have a substantial macro effect on the properties and behavior of the network as a whole. We therefore contend that we may want to consider the global consequence of link prediction on the network structure when assessing a link prediction algorithm.

We may moreover in fact want to target specific global effects in our link prediction methods. Contact recommendation functionalities nowadays account for an increasing fraction of the online social network growth; link prediction therefore represents an opportunity to favor trends towards desirable global properties in the evolution of a network, beyond (and in addition to) the short-term micro level value to be procured by the recommended links. The impact of recommendation can be quite important if we further consider the dynamic and recursive nature of social network growth.

The relation between link prediction and network evolution can be in fact obvious at the problem-statement level, and both views are naturally related in the literature: understanding how a network grows, and assessing the probability of any possible link to form, are very closely related tasks. Link prediction and network growth modeling have hence been seen as equivalent problems to some level. But how one (link prediction) can impact the other (network evolution) is yet to be studied; and the effect on network evolution has barely been considered, to the best of our knowledge, as part of the utility of the prediction algorithms to be evaluated.

In this paper, we discuss and explore several possible perspectives in the proposed direction. First, the social network analysis field provides a profuse array of concepts, metrics and analytic methods to assess the properties of the effect of link recommendation on a social network. We hence explore using such notions and measures to define new evaluation metrics for link prediction. Moreover, the recommender systems field has developed over recent years a clear awareness that accuracy alone is just a rather partial view on the value of recommendation: novelty and diversity perspectives can be as important —at both the macro and micro levels. We therefore likewise consider the adaptation of outcomes from that area to the evaluation of link recommendation. We find that, at more than one level, the global network analysis dimension of edge prediction links to similar principles as lay beneath the novelty and diversity perspectives.

2   Related Work

Many different approaches to link prediction have been researched in the literature. Most methods can be broadly classed in either of three categories: approaches based on the similarity between people [21], classical machine learning algorithms [22], and statistical network evolution models [13]. Link prediction can be applied to any type of network, yet the problem has greatly gained importance with the explosion of online social networks, where prediction is applied to recommend people to befriend or follow [12, 14, 15, 31].

Link prediction and contact recommendation have so far essentially targeted the accuracy of the predictions. Incipient research has nonetheless considered the effects of contact recommendation algorithms on global properties of the network. We can distinguish two main perspectives in this scope. The first one focuses on the measurement of the effects of recommender systems on the structure of networks. The effect on metrics such as the clustering coefficient [8, 17, 30], the number of connected components [17] or the degree distribution [8] have been analyzed. The second line considers influencing the network growth towards some desired properties. In particular, Parotsidis [27] seeks to minimize the expected path length between the target user and the rest of the network; and Wu et al. [34] seek to maximize the modularity of the network. In this paper, we aim to broaden the perspective undertaken in such initial research, towards a wider range of network metrics, and dimensions beyond accuracy, such as novelty and diversity.

3 Notation

We shall use the following notation in the rest of the paper. We denote as $G = \langle U, E \rangle$ the graph structure of a social network, where U represents the set of people in the network, and $E \subset U_*^2 = \{(u, v) \in U^2 | u \neq v\}$ represents the relations between them. We denote by $\Gamma(u)$ the set of people to which a person $u \in U$ is connected. In directed networks, we shall differentiate between the incoming and outgoing neighborhoods $\Gamma_{in}(u)$ and $\Gamma_{out}(u)$.

The link prediction problem can be stated as identifying the subset of links $\hat{E} \subset (U_*^2 - E)$ that are not observed but present in the network, or will form in the future, or would be useful to add –whatever the variant of the problem is. From a recommendation perspective, we shall denote by $\widehat{\Gamma}_{out}(u)$ the set of people involved in the predicted arcs going out from u, i.e. $\widehat{\Gamma}_{out}(u) = \{v \in U | (u, v) \in \hat{E}\}$. And we shall refer to the graph including only the recommended links as $\hat{G} = U, \hat{E}$.

4 Social Network Analysis

One way to assess the effect of a prediction algorithm on the network is to consider the extension of the network $G' = \langle U, E' \rangle$, with $E' = E \cup \hat{E}$, by a certain subset $\hat{E}$ of predicted links (for instance, the union of the top k predicted outgoing links in the ranking for each person u), as if the party the prediction is delivered to (e.g. the users of an online social network) accepted all the links in $\hat{E}$. Hence, any network metric applied to G' can be taken as a metric on the prediction method.

The social network analysis field is rich in metrics and concepts to characterize and measure network properties in many different angles. We summarize here some classical metrics we find of potential interest for the perspective under discussion. We suggest straightforward adaptations for our purpose, as well as further elaborations in some cases.

4.1 Distance-Based Metrics

An effect of recommendation, inasmuch as it increases the network density, is a general reduction of distances in the augmented graph. We may hence consider the metrics that measure this effect in different ways. Two common distance metrics are the average (ASL) and the maximum distance (diameter) over all pairs of people. We may also consider the farthest distance (eccentricity) for each person, averaged over all people. More-over, in a recommendation perspective, we can measure the average distance between the people involved in predicted links in the original graph. We define reciprocal versions of the metrics when appropriate, in such a way that high values "are good" (in the sense that they reflect a possibly desired property).

- **Average reciprocal shortest path length:** $\mathrm{ARSL}(\mathcal{G}') = \frac{1}{|\mathcal{U}|(|\mathcal{U}|-1)} \sum\limits_{u,v \in \mathcal{U}} \frac{1}{\delta'(u,v)}$

  where $\delta'(u, v)$ denotes a shortest-path distance in the extended network $\mathcal{G}'$.

- **Reciprocal diameter:** $\mathrm{RD}(\mathcal{G}') = 1/\max_{u \in \mathcal{U}} ecc(u)$

  where the eccentricity $ecc(u) = \max_{v \in \mathcal{U}:\delta'(u,v)<\infty} \delta'(u, v)$ of a node u is defined as the distance to the farthest accessible node from u in the network [9].

- **Reciprocal average eccentricity:** $\mathrm{RAE}(\mathcal{G}') = |\mathcal{U}| / \sum\limits_{u \in \mathcal{U}} ecc(u)$

- **Mean prediction distance:** $\mathrm{MPD}(\hat{E}|\mathcal{G}) = |\hat{E}| \bigg/ \sum\limits_{(u,v)\in\hat{E}} \frac{1}{\delta(u,v)} - 2$

  Where $\delta(u, v)$ denotes the shortest distance in the original network $\mathcal{G}$ (before prediction). MPD computes the harmonic mean of the prediction distances, subtracting 2 to set the metric minimum value at 0 (as $\delta(u, v) \geq 2 \forall (u, v) \in \hat{E}$, since $\delta(u, v) < 2 \Rightarrow (u, v) \in E \vee u = v$, in which case the link is not considered for prediction: $(u, v) \notin \hat{E}$).

Distance shortening is likely a desirable effect in most cases, as it makes people easier to reach from each other through a smaller number of hops through common acquaintances. The different ways to average the distances provides nuances in the perspective with which distance is accounted for.

ARSL, RD and RAE range in (0, 1], and MPD takes values in [0, ∞], reaching value ∞ when all the predicted links point to previously inaccessible people. It is easy to see that ARSL and MPD are defined in such a way that so-called global bridges [11], if any, between previously separate connected components are rewarded as the ideal case (where infinite distances are reduced to distance 1), whereas RD and RAE just ignore such improvements and just consider distance improvements within components. MPD measures in a quite direct way how the predicted links bring people far from their usual social environment, which can be seen as a measure of novelty from a contact recommendation perspective. We suggest the harmonic instead of the arithmetic mean because it can take in infinite distances.

4.2 Structural Diversity

Notions of structural diversity have been a profuse object of study in the field of complex networks [17]. From the simplest perspective, the degree distribution can be seen as a primary sign of connective diversity: a very skewed distribution reflects a concentration of links around a few highly connected people, whereas in a flatter distribution each person has a more distinctive social circle of her own, and is exposed to different interactions than other people are. The "flatness" of the degree distribution can be summarized by a single number using the Gini index, which we can reverse into the **degree Gini complement**:

$$\mathrm{DGC}(\mathcal{G}') = 1 - \frac{1}{|\mathcal{U}| - 1} \sum_{i=1}^{|\mathcal{U}|} (2i - |\mathcal{U}| - 1) \frac{|\Gamma'(u_i)|}{|E'|}$$

where people u_i in the above definition are ordered by non-decreasing degree $|\Gamma'(u_i)|$, and Γ' represents neighborhoods in the extended graph $\mathcal{G}'$. The same as we did for distance-based metrics, we take the complement of the Gini index, ranging in $[0, 1]$, in such a way high values indicate that the edges are evenly distributed, while values near zero indicate strong link concentration. In directed networks it makes also sense to compute indegree and outdegree versions IDGC and ODGC.

Richer notions of structural diversity have been studied, related to the concept of weak tie. Granovetter hypothesized that such links provide more novel information that strong ties [11]. In sociology, the strength of a link is defined as a combination of the amount of time spent on the relation, the emotional intensity, intimacy and reciprocal services that characterize the link. Strong links represent e.g. ties with family or close friends while weak edges correspond to more occasional acquaintances. Measures of link strength can also be defined based just on topological properties in the network, and can be related in some way or other to the sociological notion of weak tie [10, 11]. Such measures are typically related to notions of redundancy: a tie is weak inasmuch as it is not redundant to other links around it; it carries a somehow exclusive (and hence valuable) connection between specific people or regions of the network. Such measures can be broadly divided in two categories: global and local.

Local Notions. Local notions of weak tie consider the direct environment of a link to assess its strength. In this aim Granovetter considered a local weak link notion [11]: local bridges are links between people who do not have any common neighbors. We find this definition rather binary and restrictive, resulting in a coarse metric. The so-called link embeddedness provides a finer and more informative metric, which measures the relative overlap of the neighborhoods of its endpoints [36] as an indication of link strength:

$$\mathrm{Embeddedness}(u, v|\mathcal{G}') = \frac{|\Gamma'_{\mathrm{out}}(u) \cap \Gamma'_{\mathrm{in}}(v)|}{|\Gamma'_{\mathrm{out}}(u) \cup \Gamma'_{\mathrm{in}}(v)|}$$

This metric actually smoothly generalizes the notion of local bridge: a link is a local bridge if it has embeddedness 0. We may assess the degree to which a link prediction method suggests weak ties by measuring the **average edge weakness** of the suggested links as the complement of embeddedness:

$$\mathrm{AEW}(\hat{E}|\mathcal{G}') = \frac{1}{|\hat{E}|} \sum_{(u,v) \in \hat{E}} \left(1 - \mathrm{Embeddedness}(u, v|\mathcal{G}')\right)$$

The metric ranges in $[0, 1]$ in such a way that the higher the weakness, the higher the structural diversity brought by link prediction.

Another classical means to assess the degree of connection redundancy around a person is the clustering coefficient, which can be defined as the ratio of neighbor pairs that are connected. The global clustering coefficient of a network can be measured by averaging this coefficient over all people in the network, or by an alternative global definition: the ratio of triangles in the network over the number of paths of length two. Again, we take the **clustering coefficient complement**, to get the metric values properly aligned with a notion of diversity:

$$\mathrm{CCC}(\mathcal{G}') = 1 - \frac{|\{(u, v, w)|(u, v), (v, w), (w, u) \in E'\}|}{|\{(u, v, w)|(u, v), (v, w) \in E'\}|}$$

A link prediction method brings diversity to the network to the extent that this metric gets a low value.

Global Notions. Along with the concept of local bridge, Granovetter proposed a global notion of bridge: a unique link between connected components. Again, we find this definition very restrictive in common social networks, which typically display a giant connected component [24], outside which the remaining components are rather marginal, and bridges between them are not particularly important to the network. We hence consider a relaxed definition based on work by De Meo et al. [10]: links between communities are considered weak ties, and links inside communities are considered strong. Inspired by this notion, we can consider different metrics that assess the presence of such links in the network.

A classical measure of the presence of inter-community links is the so-called modularity [24] (and reciprocally, many community detection algorithms consist in seeking partitions of $\mathcal{U}$ that minimize modularity [7]). Given a partition of the network into a set of communities $\mathcal{C}$, modularity compares the number of edges inside communities (strong links) to the expected number of strong ties we would find if the edges were placed at random:

$$\mathrm{Mod}(\mathcal{G}'|\mathcal{C}) = \frac{\sum_{u,v \in \mathcal{U}} \left(A_{uv} - |\Gamma'_{\mathrm{out}}(u)||\Gamma'_{\mathrm{in}}(v)|/|E'|\right)[c(u) = c(v)]}{|E'| - \sum_{u,v \in \mathcal{U}} |\Gamma'_{\mathrm{out}}(u)||\Gamma'_{\mathrm{in}}(v)|/|E'|[c(u) = c(v)]}$$

where $c(u) \in \mathcal{C}$ denotes the community that u belongs to, A_{uv} is equal to 1 if there is a link between users u and v, and 0 otherwise, and $[\cdot]$ is the indicator function, which is equal to 1 iff the predicate inside the brackets is true. Once again, since low modularity indicates high diversity, we linearly reorient the values into a **modularity complement** metric ranging in $[0, 1]$, providing a direct measure of structural diversity:

$$\mathrm{MC}(\mathcal{G}'|\mathcal{C}) = \left(1 - \mathrm{Mod}(\mathcal{G}'|\mathcal{C})\right)/2$$

MC provides a measure of the abundance of weak ties across communities, but it does not provide information about the distribution of the weak links over the communities. The metric does not inform whether all those links connect a single pair of communities, or several different community pairs. The issue is illustrated in Fig. 1. We may hence want to consider a finer metric that assesses how balanced is the weak link distribution. For this purpose we propose the **inter-community Gini complement**, which counts the links between each pair of different communities, and computes the (complement of the) Gini coefficient of the distribution:

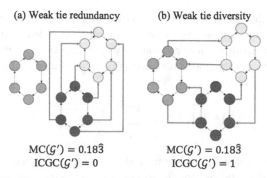

(a) Weak tie redundancy   (b) Weak tie diversity

$\text{MC}(\mathcal{G}') = 0.18\hat{3}$ $\text{MC}(\mathcal{G}') = 0.18\hat{3}$
$\text{ICGC}(\mathcal{G}') = 0$ $\text{ICGC}(\mathcal{G}') = 1$

Fig. 1. Networks with the same number of weak ties, but different link distribution. Black and red arrows represent, respectively, strong and weak ties. Nodes with the same color belong to the same community. (Color figure online)

$$\text{ICGC}(\mathcal{G}'|\mathcal{C}) = 1 - \frac{1}{M-1} \sum_{i=1}^{M} (2i - M - 1)p\big((c_1, c_2)_i | \mathcal{G}', \mathcal{C}\big)$$

where $M = |\mathcal{C}|(|\mathcal{C}| - 1)$ is the number of pairs of (different) communities in the partition ($M = |\mathcal{C}|(|\mathcal{C}| - 1)/2$ if $\mathcal{G}'$ is undirected), $(c_1, c_2)_i$ is the i-th pair of communities with the smaller number of links between them, and $p\big((c_1, c_2)|\mathcal{G}', \mathcal{C}\big)$ is the probability of randomly selecting a weak tie between that pair of communities:

$$p\big((c_1, c_2)|\mathcal{G}', \mathcal{C}\big) = \frac{|\{(u, v) \in E'|c(u) = c_1 \wedge c(v) = c_2\}|}{|\{(u, v) \in E'|c(u) \neq c(v)\}|}$$

This metric has the extreme value 0 when only two communities have links across them, and 1 when every two pairs of communities have the same amount of crossing links. However, it does not inform of the total number of weak ties.

5 Novelty and Diversity

Diversity is a rich concept that is studied in many different disciplines. Pertinent to our present focus, the information retrieval and recommender systems fields have developed notions of their own in this scope [2, 4, 6, 32], which can be meaningful in the link prediction context as well. We hence consider their adaptation in a perspective where link prediction is seen as a contact recommendation task, targeted to the social network users.

5.1 Novelty

Novelty is a primary concern to recommender systems in most common scenarios where recommendation is tied to a purpose of discovery [4]. The most common novelty notion refers to recommending minority items in the long tail of the popularity distribution. In our case this means predicting links to people with little or moderate social involvement.

A **long-tail novelty** metric can be formalized as the prior probability that a random person in the network was not acquainted to some of the recommended people to some other random user. This probability can be estimated by the proportion of people linking (in the original network $\mathcal{G}$) to recommended persons v, that is, $p(\neg known|v) = 1 - |\Gamma_{in}(v)|/|\mathcal{U}|$. The metric is hence defined as:

$$\text{LTN}\left(\hat{E}|\mathcal{G}\right) = \frac{1}{|\hat{E}|} \sum_{(u,v)\in\hat{E}} \left(1 - \frac{|\Gamma_{in}(v)|}{|\mathcal{U}|}\right)$$

which is inversely equivalent to the average indegree of the predicted contacts. This metric was proposed as the *expected popularity complement* in the context of recommender systems [4, 32].

While LTN measures novelty from a global perspective (how novel are links to anyone), it also makes sense to consider the specific novelty from the individual viewpoint of each particular target user. So-called **unexpectedness** metrics have been proposed in the evaluation of recommender systems [4], which assess the dissimilarity between the recommended items and the prior experience of the specific target user. In our case the available records of user experience simply consist of their present contacts in $\mathcal{G}$:

$$\text{Unexp}\left(\hat{E}|\mathcal{G}\right) = \frac{1}{|\hat{E}|} \sum_{(u,v)\in\hat{E}} \frac{1}{|\Gamma_{out}(u)|} \sum_{w\in\Gamma_{out}(u)} d(v, w)$$

where the distance $d(v, w)$ between users can be defined in any meaningful way for the domain at hand. Measures based on path distance in the network would be somewhat redundant to the metrics suggested in Sect. 4.1. Dissimilarity in terms of the social neighborhoods (e.g. Jaccard distance) is generally not the most informative option either, as it would typically represent a close opposite of the objective function of many prediction algorithms, and would hence tend to yield somewhat tautologically low values. Dis-similarity measures based on side-information about users are usually more meaningful.

LTN and unexpectedness can measure how much the recommended contacts takes target users far from their comfort zone, hence bringing opportunities for broadening and diversifying their social experience.

5.2 Diversity

Recommendation Perspective. From a recommendation perspective, the diversity of a set of predicted links refers to how different are from each other the people recommended at the other end of the links, for a given target user. This is commonly measured by the **intra-list dissimilarity** [4], defined as the average pairwise distance between the people recommended to each target user:

$$\text{ILD}\left(\hat{\mathcal{G}}\right) = \frac{1}{|\hat{E}|} \sum_{(u,v)\in\hat{E}} \sum_{w\in\hat{\Gamma}_{out}(u)} \frac{d(v, w)}{|\hat{\Gamma}_{out}(u)|}$$

where $d(v, w)$ is a dissimilarity measure between users, and can be defined in any meaningful way. Again, distance functions on user features tend to be more informative than measures based on the network structure around the users.

The second important diversity notion in recommendation concerns a global perspective and has often be referred to as *diversity of sales* [4]. In our context it can be defined as how evenly are the recommendations distributed over all users, as opposed to being concentrated over a few people who are recommended to everyone. Again, the Gini index is a suitable summary metric to assess this aspect, which we use to define the **prediction Gini complement**:

$$
\mathrm{PGC}\left(\hat{\mathcal{G}}\right) = 1 - \frac{1}{|\mathcal{U}| - 1} \sum_{i=1}^{|\mathcal{U}|} (2i - |\mathcal{U}| - 1) \frac{\left|\hat{\Gamma}_{\mathrm{in}}(v_i)\right|}{\left|\hat{E}\right|}
$$

where v_i represents the i-th user by non-decreasing number of times $\left|\hat{\Gamma}_{\mathrm{in}}(v_i)\right|$ she is recommended. This metric is equal to 1 when all users are recommended equally often, and 0 when all the predicted links point to the same single user.

Information Retrieval Perspective. A related but different take on diversity has been developed in search-oriented information retrieval, that considers returning diverse results considering the different possible intents or *aspects behind* an ambiguous search query [35]. Although link prediction does not involve explicit queries, it is possible to adapt this perspective by matching users in the network to queries and documents. The notion of aspect is abstract, and it can be particularized in many ways. We suggest considering latent communities as the equivalent of query aspects, whereby we can adapt all the aspect-based diversity metrics from IR.

The simplest metric, *subtopic recall*, which we may rename as **community recall** in our context, counts and averages the ratio of communities covered by the people recommended to each target user [35]:

$$
\mathrm{CRecall}\left(\hat{\mathcal{G}}|\mathcal{C}\right) = \frac{1}{|\mathcal{U}||\mathcal{C}|} \sum_{u \in \mathcal{U}} \left| \bigcup_{v \in \hat{\Gamma}_{\mathrm{out}}(u)} c(v) \right|
$$

where $\mathcal{C}$ is the set of communities and $c(v)$ is the community that user v belongs to.

A more elaborate approach to aspect-based evaluation is the so-called intent-aware scheme, in which one of the most meaningful and widely used metrics is **ERR-IA** [5]. This metric weighs down the added value of correctly predicted links in the ranking when the community of the recommended endpoint already occurs above in the ranking:

$$
\mathrm{ERR\text{-}IA}\left(\hat{E}|\mathcal{G}, E_{\mathrm{test}}, \mathcal{C}\right) = \frac{1}{|\mathcal{U}|} \sum_{u \in \mathcal{U}} \sum_{c \in \mathcal{C}} p(c|u) \, \mathrm{ERR\text{-}IA}(u, c)
$$

$$
\mathrm{ERR\text{-}IA}(u, c) = \sum_{k=1}^{\left|\hat{\Gamma}_{\mathrm{out}}(u)\right|} \frac{1}{k} p(\mathrm{rel}|v_k, c) \prod_{j=1}^{k-1} \left(1 - p(\mathrm{rel}|v_j, c)\right)
$$

where v_k is the user at position k in the ranking of recommended links for user u, $p(\text{rel}|v, c)$ is commonly defined as $p(\text{rel}|v, c) = 0.5 \cdot [(u, v) \in E_{\text{test}} \wedge c(v) = c]$, and E_{test} represents the set of test links (held out from the prediction algorithms) with which the accuracy of link prediction is evaluated. The probability $p(c|u)$ that a community is pertinent to a user can be estimated by the ratio of followers of u that belong to c:

$$p(c|u) = \frac{|\{v \in c(u)|(u, v) \in E \cup E_{\text{test}}\}|}{\sum_{c' \in \mathcal{C}} |\{v \in c'(u)|(u, v) \in E \cup E_{\text{test}}\}|}$$

6   Empirical Observation

In order to get a first feeling of the suggested metrics, we run a short experiment where we apply them to a set of state of the art link prediction algorithms over a sample of Twitter data.

6.1   Data

We use in our test the implicit dynamic network induced by the interactions between Twitter users, i.e. a link $(u, v) \in E$ if u retweets, mentions or replies v. We retrieve the data by a snowball sampling approach using the Twitter REST API. Starting from a seed user, we extract a selection of tweets published by that user. Then, we extract his social neighborhood as the set of outgoing interaction links present in the retrieved tweets. Then, all those users are added to the sample, and the procedure continues with the next retrieved user, until a desired number of users is retrieved. In our setup, we obtained 10,000 different users, and all their tweets published between the June 16th and July 16th 2015. The details of the collected dataset are shown in Table 1.

The link prediction task is set up for evaluation by means of a temporal split where the links dated prior to 9th July 2015 form the training set E of edges, and the links after that date are held out as test data E_{test}. The date of a link is defined as the timestamp of the first retrieved interaction between the users involved in the link. In fact, among all the metrics discussed here, only ERR-IA uses the test links –any pure accuracy metric, such as precision, naturally uses the test set as well.

We exclude reciprocating links from any prediction, as an obvious guess –the exceedingly high reciprocation ratio in Twitter would otherwise make the prediction task trivial; moreover Twitter already sends notifications anytime a new link is created (thus making an additional recommendation redundant).

For unexpectedness and ILD, we use as dissimilarity metric the complement of the *tf-idf* cosine similarity, using the concatenated text of the tweets posted by each user. Finally, for the community-based metrics, we tested different community detection algorithms, and we observed that the results are rather insensitive to the choice of algorithm (as al-ready noted by De Meo et al. [10]). We will report the results using the Louvain method [3], one of the best known and most effective algorithms in the literature.

Table 1. Twitter dataset details.

#Users $|\mathcal{U}|$	9,528
#Training edges $|E|$	170,425
#Test edges $|E_{\text{test}}|$	54,355

Table 2. Parameter settings for the algorithms

User CF	$k = 120$	MCN	$\Gamma_{\text{und}}(u), \Gamma_{\text{in}}(v)$
Item CF	$k = 300$	Pers. PR	$r = 0.4$
Implicit MF	$k = 260, \lambda = 150, \alpha = 40$	Matrix forest	$\alpha = 0.001$
SALSA	Authorities, $\alpha = 0.99$	Jaccard	$\Gamma_{\text{und}}(u), \Gamma_{\text{in}}(v)$
Local path	$\beta = 0.1, l = 3$	Katz	$\beta = 0.1$
Adamic	$\Gamma_{\text{und}}(u), \Gamma_{\text{in}}(v), \Gamma_{\text{und}}(w)$	Global LHN	$\lambda = 0.4$

6.2 Link Prediction Algorithms

We test the metrics on 15 different link prediction methods. Most of these algorithms have free parameters that we have tuned by simple grid search, targeting P@10; the resulting parameter settings are shown in Table 2 in the same notation as in [28]. We can classify the tested algorithms into four different families.

Neighborhood-Based. We implement three algorithms in this group: one that ranks links according to the number of users in the intersection of neighborhoods [21] (most common neighbors, MCN), the Jaccard similarity of the users' neighborhoods [21], and the Adamic-Adar coefficient [1, 21].

Path-Based. We implement four different methods: the Katz algorithm [19, 21] and a derivative algorithm, local path index [23]; the global Leicht-Holme-Newman (LHN) similarity index [20, 23]; and the matrix forest index approach [23].

Random Walks. We implement personalized PageRank [21, 33], and the personalized SALSA algorithm [12] applied in the Twitter "Who-to-follow" service.

Recommendation Algorithms. We adapt several recommendation methods to the link prediction task, including: user-based and item-based nearest-neighbor collaborative filtering (CF) [25]; a matrix factorization algorithm (Implicit MF) [16]; and a content-based approach that uses the text of tweets published by users [15].

In addition to all those algorithms, we include random link prediction, and popularity-based prediction, where the top most connected people are recommended to everyone.

As prediction thresholding method to select the set of predicted edges $\hat{E}$, we select the top k outgoing links as ranked by the predictor for each user in the network. In other words, we apply ranking cutoffs to the link prediction seen as a recommendation task targeted to the network users. To reflect this, we may append "@k" to all the metrics. In the results reported here, we take $k = \left|\hat{\Gamma}_{\text{out}}(u)\right| = 10$. Then, to compute the network analysis metrics, we add $\hat{E}$ to the original graph, as described earlier in Sect. 4.

6.3   Results

We begin by observing in Fig. 2 how the metrics correlate to each other, measured by the pairwise Pearson correlation over the set of 15 tested algorithms (the columns of Table 3). We easily spot several groups of metrics that seem to capture similar things.

ILD correlates with unexpectedness, which means that recommendations comprising a variety of users tend to be also different (on average) to the present contacts of the target user. AEW, CCC, and to lesser extent MC, are also correlated to each other, confirming the coherence of weak-tie and link-redundancy metrics. However, ICGC, also a weak-tie metric, seems to work in a different direction to the latter. We attribute this to the fact that long-tail recommendations (as measured by LTN) balance the distribution of cross-links over community pairs (as measured by ICGC), at the same time that LTN works against AEW and CCC as we discuss below.

Distance-based, Gini-based, community-based (including MC), and long-tail metrics also seem to roughly form a cluster of coherent measures, showing that they capture related sides of similar notions: connecting communities shortens distances between many users, as does avoiding link concentration. LTN and ICGC are however at the "periphery" of this cluster, and in fact correlate negatively with ARSL and MC. This is probably because connecting low-degree users (high LTN) does not shorten distances as much as linking to network hubs does. LTN seems to oppose CCC and AEW as well: links to low-degree users tend to be stronger than links to hubs, possibly because a) they contribute a smaller neighborhood size in the denominator of embeddedness for AEW, and b) long-tail people tend to have a low number of outgoing links as well, creating fewer unclosed triads for CCC.

Finally, precision correlates negatively with most novelty and diversity metrics, reflecting a general tradeoff already observed in the recommender systems field [4].

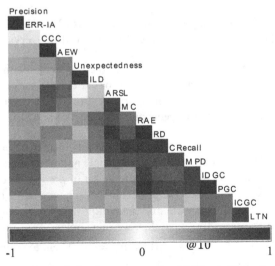

Fig. 2. Pairwise pearson correlation between metrics (@10 cutoff) for the values in Table 3.

Table 3. Metric values for a set of link prediction algorithms on the Twitter dataset described in Table 1. Column cells are colored from white (worst) to blue (best values), excepting the training graph, and saturating at the second highest value when random prediction has the top score (to avoid distorting the color scale). The best value of each metric is highlighted in bold. All metrics are at a @10 cutoff. (Color figure online)

	Prec.	ARSL	RD	RAE	MPD	IDGC	AEW	CCC	MC	ICGC	LTN	Unexp.	ILD	PGC	CRecall	ERR-IA
Training graph	–	0.256	0.077	0.150	–	0.161	–	0.940	0.146	0.170	–	–	–	–	–	–
User-based CF	**0.068**	0.293	0.111	0.166	0.257	0.119	0.982	0.980	0.155	0.167	0.939	**0.931**	0.809	0.019	0.219	**0.087**
Implicit MF	0.063	0.293	0.111	0.148	0.378	0.117	0.980	0.977	0.155	0.178	0.957	0.871	0.766	0.029	0.238	0.077
Item-based CF	0.059	0.280	0.100	0.149	0.236	0.135	0.976	0.977	0.147	0.159	0.945	0.912	0.774	0.033	0.161	0.075
Pers. SALSA	0.058	0.316	0.125	0.159	0.387	0.112	0.985	0.982	0.166	0.167	0.928	0.861	0.745	0.011	0.238	0.072
Local path ind.	0.051	0.297	0.111	0.151	0.270	0.114	0.982	0.979	0.163	0.172	0.939	0.851	0.728	0.014	0.207	0.064
Adamic-Adar	0.051	0.301	0.125	**0.168**	0.211	0.135	0.969	0.975	0.149	0.170	0.958	0.846	0.762	0.056	0.223	0.060
MCN	0.048	0.299	0.125	0.155	0.207	0.132	0.971	0.975	0.146	0.169	0.959	0.833	0.737	0.045	0.204	0.057
Pers. PageRank	0.045	0.318	**0.143**	0.167	0.209	0.124	0.979	0.983	0.182	0.181	0.949	0.868	0.796	0.029	**0.311**	0.051
Matrix forest	0.039	0.288	0.111	0.161	0.163	0.166	0.955	0.974	0.160	0.182	0.979	0.869	0.764	0.120	0.266	0.046
Popularity	0.023	**0.357**	0.143	0.167	0.755	0.104	**0.997**	**0.989**	**0.295**	0.124	0.884	0.829	0.707	0.001	0.250	0.029
Jaccard	0.017	0.285	0.111	0.163	0.241	0.217	0.930	0.965	0.146	0.183	0.996	0.855	0.774	0.204	0.231	0.021
Content-based	0.013	0.316	0.111	0.147	0.731	0.253	0.948	0.965	0.156	0.190	0.997	0.890	0.710	0.233	0.238	0.018
Katz	0.010	0.296	0.111	0.151	0.706	0.116	0.985	0.984	0.261	0.180	0.974	0.900	0.784	0.014	**0.331**	0.013
Global LHN	0.001	0.299	0.100	0.141	**0.978**	0.221	0.958	0.977	0.146	0.170	**1.000**	0.784	0.628	0.085	0.179	0.001
Random	0.001	0.354	**0.200**	**0.241**	**1.929**	**0.439**	0.996	0.984	0.280	**0.200**	0.998	0.896	**0.838**	**0.823**	**0.497**	0.000

ERR-IA however takes only relevant recommendations into account, whereby it is known to strongly correlate with precision-oriented metrics. ILD, unexpectedness and AEW.

Table 3 shows the detailed metric values for all the algorithms –we also show in the top row, for reference, the metric values of the original (training) graph $\mathcal{G}$ when it makes sense (i.e. for metrics that do not use the set of predicted links $\hat{E}$). We start by noticing that the most accurate methods do not stand out, in general, in other perspectives. The most effective algorithm in precision, user-based collaborative filtering, scores very low for most novelty and diversity metrics (with the exception of ERR-IA, which correlates with precision). And the most inaccurate algorithm, random prediction, trivially achieves the most diverse network structure in terms of almost every metric.

The most outstanding approaches in long-tail novelty are the Jaccard coefficient, the Global LHN index and the content-based approach. Those methods, along with Matrix Forest, are also the only algorithms that improve the IDGC of the original network. The rest of methods seem to be biased towards linking to popular users, thus producing more skewed degree distributions in the extended graph. In terms of ILD and unexpectedness, nearest-neighbor collaborative filtering and Katz stand out. As one might expect, the content-based approach, which links similar users, achieves very poor values for these metrics.

We also observe that most methods (excepting random prediction) tend to connect close people in the network, as reflected in MPD. The algorithms that reach farthest nodes include popularity (highly connected people are not necessarily close to arbitrary target users) and path-based approaches such as Global LHN or Katz. Connecting to popular people also reduces the global distances in the network, as reflected by ARSL, RD and RAE –and PageRank has a similar effect, as it also tends to recommend hubs.

We can also see that links to hubs (popularity) tend to be weak according to AEW and CCC. This is because, on the one hand, AEW is heavily normalized by the neighborhood size, hence resulting in low values for popular people. On the other hand, indegree hubs tend to have a high outdegree; linking to them hence creates many new unclosed triads. This trend drags along the popularity-biased algorithms, such as the user-based CF, and certain path-based algorithms. However in terms of community-based metrics, collaborative filtering and neighborhood methods produce the lowest MC values, that is, the smallest number of community-based weak ties. This is to be expected, since near nodes are less likely to belong to different communities. The disagreement between MC and ICGC on popularity-based recommendation is most revealing as to the nuance of each metric. Links to hubs often cross communities and are hence seen as weak; yet the linked communities are most often the same few ones: the communities of the top k most connected (recommended) people, and hence the community connection diversity is poor according to ICGC. Both metrics otherwise often agree; for instance the Katz algorithm scores quite highly for both, and memory-based CF is rather low on both metrics.

7 Conclusions

Prediction accuracy seems like a rather partial perspective for link prediction considering the new (quantitative and qualitative) dimensions and role that social networks are acquiring, both as a service, a communication platform and a business. We find it natural to consider further perspectives when setting the target for link prediction and recommendation technology. In this paper we reflect on such perspectives and briefly explore some possibilities in this direction. Further metrics can be explored beyond the ones we test here. The metrics can be explicitly targeted either by devising new prediction algorithms that take the new dimensions into account, or by a post-prediction optimization of the output of an initial accuracy-oriented prediction algorithm, taking the desired metric as a second objective. This can be achieved by greedy re-ranking, multi-objective optimization, etc. [4, 18].

While the benefit of accuracy is easy to motivate, we still need to understand better what the network perspectives discussed here imply in terms of their desirability and value for the people in the network, or any other concerned party (platform owner, network data consumers, etc.). For instance, shortening distances seems good for everyone: anyone can reach more people through fewer introductions by common friends [24]. Connecting distant people exposes them to the risk of an enriching experience. Enhancing the degree equality or promoting long-tail users helps avoid the disengagement of less involved people, and the saturation of hubs. Weak links may alleviate social bubbles [26] and/or enhance the speed and diversity of the information flow through the network [10, 29, 36]. Exclusive links between communities may bring strategic value [11], and so forth. This is certainly domain dependent, but can probably be studied also at some level of abstraction, which we envisage as future work.

References

1. Adamic, L.A., Adar, E.: Friends and neighbors on the web. Soc. Netw. **25**(3), 211–230 (2003)

2. Agrawal, R., Gollapudi, S., Halverson, A., Ieong, S.: Diversifying search results. ACM WSDM **2009**, 5–14 (2009)
3. Blondel, V., Guillaume, J., Lambiotte, R., Lefebvrem, E.: Fast unfolding of communities in large networks. J. Stat. Mech. **10**, P10008 (2008)
4. Castells, P., Hurley, N.J., Vargas, S.: Novelty and diversity in recommender systems. In: Ricci, F., Rokach, L., Shapira, B. (eds.) Recommender Systems Handbook, pp. 881–918. Springer, Boston, MA (2015). https://doi.org/10.1007/978-1-4899-7637-6_26
5. Chapelle, O., Shihao, J., Liao, C., Velipasaoglu, E., Lai, L., Wu, S.: Intent-based diversification of web search results: metrics and algorithms. Inf. Ret. **14**(6), 572–592 (2011)
6. Clarke, C., et al.: Novelty and diversity in information retrieval evaluation. ACM SIGIR **2008**, 659–666 (2009)
7. Clauset, A., Newman, M., Moore, C.: Finding community structure in very large networks. Phys. Rev. E **70**(6), 1–6 (2004)
8. Daly, E.M., Geyer, W., Millen, D.R.: The network effects of recommending social connections. ACM RecSys **2010**, 301–304 (2010)
9. Dankelmann, P., Goddard, W., Swart, C.: The average eccentricity of a graph and its subgraphs. Utilitas Math. **65**, 41–52 (2004)
10. De Meo, P., Ferrara, E., Fiumara, G., Provetti, A.: On facebook, most ties are weak. Commun. ACM **57**(11), 78–84 (2014)
11. Granovetter, M.: The strength of weak ties. Am. J. Sociol. **78**(6), 1360–1380 (1973)
12. Goel, A., Gupta, P., Sirois, J., Wang, D., Sharma, A., Gurumurthy, S.: The who-to-follow system at twitter: strategy, algorithms and revenue impact. Interfaces **45**(1), 98–107 (2015)
13. Guimerà, R., Sales-Pardo, M.: Missing and spurious interactions and the reconstruction of complex networks. PNAS **106**(52), 22073–22078 (2009)
14. Guy, I.: Social recommender systems. In: Ricci, F., Rokach, L., Shapira, B. (eds.) Recommender Systems Handbook, 2nd edn, pp. 511–543. Springer, Boston (2015). https://doi.org/10.1007/978-1-4899-7637-6_15
15. Hannon, J., Bennet, M., Smyth, B.: Recommending Twitter users to follow using content and collaborative filtering approaches. ACM RecSys **2010**, 199–206 (2010)
16. Hu, Y., Koren, Y., Volinsky, C.: Collaborative filtering for implicit feedback datasets. ICDM **2008**, 263–272 (2008)
17. Huang, X., Tiwari, M., Shah, S: Structural diversity in social recommender systems. In: RSWeb Workshop at ACM RecSys 2013, CEUR Workshop Proceedings, vol. 1066 (2013)
18. Hurley, N., Zhang, M.: Novelty and diversity in Top-N recommendation – analysis and evaluation. ACM Trans. Internet Technol. **10**(4), 1–30 (2011)
19. Katz, L.: A new status index derived from sociometric analysis. Psychometrika **18**(1), 39–43 (1953)
20. Leicht, E., Holme, P., Newman, M.: Vertex similarity in networks. Phys. Rev. E **73**(2), 026120 (2006)
21. Liben-Nowell, D., Kleinberg, J.: The link-prediction problem for social networks. J. Am. Soc. Inf. Sci. Technol. **58**(7), 1019–1031 (2007)
22. Lichtenwalter, R., Lussier, J., Chawla, N.: New perspectives and methods in link prediction. ACM KDD **2010**, 243–252 (2010)
23. Lü, L., Zhou, T.: Link prediction in social networks: a survey. Phys. A **390**(6), 1150–1170 (2010)
24. Newman, M.: Networks: An Introduction. Oxford University Press, Oxford (2010)
25. Ning, X., Desrosiers, C., Karypis, G.: A comprehensive survey of neighborhood-based recommendation methods. In: Ricci, F., Rokach, L., Shapira, B. (eds.) Recommender Systems Handbook, 2nd edn, pp. 37–76. Springer, Boston (2015). https://doi.org/10.1007/978-1-4899-7637-6_2

26. Pariser, E.: The Filter Bubble. Penguin Books, New York, USA (2012)
27. Parotsidis, E., Pitoura, E., Traparas, P.: Centrality-aware link recommendations. ACM WSDM **2016**, 503–512 (2016)
28. Sanz-Cruzado, J., Castells, P.: Contact recommendations in social networks. In: Collaborative Recommendations, pp. 519–569. World Scientific Publishing, Singapore (2018)
29. Sanz-Cruzado, J., Castells, P.: Enhancing the structural diversity in social networks by recommending weak ties. ACM RecSys **2018**, 233–241 (2018)
30. Su, J., Sharma, A., Goel, S.: The effect of recommendations on network structure. In: WWW 2016, pp. 503–512 (2016)
31. Tang, J., Hu, X., Liu, H.: Social recommendation: a review. Soc. Netw. Anal. Min. **3**(4), 1113–1133 (2013)
32. Vargas, S., Castells, P.: Rank and relevance in novelty and diversity metrics for recommender systems. ACM RecSys **2011**, 109–116 (2011)
33. White, S., Smyth, P.: Algorithms for estimating relative importance in networks. ACM KDD **2003**, 266–275 (2003)
34. Wu, J., Zhang, G., Ren, Y.: A balanced modularity maximization link prediction model in social networks. Inf. Process. Manag. **53**(1), 295–307 (2017)
35. Zhai, C., Cohen, W., Lafferty, J.: Beyond independent relevance: methods and evaluation metrics for subtopic retrieval. ACM SIGIR **2003**, 10–17 (2003)
36. Zhao, J., Wu, J., Xu, K.: Weak ties: subtle role of information diffusion in online social networks. Phys. Rev. E **82**(1), 016105 (2010)

A Novel Similarity Measure for Group Recommender Systems with Optimal Time Complexity

Guilherme Ramos[1,2]($\boxtimes$) and Carlos Caleiro[2]

[1] Department of Electrical and Computer Engineering, Faculty of Engineering,
University of Porto, Porto, Portugal
guilhermeramos21@gmail.com
[2] SQIG - Instituto de Telecomunicações, Department of Mathematics,
Instituto Superior Técnico, University of Lisbon, Lisbon, Portugal
carlos.caleiro@tecnico.ulisboa.pt

Abstract. Once we subscribe to an e-commerce portal, or to a social media website, we interact with multiple brands and with content from numerous providers. However, a unique user profile is created, containing all our preferences. Suppose that a company wants to understand who are its customers. It wants to treat costumers as a target, and understand what campaigns the company should run on them. On the one hand, an approach that clusters the users and performs group recommendations would be useful, while on the other hand, a generic user profile would not be helpful, since the preferences in it are not specific for a brand. Hence, we have to determine multiple user clusterings (one for each brand). This task makes the problem of producing group recommendation challenging, since little and very sparse information about the users is available, and for each pair of users we have to detect as many similarities as the brands existing in the system. To tackle this problem, in this paper, we introduce a novel and optimal measure to compute the similarity between users, based on Kolmogorov complexity. Further, we test it in the group recommendation scenario. The results show that our similarity measure can provide similar accuracy when compared to classical measures, but with significant performance gains, having a strictly lower time complexity than the state-of-the-art similarity measure.

Keywords: Group recommendation · Similarity measure ·
Kolmogorov complexity · Collaborative filtering · Recommender systems

1 Introduction

Our online experience can tell much about our preferences. Indeed, from the analysis of browsing sessions to the comments, likes, and ratings we leave, lots of implicit and explicit traces are available on the Web. These preferences are

© Springer Nature Switzerland AG 2020
L. Boratto et al. (Eds.): BIAS 2020, CCIS 1245, pp. 95–109, 2020.
https://doi.org/10.1007/978-3-030-52485-2_10

usually stored in a user profile and can be exploited by those running services, such as e-commerce websites or social media platforms, to provide us tailored services, like recommendations.

Given that the experience of users on the Web is usually individual, these services are single users' tailored. Group recommendation operates in contexts in which more than one person is involved in the recommendation process [4]. This area usually focuses on offline scenarios, in which people have to experience something together (e.g., a group that goes to dinner, or watches a movie).

Suppose that a brand wants to run an advertising campaign specific to its customers. The usual way of doing it would be targeting a group of users, and recommend them a set of possibly interesting products. Usually, we base this targeting on users' global preferences, i.e., on the whole user's profile. However, it is not trivial to understand how the users interacted with the items of a specific brand. Indeed, the preferences contained in the user profiles are available only to persons who are running an e-commerce website. This website should provide a personalized service to the brand, by extracting segments of users, based only on how they interacted with that brand.

We can effectively employ group recommendation in this scenario, by first analyzing how the users interacted with a brand and detecting groups of users, and by providing group recommendation to these groups, treating them as a target.

Open Problem and Scientific Contribution. Group recommendation is naturally considered a challenging area [21, 37], due to the fact that we have to take into account multiple preferences in the recommendation process. Hence, the problem we are tackling is even more challenging. Indeed, the information about the user preferences becomes even more sparse than the usual recommendation scenarios, and detecting brand-specific groups is not trivial. This problem is due to the fact that the similarity for each pair of users does not have to be detected just once, considering the whole profile, but once for each brand. Hence, we need a fast similarity measure, able to deal both with the fact that the group recommendation problem has to be solved multiple times, and with the continuous evolution of the user preferences.

In this paper, we propose a new similarity measure to group users. This similarity has lower time and space complexity than the state-of-art Pearson correlation similarity measure that presents statistically the same root mean-squared-error results (RMSE) when tested in offline datasets. More specifically, our contributions are the following:

- we propose a novel similarity measure based on Kolmogorov complexity that detects the similarity for the users in an efficient and effective way;
- we show that our measure has lower and optimal time complexity than the state-of-the-art measure used to compute the similarities between users (Pearson's correlation);
- we embed our measure in a group recommender system, and test its effectiveness on two real-world datasets.

Paper Structure. The paper is organized as follows. In Sect. 2, we present related work in group recommendation. In Sect. 3, we introduce the notation we use in the manuscript. In Sect. 4, we propose a novel similarity measure. In Sect. 5, we analyze the computational complexity of the proposed similarity measure. In Sect. 6, we describe the setup of our group recommender system, and we test it in Sect. 7. In Sect. 8, we conclude the paper and draw avenues for further research.

2   Related Work

Group recommender systems provide suggestions in contexts in which the objective of the recommendations is not an individual, but multiple users [2–4,28].

Group recommender systems naturally adapt to any scenario that involves a group of users. Indeed, approaches have been developed for people who perform activities together, such as going to the cinema [33], planning a travel [1,15,30], watching TV [17,42], or working out in a gym [29] (to name a few).

Providing group recommendations in online scenarios is an approach that has been explored, mostly taking advantage of social networks [36,38]. Recent literature has also shown that the offline interaction between the users can help moving from individual to group preferences [16].

Previous approaches have dealt with the detection of cluster for group recommendation purposes [7,10], by analyzing how to deal with the curse of dimensionality when clustering the users [6,13], how to build the predictions [8,11,12], and how to model the group preferences [5,9]. As highlighted in the Introduction, these approaches deal with a unique a user profile and do not separately consider the different preferences of the users.

It is also worth highlighting that Ntoutsi et al., in [32], previously introduced the concept of fast group recommendation. By "fast" the authors meant that the users are clustered in order to speed up the computation when the neighbors are selected at the prediction stage. However, the group recommender system is run once for the whole dataset, so this would not solve the problem tackled in this paper. However, a comparison with this approach will be presented in Sect. 7.

As this analysis of the literature shows, no approach in the literature performed group recommendation at subsets of the dataset, thus facing the efficiency and effectiveness problems at the same time. Moreover, our approach is the first where recommendations may be provided and consumed online.

3   Preliminaries and Notation

We first introduce some notation to make the paper self-contained, and then we propose a similarity to group users for group recommender systems.

We denote the *set of users* by $\mathcal{U} = \{u_1, ..., u_N\}$, the *set of items* by $\mathcal{I} = \{i_1, ..., i_M\}$, and the $N \times M$ matrix of ratings by R, where R_{ui} denotes the rating that user u gave to item i. The entries take values on the set of allowed ratings together with a special value denoting the absence of rating, $\perp$ (in this paper, $\perp$ is either 0 or 99, depending on the dataset). We denote the set of given ratings by $\mathcal{R}$, that is the set of triples (user, item, rating), and it corresponds to the entries of R different from the special number. The set $\mathcal{U}_i = \{u : R_{ui} \neq \perp$ and $u \in \mathcal{U}\}$ denotes the *set of users that rated item i*. The set $\mathcal{I}_u = \{i : R_{ui} \neq \perp$ and $ui \in \mathcal{I}\}$ denotes the *set of items user u rated*. Analogously, we denote the set of items that users u and v, $u, v \in \mathcal{U}$, rated in common by $\mathcal{I}_{u,v} = \mathcal{I}_u \cap \mathcal{I}_v$. We adopt standard notation to denote matrices and vectors. For a matrix R, we denote the uth row of R by R_u, the ith column of R by R_i^{T}, and the ith column of the uth row by R_{ui}. Given a vector $X \in \mathbb{R}^n$, we denote by $\bar{X}$ the average of the vector, i.e.,

$$\bar{X} = \frac{\sum_{i=1}^n X_i}{n}. \tag{1}$$

Further, we denote by σ_X the standard deviation of the vector X, i.e.,

$$\sigma_X = \sqrt{\frac{\sum_{i=1}^n (X_i - \bar{X})^2}{n-1}}. \tag{2}$$

Given a set of objects $\mathcal{X}$, a *similarity* is a function $s : \mathcal{X} \times \mathcal{X} \to [0,1]$ such that whenever $x \in \mathcal{X}$, $s(x,x) = 1$. Further, given two vectors with dimension n, x and y, we denote by $x \odot y$ the vector whose entries are the product of the entries of x and y, i.e., $x \odot y = (x_1 y_1, \ldots, x_n y_n)$.

Let $\Sigma = \{w_1, \ldots, w_k\}$ be a finite alphabet (a set of characters). A word is an element in Σ^*, i.e., a sequence of characters, such that the empty word $\varepsilon \in \Sigma^*$ and if $x, y \in \Sigma^*$ are two words, then its *concatenation* xy is also a word, i.e., $xy \in \Sigma^*$. The length of a word $x \in \Sigma^*$ is inductively defined as $|x| = 0$ if $x = \varepsilon$ and $|x| = 1 + |z|$ if $x = wz$, with $w \in \Sigma$ and $z \in \Sigma^*$.

The Pearson product-moment correlation coefficient [24], or Pearson similarity, is the standard to measure the similarities between users [40]. Given two vectors $X, Y \in \mathbb{R}^n$, the Pearson similarity between the two vector is given by

$$Pearson(X,Y) = \frac{\sum_{i=1}^n (X_i - \bar{X}) \cdot (Y_i - \bar{Y})}{(n-1) \cdot \sigma_X \cdot \sigma_Y}. \tag{3}$$

4   The Kolmogorov-Based Similarity

In this section, we present a new similarity measure, inspired by the notion of Kolmogorov complexity [14], from information theory. Given the description of a string, x, its *Kolmogorov complexity*, $K(x)$, is the length of the smallest computer program that outputs x. In other words, $K(x)$ is the length of the smallest compressor for x. Although Kolmogorov complexity is non-computable, there are efficient and computable approximations by compressors. Let C be a compressor and $C(x)$ denote the *length of the output string* resulting from the compression of x using C. In [25], the authors presented the *normalized compression distance* between two strings x and y:

$$NCD(x,y) = \frac{C(xy) - \min\{C(x), C(y)\}}{\max\{C(x), C(y)\}},$$

where string xy is the concatenation of x and y. We can readily design a similarity measure from the NCD by considering that when the distance is 0 the similarity is 1 and vice-versa, that is, the similarity between strings x and y is $1 - NCD(x, y)$. The main drawback of using NCD in a similarity measure is that, to compute the similarity between two strings, we need to compute their individual compressions, and also the compression of their concatenation. In other words, the time complexity of NCD is $\mathcal{O}(|x| + |y|)$.

Inspired by the NCD, but in order to reduce its computational complexity, we propose another similarity measure. This similarity also makes use of Kolmogorov complexity.

Kolmogorov-Based Similarity. *We define the* Kolmogorov-based similarity *between strings x and y as*

$$KS(x, y) = \frac{1}{1 + |C(x) - C(y)|}. \tag{4}$$

In the context of this work context, the string x is the string with the pairs of items and ratings, given by a user, or the pairs of items and ratings estimated/predicted for that user. To compress the description strings, we use the standard *Python* function, from the *numpy* package, *savez_compressed*. Intuitively, both the similarity based on the NCD and the Kolmogorov similarity KS we propose measure how related are the compactest descriptions of a pair of users or a pair of items.

While we are aware that the KS measure could also be employed to compute the similarity between users in the single-user recommendation scenario, analyzing its effectiveness in that case would beyond the scope of this paper and this study is left as future work.

The presented Pearson similarity and the KS have, here, the same purpose. However, it is not easy to compare them mathematically, although we are able to compare them in terms of computational complexity.

5 Complexity Analysis

Now, we compare the theoretical time and space complexity that we need to compute the Pearson and the KS similarities between every pair of users.

Lemma 1. *Let $\mathcal{U} = \{u_1, \ldots, u_n\}$ be a set of users, $\mathcal{I} = \{i_1, \ldots, i_m\}$ a set of items and $\mathcal{R}$ a set of ratings given by users to items. The time and space complexity of computing the Pearson similarity of each pair of users are $\mathcal{O}(mn^2)$ and $\mathcal{O}(n)$, respectively.*

Proof. First, we compute and store the mean and standard deviation of the ratings for each user. It takes $\mathcal{O}(m)$ time to compute expression 1 for each user. Therefore, we need $\mathcal{O}(nm)$ time to compute the mean vector of the ratings of all users and $\mathcal{O}(n)$ space to store it. Having the mean vector, we may compute the standard deviation, expression 2, also in $\mathcal{O}(nm)$ times and store it in $\mathcal{O}(n)$

space. Now, we need to compute expression 3. For a pair of users ratings, having the vector of means and the vector of standard deviation stored, we need $\mathcal{O}(m)$ time to compute the Pearson similarity between the pair of users. To compute the Pearson similarity of every pair of users, $\mathcal{O}(n \times n)$ pairs, we need $\mathcal{O}(mn^2)$ time.

Lemma 2. *Let* $\mathcal{U} = \{u_1, ..., u_n\}$ *be a set of users,* $\mathcal{I} = \{i_1, ..., i_m\}$ *a set of items and* $\mathcal{R}$ *a set of ratings given by users to items. The time and space complexity of computing the Kolmogorov-based similarity (LS) of each pair of users are* $\mathcal{O}(\max\{n^2, nm\})$ *and* $\mathcal{O}(n)$, *respectively.*

Proof. First, we compute, and store, the compression size of each set of ratings of each user. For each user, the set of ratings has $\mathcal{O}(m)$ size, and we can compute its compression in $\mathcal{O}(m)$ times, using [41], for instance. The $\mathcal{O}(n)$ compressions for each user take $\mathcal{O}(nm)$ time and $\mathcal{O}(n)$ space to store them. Now, we can compute the KS between a pair of users in $\mathcal{O}(1)$ time, using expression 4 and the stored values of the previous step. Finally, to compute the KS similarity for each pair of users, $\mathcal{O}(n^2)$ pairs, hence we need $\mathcal{O}(\max\{n^2, nm\})$ time.

Notice that for the Pearson similarity we need $2n$ space to store the vector of means and the vector of the standard deviation of the users' ratings. For KS, we need only n space to store the size of the compressions of the set of ratings that each user gave. The time complexity of KS contrasts with the one of Pearson similarity, because we need less an order of operations, as we summarize in Table 1.

Table 1. Time and space complexity of the similarities.

	PEARSON	KS
TIME	$\mathcal{O}(mn^2)$	$\mathcal{O}(\max\{n^2, nm\})$
SPACE	$\mathcal{O}(n)$	$\mathcal{O}(n)$

Lemma 3. *If* $n \geq m$, *then KS has optimal time complexity.*

Proof. To compute the similarity between each pair of users we always need to compute at least $\frac{n^2}{2}$ ($\mathcal{O}(n^2)$) values. If $n \geq m$ then $\mathcal{O}(\max\{n^2, nm\}) = \mathcal{O}(n^2)$. Therefore, the time complexity is optimal.

6   The Group Recommender System

Here, we present the group recommender algorithm we use in this work, Algorithm 1.

In particular, in this work, we use as the prediction function *Pred* the benchmark SVD algorithm for matrix completion, see [31]. It has time complexity of

---

Algorithm 1. Group Recommender System.

1: **input**: ratings' matrix R, number of clusters k, a similarity measure s, and rating prediction function $Pred$
2: **compute** $P = Pred(R)$
3: **compute** similarity of each pair of users with function s
4: **compute** G the k groups of users, clustered by similarities
5: **group** estimated ratings in P for each group as the average of predictions
6: **output**: Recommendation list for each group in G

$\mathcal{O}(\min\{mn^2, m^2n\})$ [19]. Also, for a comparison, we test the k-nearest neighbors algorithm (KNN) as the prediction function $Pred$, see [23], with time complexity of $\mathcal{O}(m^2n)$.

Further, we use a polynomial time approximation of the k-means clustering algorithm. The k-means Algorithm [26] is, in general, NP-hard for a generic number of clusters k, even in the plane, see [27]. In practice, k-means may be approximated by Lloyd's heuristic algorithm [18], which has time complexity of $\mathcal{O}(nkdi)$, where k is the number of clusters, d is the dimension of the elements that we are clustering, and i is the number of iterations needed until convergence, which is usually small. In our case $d = 1$, and the number of clusters k is a parameter of Algorithm 1.

Theorem 1. *Let i denote the number of iterations that Lloyd's algorithm takes to compute the users' clusters. Let n be the number of users, m the number of items and k the number of users' groups. The time complexity of Algorithm 1, using SVD as the Pred algorithm of step 2, is:*

– *$\mathcal{O}(mn^2 + nki + km\log m)$, using Pearson similarity;*
– *$\mathcal{O}(\min\{mn^2, m^2n\} + \max\{n^2, mn\} + nki + km\log m)$, using KS.*

Proof. The time complexity of Algorithm 1 is the sum of the time complexities of each step. The SVD step, step 2, takes time of $\mathcal{O}(\min\{mn^2, m^2n\})$. The Lloyd's algorithm, the clustering step 4, takes $\mathcal{O}(nki)$, where i is the number of iterations needed until convergence. If we user the Pearson similarity in step 3, by Lemma 1, we need $\mathcal{O}(mn^2)$ time to compute the similarities between every pair of users. This yields a total time of $\mathcal{O}(n^2m+nki))$, because $mn^2 \geq \min\{mn^2, m^2n\}$. If we use the KS in step 3, by Lemma 2, we need $\mathcal{O}(\max\{n^2, mn\})$ time to compute the similarities between every pair of users, and $\max\{n^2, mn\} < \min\{mn^2, m^2n\}$. Step 4 takes $\mathcal{O}(mn)$ to average the ratings' estimations for the users of each group. Step 5 takes $\mathcal{O}(km\log m)$ to sort the ratings' prediction for each of the k groups. Hence, the total amount of time is $\mathcal{O}(n^2m + nki + km\log m)$ and $\mathcal{O}(\min\{mn^2, m^2n\} + \max\{n^2, mn\} + n^2i + km\log m)$ when using Pearson similarity and KS, respectively.

In fact, Theorem 1 states that the complexity order of Algorithm 1 is strictly better when using KS whenever $n > m$, otherwise it has the same order than when using the Pearson similarity. However, we notice that if we compare not only the complexity order but also the exact complexity, we have the following. When we use Pearson similarity, the total amount of time is $c_1 mn^2 + c_2 \min\{mn^2, m^2n\} + c_3 nki + c_4 km \log m$, for some non zero constants $c_1, c_2, c_3, c_4 \in \mathbb{R}^+$. When we use KS, the total amount of time is $c_2 \min\{mn^2, m^2n\} + c_3 nki + c_4 km \log m + c'mn + c'' \max\{n^2, nm\}$, for the same $c_2, c_3, c_4 \in \mathbb{R}^+$ as in the Pearson's scenario, and $c', c'' \in \mathbb{R}^+$. Therefore, the time complexity is always strictly better in the case that we use KS.

Observe that if, instead of using the SVD algorithm in step 2 of Algorithm 1, we use the KNN algorithm then the time complexity is the following. Using the Pearson similarity, we get $\mathcal{O}(mn^2 + m^2n + nki + km \log m)$, and using KS we always obtain a better complexity order of $O(m^2n + nki + km \log m + \max\{n^2, nm\})$.

7   Experimental Setup

In this section, we test our similarity measure in two real-world datasets. We use the MovieLens 100k (ML–100k) and the MovieLens 1M (ML–1M), available in http://movielens.umn.edu, and both datasets have ratings in $\{1, ..., 5\}$, with $\perp = 0$. The choice of two relatively-small and very sparse datasets was made to simulate our scenario, in which group recommendations have to be computed for medium- and large-sized companies. In other words, to reconnect to the example presented in the Introduction, we are treating each dataset as a company, with its individual customers and items. Given the information about the preferences of the users for that company, we study how efficient and effective it is to produce group recommendations with our similarity measure (KS) and with the state-of-the-art one (Pearson).

All experiments were done in a 3.33GHz Six-core Intel Xeon, with 6GB 1333MHz RAM, using Python 3, and with OS X 10.13. We use the *Surprise scikit* [20] to compute the individual predictions with the SVD algorithm and the KNN algorithm, step 2 of Algorithm 1. Further, to compute the Pearson similarity we use the *pearsonr* function from the Python package *scipy.stats*. A Python 3 implementation of Algorithm 1 is available at https://fenix.tecnico.ulisboa.pt/homepage/ist164938/group-recommender-system.

Table 2. Datasets details.

	ML–100 k	ML–1 M
$|\mathcal{U}|$	983	6040
$|\mathcal{I}|$	1682	3952
$|\mathcal{R}|$	100,000	1,000,000

7.1   Evaluation Measure

To evaluate and compare the performance of the proposed algorithm, Algorithm 1, we use the 5-fold-cross-validation method. For the ML–100k, the dataset already provides a set of 5 train and test files. For the ML–1M we randomly split the original dataset in a set of 5 train/test files (Table 2).

We use the *root-mean-square error (RMSE)* [22] to evaluate the performance of the proposed group recommender algorithm. It measures the difference between the estimated missing values and the original values as we detail next. Let R be the original ratings matrix, and let R^* be the train set, equal to R except on the missing entries of the test set $\mathcal{T}$, where it has the value $\perp$. Let $\hat{R}_{ui}$ denote the estimated rating of the group where user u belongs for item i, and $\hat{R}$ the matrix with all the estimated ratings. The RMSE is given by

$$RMSE(R, \hat{R}) = \sqrt{\frac{1}{|\mathcal{T}|} \sum_{(u,i) \in \mathcal{T}} (R_{ui} - \hat{R}_{ui})^2}. \tag{5}$$

7.2   Experimental Results

Now, we present the experimental results of Algorithm 1. We test the users' clustering/grouping phase using the Pearson similarity versus our proposed Kolmogorov-based similarity (KS). For the ratings' prediction phase, step 2 of Algorithm 1, we tested with the SVD and the KNN algorithms[1].

Figure 1 and Fig. 2 depict the RMSE 5 evolution (yy axis) with the number of users' groups (xx axis) as the average of a 5-fold-cross-validation method. The blue points correspond to using the Pearson similarity and the yellow points to using the KS.

Next, we test that the results depicted in Fig. 1 and Fig. 2 are not related with the prediction algorithm (SVD), step 2 of Algorithm 1. For this purpose, we replace the SVD by the KNN algorithm, and we obtain the results in Figs. 3 and Fig. 4.

We obtain better RMSE results when using SVD for the ratings' prediction phase than when using KNN, which is expected. More important, we get the same behavior in the evolution of the RMSE with the number of groups for the KS and the Pearson similarity, when using either the SVD or the KNN in the prediction step.

We can see in Figs. 1–4 that the RMSE results when using the Pearson similarity or the KS are very close. Hence, we test the null hypothesis (H_0) that the differences we obtain in the results are due to randomness. We compare the two means for the 5-fold tests of each different group size with the Student's

---

[1] In order to speed up the process furthermore and embrace the concept of fast group recommendation proposed by Ntoutsi et al. [32], we also considered an alternative to the KNN approach, in which the neighbors were only selected inside the cluster of the target user. However, results show that, in our context, the effectiveness decreases. These results are not presented, to improve the readability of the paper.

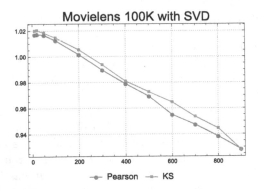

Fig. 1. RMSE evolution with the number of users' groups of a 5-fold-cross-validation method, using Algorithm 1 with SVD for its step 2, with Pearson similarity (blue points) and KS (yellow points) for the ML-100K.

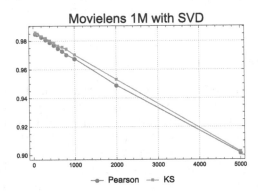

Fig. 2. RMSE evolution with the number of users' groups of a 5-fold-cross-validation method, using Algorithm 1 with SVD for its step 2, with Pearson similarity (blue points) and KS (yellow points) for the ML-1M.

t-test [34]. For both datasets, we obtained p-values larger than 0.05 and, thus, we must accept the H_0. In other words, the RMSE results depicted in Fig. 1 and Fig. 2, and the ones depicted in Fig. 3 and Fig. 4 are, essentially, the same.

Finally, in Table 3, we present average and standard deviation of the time that Algorithm 1 spends in step 3, the computation of the similarities between each pair of users, also using a 5-fold-cross-validation method. Table 3 compares, in practice, the time complexity results of Lemma 1 and Lemma 2, which are part of Algorithm 1 and responsible for the difference of the two cases of time complexity in Theorem 1. Recall that, to compute the similarity of each pair of users, we need $\mathcal{O}(mn^2)$ time using the Pearson similarity, and $\mathcal{O}(n^2)$ using KS. In practice, we notice that for the ML-100k the KS takes a few seconds against the 2 min needed in the Pearson similarity case. Further, for the ML-1M the gain is even more notorious because KS takes only about 1 min versus more than 3 h needed for the Pearson similarity scenario.

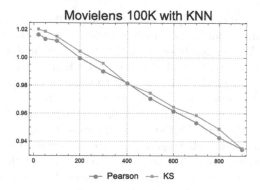

Fig. 3. RMSE evolution with the number of users' groups of a 5-fold-cross-validation method, using Algorithm 1 with KNN for its step 2, with Pearson similarity (blue points) and KS (yellow points) for the ML-100K. (Color figure online)

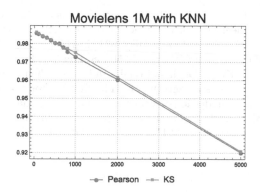

Fig. 4. RMSE evolution with the number of users' groups of a 5-fold-cross-validation method, using Algorithm 1 with KNN for its step 2, with Pearson similarity (blue points) and KS (yellow points) for the ML-1M. (Color figure online)

Table 3. Average and standard deviation of the computation time of the similarities between every pair of users in a 5-fold cross validation.

	ML–100K	ML–1M
Pearson	2'5.1710" ± 1.1862"	3h23'20.3505" ± 10'29.6983"
KS	**4.5608" ± 0.0688"**	**1'13.9046" ± 3.1560"**

8   Conclusions

In this paper, we tackled the problem of producing brand-specific group recommendations, i.e., recommendations to groups of users, considering only the preferences expressed for a specific brand. Since we need to compute the similarity for a pair of users multiple times, we devised a novel and fast to compute similarity measure, the Kolmogorov-based similarity (KS). Our similarity measure has better (and optimal) theoretical computational complexity than the state-of-the-art Pearson similarity, which is widely used in the group recommendation community. We tested these similarity measures in the context of group recommendation in two real-world datasets. The RMSE that we obtained for both similarities is statistically the same, up to some randomness. For the larger dataset, the computation of users' similarities, took 1 min, using the KS, while it took more than 3 h when using the Pearson similarity. In future work, we will analyze the obtained clusters. This analysis allows us to explain to a brand what are the characteristics of each targeted group, in terms of users' preferences. Also as future work, we would like to study the relation of the KS with known Kolmogorov-based distances, see [25] and references therein, and also to explore using different compressors to compute KS. Finally, we would like to study the effect that bribing users to rate items has in group recommender systems, following the approaches of [35,39].

Acknowledgments. G. Ramos is with Department of Electrical and Computer Engineering, Faculty of Engineering, University of Porto, Portugal. This work was supported in part by FCT project POCI-01-0145-FEDER-031411-HARMONY. Further, this work was developed under the scope of R&D Unit 50008, financed by the applicable financial framework (FCT/MEC through national funds and when applicable co-funded by FEDER - PT2020 partnership agreement). The first author acknowledges the support of the DP-PMI and Fundação para a Ciência e a Tecnologia (Portugal), through scholarship SFRH/BD/52242/2013 and the support of Instituto de Telecomunicações through the research grant - BIM/N°154 - 16/11/2017 - UID/EEA/50008/2017.

References

1. Ardissono, L., Goy, A., Petrone, G., Segnan, M., Torasso, P.: Intrigue: personalized recommendation of tourist attractions for desktop and hand held devices. Appl. Artif. Intell. **17**(8–9), 687–714 (2003)
2. Boratto, L.: Group recommender systems. In: Sen, S., Geyer, W., Freyne, J., Castells, P. (eds.) Proceedings of the 10th ACM Conference on Recommender Systems, Boston, MA, USA, 15–19 September 2016, pp. 427–428. ACM (2016)
3. Boratto, L.: Group recommender systems: state of the art, emerging aspects and techniques, and research challenges. In: Ferro, N., et al. (eds.) ECIR 2016. LNCS, vol. 9626, pp. 889–892. Springer, Cham (2016). https://doi.org/10.1007/978-3-319-30671-1_87
4. Boratto, L., Carta, S.: State-of-the-art in group recommendation and new approaches for automatic identification of groups. In: Soro, A., Vargiu, E., Armano, G., Paddeu, G. (eds.) Information Retrieval and Mining in Distributed Environments. Studies in Computational Intelligence, vol. 324, pp. 1–20. Springer, Heidelberg (2011). https://doi.org/10.1007/978-3-642-16089-9_1
5. Boratto, L., Carta, S.: Modeling the preferences of a group of users detected by clustering: a group recommendation case-study. In: Akerkar, R., Bassiliades, N., Davies, J., Ermolayev, V. (eds.) 4th International Conference on Web Intelligence, Mining and Semantics (WIMS 14), WIMS 2014, Thessaloniki, Greece, 2–4 June 2014, pp. 16:1–16:7. ACM (2014)

6. Boratto, L., Carta, S.: Using collaborative filtering to overcome the curse of dimensionality when clustering users in a group recommender system. In: Hammoudi, S., Maciaszek, L.A., Cordeiro, J. (eds.) ICEIS 2014 - Proceedings of the 16th International Conference on Enterprise Information Systems, Volume 2, Lisbon, Portugal, 27–30 April 2014, pp. 564–572. SciTePress (2014)

7. Boratto, L., Carta, S.: ART: group recommendation approaches for automatically detected groups. Int. J. Mach. Learn. Cybernet. **6**(6), 953–980 (2015). https://doi.org/10.1007/s13042-015-0371-4

8. Boratto, L., Carta, S.: The rating prediction task in a group recommender system that automatically detects groups: architectures, algorithms, and performance evaluation. J. Intell. Inf. Syst. **45**(2), 221–245 (2014). https://doi.org/10.1007/s10844-014-0346-z

9. Boratto, L., Carta, S., Fenu, G.: Discovery and representation of the preferences of automatically detected groups: exploiting the link between group modeling and clustering. Future Gener. Comput. Syst. **64**, 165–174 (2016)

10. Boratto, L., Carta, S., Fenu, G.: Investigating the role of the rating prediction task in granularity-based group recommender systems and big data scenarios. Inf. Sci. **378**, 424–443 (2017)

11. Boratto, L., Carta, S., Fenu, G., Mulas, F., Pilloni, P.: Influence of rating prediction on group recommendation's accuracy. IEEE Intell. Syst. **31**(6), 22–27 (2016)

12. Boratto, L., Carta, S., Fenu, G., Mulas, F., Pilloni, P.: Influence of rating prediction on the accuracy of a group recommender system that detects groups. IEEE Intell. Syst., 1 (2017)

13. Boratto, L., Carta, S., Satta, M.; Groups identification and individual recommendations in group recommendation algorithms. In: Picault, J., Kostadinov, D., Castells, P., Jaimes, A. (eds.) Proceedings of the Workshop on the Practical Use of Recommender Systems, Algorithms and Technologies, PRSAT 2010, Barcelona, Spain, 30 September 2010, vol. 676 of CEUR Workshop Proceedings, pp. 27–34 (2010). CEUR-WS.org

14. Cover, T.M., Thomas, J.A.: Elements of Information Theory. Wiley, New York (2012)

15. De Pessemier, T., Dhondt, J., Vanhecke, K., Martens, L.: TravelWithFriends: a hybrid group recommender system for travel destinations. In Proceedings of the Workshop on Tourism Recommender Systems, in Conjunction with the 9th ACM Conference on Recommender Systems, pp. 51–60 (2015)

16. Delic, A., et al.: Observing group decision making processes. In: Proceedings of the 10th ACM Conference on Recommender Systems, RecSys 2016, pp. 147–150. ACM, New York (2016)

17. Goren-Bar, D., Glinansky, O.: Fit-recommend ing TV programs to family members. Comput. Graph. **28**(2), 149–156 (2004)

18. Hartigan, J.A., Wong, M.A.: Algorithm as 136: a k-means clustering algorithm. J. Roy. Stat. Soc. Ser. C (Appl. Stat.) **28**(1), 100–108 (1979)

19. Holmes, M., Gray, A., Isbell, C.: Fast svd for large-scale matrices. In: Workshop on Efficient Machine Learning at NIPS, vol. 58, pp. 249–252 (2007)

20. Hug, N.: Surprise, a Python library for recommender systems (2017). http://surpriselib.com

21. Jameson, A., Smyth, B.: Recommendation to groups. In: Brusilovsky, P., Kobsa, A., Nejdl, W. (eds.) The Adaptive Web. LNCS, vol. 4321, pp. 596–627. Springer, Heidelberg (2007). https://doi.org/10.1007/978-3-540-72079-9_20

22. Koren, Y.: Factorization meets the neighborhood: a multifaceted collaborative filtering model. In: Proceedings of the 14th ACM SIGKDD International Conference on Knowledge Discovery and Data Mining, pp. 426–434. ACM (2008)
23. Koren, Y.: Factor in the neighbors: scalable and accurate collaborative filtering. ACM Trans. Knowl. Discovery Data (TKDD) **4**(1), 1 (2010)
24. Lee Rodgers, J., Nicewander, W.A.: Thirteen ways to look at the correlation coefficient. Am. Stat. **42**(1), 59–66 (1988)
25. Li, M., Chen, X., Li, X., Ma, B., Vitányi, P.M.: The similarity metric. IEEE Trans. Inf. Theory **50**(12), 3250–3264 (2004)
26. MacQueen, J., et al.: Some methods for classification and analysis of multivariate observations. In: Proceedings of the Fifth Berkeley Symposium on Mathematical Statistics and Probability, Oakland, CA, USA, vol. 1, pp. 281–297 (1967)
27. Mahajan, M., Nimbhorkar, P., Varadarajan, K.: The planar k-means problem is NP-hard. In: Das, S., Uehara, R. (eds.) WALCOM 2009. LNCS, vol. 5431, pp. 274–285. Springer, Heidelberg (2009). https://doi.org/10.1007/978-3-642-00202-1_24
28. Masthoff, J.: Group recommender systems: aggregation, satisfaction and group attributes. In: Ricci, F., Rokach, L., Shapira, B. (eds.) Recommender Systems Handbook, pp. 743–776. Springer, Boston, MA (2015). https://doi.org/10.1007/978-1-4899-7637-6_22
29. McCarthy, J.F., Anagnost, T.D.: MusicFX: an arbiter of group preferences for computer supported collaborative workouts. In: Poltrock, S.E., Grudin, J. (eds.) CSCW 1998, Proceedings of the ACM 1998 Conference on Computer Supported Cooperative Work, Seattle, WA, USA, 14–18 November 1998, pp. 363–372. ACM (1998)
30. McCarthy, K., Salamó, M., Coyle, L., McGinty, L., Smyth, B., Nixon, P.: Cats: a synchronous approach to collaborative group recommendation. In: Sutcliffe, G., Goebel, R. (eds.) Proceedings of the Nineteenth International Florida Artificial Intelligence Research Society Conference, Melbourne Beach, Florida, USA, 11–13 May 2006, pp. 86–91. AAAI Press (2006)
31. Mnih, A., Salakhutdinov, R.R.: Probabilistic matrix factorization. In: Advances in Neural Information Processing Systems, pp. 1257–1264 (2008)
32. Ntoutsi, E., Stefanidis, K., Nørvåg, K., Kriegel, H.-P.: Fast group recommendations by applying user clustering. In: Atzeni, P., Cheung, D., Ram, S. (eds.) ER 2012. LNCS, vol. 7532, pp. 126–140. Springer, Heidelberg (2012). https://doi.org/10.1007/978-3-642-34002-4_10
33. O'Connor, M., Cosley, D., Konstan, J.A., Riedl, J.: PolyLens: a recommender system for groups of users. In: Prinz, W., Jarke, M., Rogers, Y., Schmidt, K., Wulf, V. (eds.) Proceedings of the Seventh European Conference on Computer Supported Cooperative Work, Bonn, Germany, 16–20 September 2001, pp. 199–218. Kluwer (2001)
34. O'Mahony, M.: Sensory Evaluation of Food: Statistical Methods and Procedures, vol. 16. CRC Press, Boca Raton (1986)
35. Ramos, G., Boratto, L., Caleiro, C.: On the negative impact of social influence in recommender systems: a study of bribery in collaborative hybrid algorithms. Inf. Process. Manag. **57**(2), 102058 (2020)
36. Recalde, L., Mendieta, J., Boratto, L., Teran, L., Vaca, C., Baquerizo, G.: Who you should not follow: extracting word embeddings from tweets to identify groups of interest and hijackers in demonstrations. IEEE Trans. Emerging Top. Comput., 1 (2017)

37. Alhajj, R., Rokne, J. (eds.): Encyclopedia of Social Network Analysis and Mining. Springer, New York (2014). https://doi.org/10.1007/978-1-4614-6170-8
38. Sánchez, L.Q., Díaz-Agudo, B., Recio-García, J.A.: Development of a group recommender application in a social network. Knowl. Based Syst. **71**, 72–85 (2014)
39. Saúde, J., Ramos, G., Caleiro, C., Kar, S.: Reputation-based ranking systems and their resistance to bribery. In: 2017 IEEE International Conference on Data Mining (ICDM), pp. 1063–1068. IEEE (2017)
40. Brusilovsky, P., Kobsa, A., Nejdl, W. (eds.): The Adaptive Web. LNCS, vol. 4321. Springer, Heidelberg (2007). https://doi.org/10.1007/978-3-540-72079-9
41. Williams, R.N.: An extremely fast ziv-lempel data compression algorithm. In: Data Compression Conference, DCC 1991, pp. 362–371. IEEE (1991)
42. Yu, Z., Zhou, X., Hao, Y., Gu, J.: TV program recommendation for multiple viewers based on user profile merging. User Model. User Adap. Inter. **16**(1), 63–82 (2006)

What Kind of Content Are You Prone to Tweet? Multi-topic Preference Model for Tweeters

Lorena Recalde[1(⊠)] and Ricardo Baeza-Yates[2]

[1] Information and Computer Sciences Department, National Polytechnic School,
Quito, Ecuador
lorena.recalde@epn.edu.ec

[2] Department of Information and Communication Technologies,
Universitat Pompeu Fabra, 08018 Barcelona, Spain
ricardo.baeza@upf.edu

Abstract. According to tastes, a person could show preference for a given category of content to a greater or lesser extent. However, quantifying people's amount of interest in a certain topic is a challenging task, especially considering the massive digital information they are exposed to. For example, in the context of Twitter, aligned with his/her preferences a user may tweet and retweet more about technology than sports and do not share any music-related content. The problem we address in this paper is the identification of users' implicit topic preferences by analyzing the content categories they tend to post on Twitter. Our proposal is significant given that modeling their multi-topic profile may be useful to find patterns or association between preferences for categories, discover trending topics and cluster similar users to generate better group recommendations of content. In the present work, we propose a method based on the Mixed Gaussian Model to extract the multidimensional preference representation for 399 Ecuadorian tweeters concerning twenty-two different topics (or dimensions) which became known by manually categorizing 68.186 tweets. Our experiment findings indicate that the proposed approach is effective at detecting the topic interests of users.

Keywords: Multidimensional profile · User modeling · Expectation maximization · Group recommender system · Topic modeling · Twitter

1 Introduction

People show different levels of interest in the different topics which compose the large amounts of digital information they are exposed to. Quantifying and measuring a user's degree of interest in a given piece of content and finding its correlation with his/her preference for another topic is a challenging task, especially in social media platforms where the user interests are not static. For example, people highly engaged with culture-related topics may often retweet posts about

© Springer Nature Switzerland AG 2020
L. Boratto et al. (Eds.): BIAS 2020, CCIS 1245, pp. 110–126, 2020.
https://doi.org/10.1007/978-3-030-52485-2_11

upcoming concerts, but when their favorite soccer team wins a match, they generate posts according to a sports related topic. Therefore, representing this kind of topic preferences association as a multidimensional user model, (MUM), may be useful to define how much the user shows interest in content categories as well as to group like-minded users and generate better recommendations for them.

In the context of Twitter, automatically classifying a tweet into a topic category is hard to achieve. Indeed, having a group of words that form a sentence of less than 140 characters[1] and that contains abbreviations, emoticons, URLs and mentions of other users, which in particular do not provide a relevant meaning by themselves, makes the semantic analysis a challenge. Also, during the classification work of a tweet, the capture of other words like hashtags[2], proper nouns, compound nouns and verbs lead to a better topic assignment. Accordingly, to make the implementation of the comprehension and classification tasks of a tweet possible (as the basic step to then associate topic interest to tweeters) we propose a method that merges language modeling techniques together with the Expectation Maximization algorithm [6] (EM for Mixture of Gaussians).

The strategy is independent of the users' posts language which makes it feasible to take Spanish tweets posted by Ecuadorians as our case study. Respectively, aggregating the Mixed Gaussian Model (topic soft assignments) of the target users' tweets in order to find their MUM is useful for clustering them and finding groups of users interested in the same topics and with the same level of interest. There are many research works in the field of users' topic preferences modeling. However, to the best of our knowledge, our proposal represents the first attempt to quantify the degree of responsibility a topic has over a given tweeter. That is to say, the method allows to identify the percentage in which each category (*i.e.*, topic) takes part in the user profile. Given this real-world application scenario, our scientific contributions are:

- A method to define the multidimensional user model MUM for tweeters, which can be further applied to cluster like-minded users and design group recommendations.
- An evaluation of the accuracy of the proposed method considering, in terms of a comparative analysis, a baseline approach which takes a *ground-truth dataset* of labeled tweets. In such way, the MUM approach is compared to the results of a traditional machine learning classifier.
- A detailed validation of our approach that shows its effectiveness in modeling users. We show that similar tweeters, whose profiles were modeled with MUM, are effectively grouped together.

In summary, in this paper we propose a novel method for unsupervised and topic-based "soft" classification of tweets. This approach is used to model Twitter users. The remainder of the paper is organized as follows. Section 2 summarizes the context of the present research and related literature; moreover, we

---

[1] When the dataset was collected Twitter posts were limited to 140 characters. Currently, the length of a tweet may be up 280 characters.

[2] Users can add some words prefixed by the symbol # to their tweets and they are identified as hashtags.

draw a comparison to our proposal; Sect. 3 describes our approach; in Sect. 4 we present the experimental framework and the obtained results. Finally, some observations, findings and future directions are discussed in Sect. 5.

2   Related Work

Modeling users' profiles is essential to find the topics they enjoy consuming and provide users with meaningful information, in this section we present related works considering *Tweeters Modeling for Recommender Systems* whose aim is to link tweeters with the corresponding content/items. Later, *Group Formation and Group Recommendation* is detailed due to the further application of our approach in this area. Finally, as our proposal is based on the use of EM to find the *degree of responsibility* [20] a topic has over a tweet, *Tweets Classification* is also described.

2.1   Tweeters Modeling for Recommendation

Recommender systems predict if an *unseen item* is going to be of interest to a target user. To address the problem of recommendation in the Social Web such systems mine people's interactions, trust connections, previously adopted suggestions, use of self-annotated content (*i.e.* through hashtags), and group subscription, among others [9]. Tweet recommendation has been studied due to the constant threat of content overload in the users time-line. In [5], the approach makes use of three components: tweet topic level factors, user social relation factors and explicit features like authority of the tweet creator and quality of the tweet to define if a tweet can be recommended. Unlike our proposal, [5] bases the user model on the social connections and not on topics of interest. Research presented in [4] proposes a URLs recommender system for tweeters based on content sources, topic interest models of users, and social voting. Their findings show that topic relevance and social interactions were helpful in presenting recommendations. They work with the weighting scheme *TF-IDF* [17] to find the relevant topics for the user while we apply word embeddings.

In [21], Weng *et al.* propose an approach to identify and rank topic-influential Twitter users. A main step in the approach is the topics modeling per user. The authors apply Latent Dirichlet Allocation (LDA [2]) to distill the topics that tweeters are interested in. To identify the topics that are related to the user, they aggregate the tweets posted by him/her so they can be seen as a *document*. Similarly, in our approach we need to aggregate the content generated by the user. However, instead of aggregating the user's tweets we aggregate the tweets' embeddings. Furthermore, unlike applying LDA for topic modeling, we use the Mixture Gaussian Model.

2.2   Groups Formation and Recommendations

From a general perspective, the benefits of using a microblogging platform such as Twitter emerge from the activity of the users themselves. This social and data-oriented phenomenon is known as collective intelligence [11]. For example, a recommender system that tracks events liked by the users may infer that the users who attend musicals twice a month also attend plays once a month. This generalization may be done because the system learns patterns from the behavior of the whole community. In such a case, like-minded users need to be grouped and analyzed together.

A Group Recommender System supports the recommendation process by using aggregation methods in order to model the preferences of a group of people. This is needed when there is an activity (domain) that can be done or enjoyed in groups [3]. From our proposal, it may be possible to detect groups of tweeters interested in the same topics and suggest for them, for example, lists to subscribe in.

2.3 Tweets Classification

In terms of tweets classification, in [18], 5 content categories (News, Events, Opinions, Deals, and Private Messages) are proposed in order to classify short text. In this work, tweets are modeled considering 8 specific features which lead to determine the class of a tweet. For example, one of the features is *presence of time-event phrases* that, when it is true for a given tweet, might relate it to the Events category. On the other hand, when the feature *presence of slang words, shortenings* is true for a given tweet this may suggest a "Private Message class". Whereas this method works with more general categories and a supervised classifier, our proposal allows a 300-dimension representation of tweets which are later classified (with soft assignments) considering 22 categories.

In [8], the problem of hashtag prediction is investigated to recommend the users proper hashtags for their tweets. As a first step, Naïve Bayes and the Expectation Maximization algorithm are employed to classify English and non-English tweets. Later, LDA with Gibbs sampling is applied to find the tweet-topic distribution. Like our proposal, EM was employed as a means of unsupervised classification of tweets. However, we used it to model the tweets depending on the hidden topics, to then see the tweet model as a percentage allocation per topic. On the other hand, the mentioned work uses EM to identify the probability of a tweet as being writing in English and later, they do a hard class assignment.

Topic modeling with LDA-based approaches has been broadly used as means of tweet classification. Furthermore, supervised learning to classify tweets according to topics has also been studied. In [10], the authors propose a method where a group of four classifiers are trained to learn the topics for tweet categorization. They define ten topics and with the help of annotators, they classify a set of hashtags into those topics. Once the hashtags are classified, they can label tweets (containing the hashtags) with the corresponding topic. In their experiments they try to find the features and feature classes relevant to maximize the topic classification performance. The baseline method employed to validate our approach follows the same strategy in terms of supervised classification. In [22], a real-time high-precision tweet topic modeling system is proposed. A total of 300 topics are considered, and the proposal is based on an integrative inference algorithm using supervised learning. In contrast, we present a method to categorize tweets in an unsupervised manner. Our method is effective in calculating the degree of participation of a topic in a given tweet (soft clustering) and no labeled data is required.

3   Approach

In this section we present the core phases that were implemented to *i)* identify the level of responsibility that each category has over a tweet and *ii)* aggregate the user's tweets classification extracted in the former phase to then define his/her multidimensional user model *MUM*. The *MUM* approach, consists of:

1. **Tweets Modeling.** By using word2vec [14] we find a vector representation for a given tweet.
2. **Extraction of the Suitable Number of Topics.** A known technique to define the number of topics hidden in a corpus is the Elbow method [19]. We use it to decide how many dimensions our tweet/user model will have.
3. **Tweets Classification.** To define the topics' responsibility degree over a tweet we use EM. As a result, every tweet will have a vector with K dimensions where K depends on the number of topics. Every feature value of the vector is the percentage of the participation of the corresponding topic in the given tweet.
4. **Twitter Users Model.** Once the strategy to model a tweet is established as formulated in the previous phase, it is applied to the tweets of the target user. We aggregate the results to define the multidimensional user model.
5. **Grouping like-minded Users.** *MUM* provides a profile of tweeters who may be clustered in groups of homogeneous interests.

The following presents the details of our approach considering each task.

3.1   Tweets Modeling

A collection of tweets is employed to build a vector representation model for the words (vocabulary). We use a word embedding strategy based on a neural language model, *word2vec*, and its implementation *skip-gram*. The model learns to map each word into a low-dimensional continuous vector-space from its distributional properties observed in the provided corpus of tweets.

To train the model, a file that contains one tweet per row is needed. Other input parameters have to be provided: *size* or number of vector dimensions, *window* or maximum skip length between words, *sample* or threshold for how often the words occur, and *min_count* or minimum number of times a word must occur to be considered. The output of the trained model is a vector for each word in the corpus. Since the vectors are linear, we can sum several vectors to obtain a unique model representation. Therefore, in order to create a model of a *tweet* from the words in it, we sum its word vectors. Let W_t be the set of words in the considered tweet t. By taking their embeddings, w_t being the vector for a given word, we build the tweet model:

$$w'_t = \sum_{w_t \in W_t} w_t \tag{1}$$

then, the vector representation for t is w'_t.

The authors of this paper have worked in tweets modeling with word2vec in previous research projects, and the detailed methodology which covers tweets cleaning/pre-processing and text modeling is explained in [15]. It is worth mentioning that the tweets are being represented as 300-dimension vectors. The values that the parameters took in this study are reported in the Sect. 4.3 to allow our experiments to be reproduced.

3.2   Extraction of the Suitable Number of Topics

To define the number of topics in which tweeters tend to get involved, we take the w'_t or tweets representation extracted previously and try to find the appropriate number of clusters of tweets. Therefore, we may find a meaningful topic per cluster by inspecting the tweets in it (in case the clusters need to be labeled). To separate the tweets into clusters, we applied *K-Means++* [1]. This method spreads out the initial set of cluster centroids, so that they are not too close together. By applying *K-Means++*, it is possible to find an optimal set of centroids, which is required to have optimal means to initialize EM.

The intuition behind clustering is that objects within a cluster are as similar as possible, whereas objects from different clusters are as dissimilar as possible. However, the optimal clustering is somehow subjective and dependent of the final purpose of the clusters; that is to say, the level of detail required from the partitions. The clusters we obtain may suffer from a wide variation of the number of samples in each cluster (*e.g.* few tweets talking about religion and lots talking about politics) so the distribution is not normal. Nevertheless, we can select the number of clusters by using the heterogeneity convergence metric as the *Elbow* method specifies. We are required to run tests considering different K values (*i.e. number of clusters*). To measure distances between observations we use the cosine distance metric. Then, having K, we measure the intra-cluster distances between n points in a given cluster C_k and the centroid c_C of that cluster.

$$D_k = \sum_{i=1}^{n} cosineDistance(x_i, c_C)^2 \quad x_i \in C_k \ \land \ n = |C_k|$$

Finally, adding the intra-cluster sums of squares gives a measure of the compactness of the clustering:

$$het_k = \sum_{k=1}^{K} D_k \tag{2}$$

In the *Elbow* heuristic we need to visualize the curve by plotting the heterogeneity value het_k against the number of clusters K. At certain point, the gain will drop, forming an angle in the graph. Therefore, the "Elbow" of the curve will be where the heterogeneity decreases *rapidly* before this value of K, but then only *gradually* for larger values of K. The details of this analysis are presented in the experimental setup (Sect. 4.3). While doing the experiments with different K values, we need to keep track not only the heterogeneity (used to apply the Elbow method), but also the centroids c_C calculated for the clusters.

3.3 Tweets Classification: The EM Algorithm Applied over Tweets

Mixture of Gaussians is one of the probabilistic models that can be used for the soft-clustering of observations. The model assumes that all the observations are generated from a mixture of K Gaussian distributions with unknown parameters. Then, after learning the properties of the observations, each mixture component represents a unique cluster specified by its weight, mean and variance. Mixture models generalize K-Means clustering by taking into account information about the covariance structure of the data as well as the centers of the latent Gaussians.

When the number of topics, specified by the number of clusters found in the previous phase is obtained, the next step is the implementation of the Expectation Maximization (EM) algorithm. EM is sensitive to the choice of initial means. With a bad initial set of means, EM might generate clusters that span a large area and are mostly overlapping. Then, instead of initializing means by selecting random points, we take the final set of centroids calculated before (suitable set of initial means). Indeed, the initialization values for EM will be: *i)* initial means, the cluster centroids c_C extracted for the chosen K; *ii)* initial weights, we will initialize each cluster weight as the proportion of tweets assigned by K-Means++ to that cluster C_k; in other words, n/N for $n = |C_k|$ and $N = $ total number of tweets; iii) initial covariance matrix, to initialize the covariance parameters, we compute $\sum_{i=1}^{N}(x_{ij} - \mu_{C_k j})^2$ for each dimension j. When the initial parameters are set, the input for the algorithm will be the vectors which belong to the tweets that we want to model. The EM algorithm will be in charge of defining the degree of responsibility the topics will have over each tweet [20]. Then, the output after running the algorithm will be the *responsibility matrix*[3] whose cardinality is NxK. Each row of the matrix corresponds to a responsibility vector r_i, where each element is the *responsibility* cluster k takes for observation x_i: $r_i = [r_{i1}, r_{i2}, ..., r_{iK}]$. In other words, the rows of the matrix specify the extent to which the observation x_i was assigned to the different K topics (columns). For example, if the topic 0 (or cluster 0) has full responsibility over the observation the value is going to be 1. If we see shared responsibility between eight topics over another tweet, the sum of those values will be 1 (refer to Sect. 4.3 to see an example).

---

[3] Refer to the repository https://github.com/lore10/Multidimensional_User_Profile to access the code related to the EM algorithm (datasets and other files are also included).

3.4   Twitter Users Model: Extraction of the MUM

Once we have obtained the responsibility matrix, we then need to identify which tweets (rows of the matrix) correspond to the given user (noting t as a modeled tweet $\in T_u$). Thus, for the user being analyzed we will have a $|T_u|\text{x}K$ submatrix, which will be represented as U. To establish the Multidimensional User Model (MUM), we apply the following equations.

$$sum_j = \sum_{i=0}^{|T_u|-1} t_{ij} \tag{3}$$

for $j \in [0, K-1]$. Then, we sum the vector values j to obtain the total:

$$total = \sum_{j=0}^{K-1} sum_j \tag{4}$$

Finally, the model for the user (given by dimension j) will be represented as percentages:

$$MUM_j = (sum_j/total) * 100 \tag{5}$$

In conclusion, MUM is going to be a vector of K dimensions that models the given user according to the topics he/she tends to tweet about. The j values will express the extent of topic participation in the user's Twitter profile.

3.5   Grouping Like-Minded Users

One of the applications of the multi-topic model of users would be for clustering similar users to analyze audiences on Twitter. This would make it possible to target certain groups of tweeters with recommendations, and studying subtopics of interest given a group, among others. In the case of our study, grouping like-minded users was employed to evaluate the proposed approach performance. The clustering algorithm we used was K-Means++ [13], whose implementation is provided in the tool Graphlab [12] for Python (K-Means with smart centers initialization). The scalability and low cost of the algorithm to process partitions of big datasets allows this clustering approach to be used widely for many applications. To define the optimal number of groups of users, for a given dataset being analyzed, we also applied the Elbow Heuristic.

4   Experimental Framework

In this section, we detail the experimental framework which validates our proposal. We present a case study based on a real-world scenario and have divided the section as follows: First, we describe the datasets employed during the experiments; then we provide an explanation about the baseline approach used for comparison. Later, the experimental setup followed by the corresponding results are discussed.

4.1   Data Collection

To run the experiments and implement our approach we need the following:

- A set of tweets to train the word2vec model,
- A list of users and their tweets/retweets, and
- A list of users whose profile or preferred topic is well known in order to evaluate the performance of the baseline method and the proposed approach.

The detailed description of the data is provided next.

Training Corpus to Obtain the Vocabulary Model. As it was said before, we collected datasets with the aim of applying word2vec. The trained model, which was the result of the research done in [16], was used in the present work because of the advantages the dataset presented: *i)* diverse nature of content from a pool of 319,889 tweets posted by Ecuadorian users over a one month period, and *ii)* the authors have knowledge of the context involved, *i.e.* hashtags and their topics, meaning of referenced places and events, and public figures as well as the category their posts fall in. The previous research explored and validated the quality of the training dataset. Indeed, the vocabulary extracted and represented as vectors covers most of the words Ecuadorian tweeters tend to use. Therefore, it suggests that the model can be generalized for similar scenarios as the one presented in this research. Furthermore, after performing validation tests, it was found that the appropriate representation for this kind of input text (short sentences in Spanish) was of 300 dimensions.[4] The trained model corresponds to the output of the approach phase presented in Sect. 3.1, Tweets Modeling. Once these tweets were modeled we identified the number of topics involved (Sect. 3.2) and the centroids for initializing the EM algorithm. Also, the vocabulary vectors were later used to define other tweet models.

Sample of Users and Their Timeline. A set of 360 users was sampled from the list of tweeters who created the tweets in Sect. 4.1. Every tweet in the corpus has meta-data that has information about it, such as 'text' of the tweet, 'creation date', 'list of hashtags' contained in the tweet, 'user' (id number and screen name) who posted the tweet, among others. Given that we have a list of 37,628 users, we had to randomly sample 360 of them due to the Twitter API rate limits. To apply the proposed method, we extracted the last 3,200 tweets from their accounts. Finally, the amount of tweets collected from the users' timelines was 236,453.

Sample of Users for Approach Evaluation. We considered a list of 39 political figures who have worked in the government in decision-making positions or who were candidates for government positions during the 2017 elections.

---

[4] Google uses a 300 dimension vector to represent words and has published a pretrained model. This model was trained on Google news data (around 100 billion words) and contains 3 million words and phrases in the vocabulary.

Their tweets were collected during election campaigns (Nov 2016), and we validated their political profile in the platform 'Smart Participation' (Participación Inteligente).[5] The official information published there confirmed their candidature as politicians and affiliation to a political party. We queried their Twitter accounts and extracted a total list of 58,533 tweets. These tweets were added to the set previously obtained. Then, we applied our approach (Sect. 3.3) considering a dataset of 294,986 tweets in total. It is worth mentioning that those tweets belong to the 399 users. 39 of them are politicians (intentionally added to the corpus of 360 users) to test the accuracy of the proposed approach. In other words, the political figures help us to validate if after getting their *MUMs* and clusters (Sects. 3.4, 3.5), they are going to be found as similar (homogeneous profile models) and put together. In this way, we can validate that the tweets and users are being correctly modeled.

4.2   Baseline Approach

To compare the performance of the MUM approach for modeling tweeters, a baseline method is proposed by elaborating a strategy made of core techniques. What follows is a map of the steps of our approach and the decisions made to construct the baseline.

1. **Tweets Modeling.** The dataset of tweets presented in Sect. 4.1 (training corpus) was modeled by applying *TF-IDF*.
2. **Extraction of the Suitable Number of Topics.** To build a ground truth about the topics hidden in the tweets dataset and obtain a subset of classified tweets, we extracted a list of the most frequent hashtags present in the tweets. We inspect the hashtags to identify keywords corresponding to a given category. For example, the hashtags *#ecu911, #routesecu911 and #ecu911withme* lead us to define the topic *Citizens Safety and Emergencies*. As a result, 22 topics were extracted and the corresponding tweets, which contained the studied hashtags, were labeled accordingly. Usually, this manual classification technique allows the categorization of 20% of the tweets. In our case, from 319,889 tweets we classified 68,186 which correspond to 21.3%. The 22 categories define the number of dimensions the users' model will have.
3. **Tweets Classification.** In our approach, EM is used to generate a topic-soft-assignment for each tweet (Mixture of Gaussians). For the baseline approach, we will predict the *topic* of the given tweet by applying a traditional machine learning algorithm. We did a series of tests to select an appropriate classification algorithm. First, we chose three machine learning approaches used to realize *multi-class* prediction. These were logistic regression, decision trees and boosting trees. Then, we took 80% of the previously labeled tweets to be the training dataset. The rest of the tweets were used to test the models.
   As shown in Fig. 1, the Boosting Trees algorithm [7] outperformed the others, so it was chosen to classify the users' tweets. The algorithm is based on

---

[5] Voting Advice Application in Ecuador, https://participacioninteligente.org.

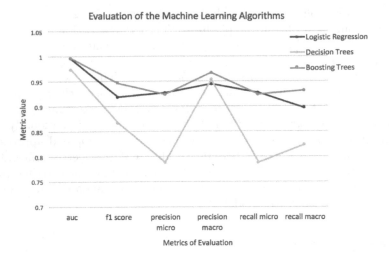

Fig. 1. Comparison of the performance of the algorithms (multi-class prediction).

a technique which combines a collection of base learners (decision tree classifiers) for predictive tasks. It can model non-linear interactions between the
features and the target. For precision and recall we calculated the micro and
macro values [23]. Micro precision/recall calculates the metrics globally by
counting the total true positives, false negatives, and false positives. On the
other hand, the macro value calculates the metrics for each label and finds
their unweighted mean (label imbalance is not considered). We use the trained
boosted trees model[6] to get the class/topic of the new observations (294,986
tweets of the 399 users with their TF-IDF representation). As output, we
obtain the *class* and the corresponding *class-probabilities*.

4. **Twitter Users Model.** The MUM method aggregates the results of the
   EM algorithm applied over the tweets of a given user. On the other hand,
   considering the baseline approach, we take the tweets of the target user T_u
   and their probabilities associated to the class prediction P_t (results of the
   boosting trees classifier). Lastly, to define the user's model M for the baseline,
   we average the probabilities obtained for each of the 22 classes:

$$M_j = avg(\sum_{i=0}^{|T_u|-1} P_t^{ij})$$

for $j \in [0, 21]$. At the end of this baseline method's stage, the users will
have a set of j values that quantify the level of preference of the user for the
corresponding 22 topics.

---

[6] https://turi.com/products/create/docs/generated/graphlab.boosted_trees_classifier.
html.

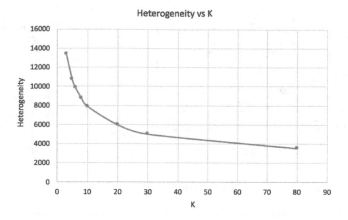

Fig. 2. Elbow Heuristic: heterogeneity vs K values.

5. **Grouping like-minded Users.** This step evaluates the performance of the baseline approach. In order to compare our method and the baseline, this step was identically applied in both MUM and M (refer to Sect. 3.5). More detail about the obtained results is given in Sect. 4.4.

4.3   Experimental Setup and Strategy

The parameters used to apply word2vec over the *training corpus* are: *size=300*, *window=5*, *sample=0* and *min_count=5*. The output of the word2vec model contains a vocabulary of 39,216 words represented as vectors. Equation 1 was applied to obtain the vectors of the tweets in the training corpus. When the set of w'_t is ready we can move on to the next phase to define the number of clusters in which the tweets are classified. We ran some experiments with different values of K (the number of clusters to find). For each given K we applied K-Means++ to cluster the tweets and after that, we calculated the heterogeneity (Eq. 2).

The results are shown in Fig. 2 where we have the heterogeneity vs K plot.[7] The Elbow Heuristic specifies that by analyzing this plot, the gain reduces significantly from $K = 3$ to $K = 20$. Besides, we see a flattening out of the heterogeneity for $K >= 30$ (overfitting for larger K). So, it might indicate that K is in a range of 20 and 30. To make a choice for K, we take into account the manual classification of the training tweets in the baseline method, where *22 topics* were found. Whereby, as the Elbow Heuristic also suggests, we consider $K = 22$. The centroids for the 22 clusters are calculated and used to initialize the *means* for EM. When applying the EM algorithm in order to get a soft topic assignment per tweet, we used the dataset of 399 users' tweets. When EM converges, we will

---

[7] For the given K we test some initialization seeds: 0, 20000, 40000, 60000, 80000. To define the centroids we took the seed that reported the minimum heterogeneity.

	Life reflections	Activism/ IdealsDefense	Economy	Politics Elections	(-) sentiment
The Ecuador is with you vicepresident @JorgeGlas ♥ we support you 👍 #JorgeFriend	2.1E-36	6.8E-19	6.1E-13	1.0E+00	1.2E-78
We'll be in #Quito supporting the #winnerTeam Lenin-Jorge ♥ no one will stop us 👍	1.9E-25	5.5E-01	2.1E-01	2.4E-01	9.6E-65
Mixed feelings 😊 #remembering🔥	2.4E-25	1.3E-81	2.5E-89	3.9E-61	1.0E+00
We are going for more 👍 https://t.co/KRcYQaLJI6	4.3E-69	9.1E-95	1.6E-98	1.0E+00	5.9E-78
The eyes show the sadness of a face.	1.0E+00	7.2E-53	8.2E-26	1.2E-35	2.3E-12
Love what you have before the life makes you love what you loose.	1.6E-14	1.6E-91	3.5E-76	9.3E-62	1.0E+00
#C7moreThan a competition a stile of life	1.0E+00	2.6E-22	1.6E-24	8.3E-33	1.2E-22
God gives the hardest fights to the best soldiers.	1.0E+00	3.6E-47	5.0E-50	2.5E-24	6.1E-06
An abnormal life.	2.2E-10	2.5E-57	1.3E-70	6.4E-50	1.0E+00
The silence and behavior say everything 😊 learn from life's lessons	1.0E+00	6.2E-71	2.7E-33	1.2E-51	3.0E-20
Dreams never end 😊	1.0E+00	6.6E-76	2.3E-46	9.2E-39	5.4E-05
Study study study despite everything 😊 😊	1.9E-11	6.4E-108	3.0E-80	1.4E-65	9.9E-01
Here, doing the thesis 😴 no sleeping 😴 http://t.co/sRWyUer2k	3.7E-11	3.3E-70	1.1E-67	4.1E-74	1.0E+00

Fig. 3. Example of topic assignment with EM algorithm.

Table 1. Summary of users clusters: Baseline and MUM methods.

Cluster ID	Total size (baseline)	Total size (MUM)	Politicians classification (baseline)	Politicians classification (MUM)
0	50	100	17	36
1	165	6	0	0
2	126	45	0	1
3	16	122	2	1
4	42	126	20	1

get the resulting responsibility matrix which is used to define the MUM of the users by implementing Eqs. 3, 4 and 5.

As an example, Fig. 3 shows 5 topics and the degree of responsibility they have over 13 tweets of a given user. This user had 698 tweets and once we extracted his/her MUM, the model presented a value of 49.1 for the topic '(-) sentiments' and 11.4 in 'life reflections' (highest category weights). The model of tweeters was finally obtained and may be used for many purposes. Actually, we cluster the users to define groups of tweeters with *similar profiles* or tastes about content topics (last phase, Sect. 3.5). By making use of heterogeneity and Elbow Heuristic we found that the users in our dataset form 5 clusters. To evaluate the behavior of our approach and the baseline, we used a set of politicians as input. The assumption behind this is that if their profile is well represented, they are going to be grouped in the same cluster. This validation is presented next.

4.4   Validation of Results

The users we take to do this validation are well-known political figures who have a position in the government or were candidates in public elections. K-Means++ was applied with the aim of validating the MUM and baseline approaches. The details about the results are presented in Table 1. In the table we see that the

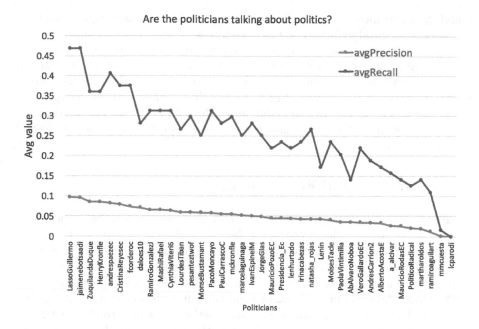

Fig. 4. Relevance of "politics" in the politicians' Twitter accounts.

case of the baseline, there are two prominent groups of politicians. One group (cluster 0) covers 44% of the total, while the other group (cluster 4) covers 51%. By analyzing the centroids of the two clusters, we identified that *cluster 4*, in contrast to *cluster 0*, groups users who tend to talk more about the economy. Compared to our approach, it is shown that MUM performance for clustering politicians has 92% of precision. From the 39 politicians, only 3 were left out of the political-related cluster. These users are *lcparodi*, *ramiroaguilart* and *mmcuesta*. By verifying their MUM (the 22 dimensions of the model) and their tweets, it is seen that their profiles are different from the rest of politicians who mostly talk about elections, economy and social issues. Instead, lcparodi tweeted about capital market and investment, ramiroaguilart posted about his interviews in radio media and talks directly to people loading his account of mentions (@); and mmcuesta because talked about recipes/food and cooking, and she promotes several enterprises.

To make a more in-depth comparison of the politicians who were clustered together and the remaining three, we performed text mining over their Twitter accounts. We consider every politician's tweets as a document; *i.e.*, there is a collection of 39 documents to be analyzed. We applied TF-IDF over this corpus and found the most relevant words for the corresponding politicians' profiles. From among the most frequent words in the whole corpus, a list of meaningful words in the context of "politics" was extracted. The list contained 16 words:

Ecuador, government, country, Ecuadorians, president, 'the people' (pueblo), job, work, city, production, laws, taxes, congress, health, justice, and citizens.

In this experiment we try to find if the previous list was present among the relevant words extracted for the politicians. We worked with the 30, 50, 100 and 200 most relevant words taken from their profiles. The results for the *average* precision and recall are shown in Fig. 4. As it is shown, the users *ramiroaguilart*, *mmcuesta* and *lcparodi* have the minimum values for both precision and recall; thus, it is proven that they did not discuss about political issues as the rest of the politicians did.

5   Conclusions and Future Work

In this research, we have proposed a method that creates a vector representation of tweets by applying word2vec. Then, by using a Mixture of Gaussians through the EM algorithm, it calculates the degree of responsibility that a set of topics have over a tweet. Finally, we aggregate the results of the tweets which correspond to a given user to define his/her multi-topic preference model.

We have validated our proposal by comparing it with the results of a baseline approach. This evaluation showed that our method was able to cluster 92% of politicians in the same group, with respect to the results of the baseline method which divided the politicians in two clusters. To understand the reasons why three politicians were not included in the political-related cluster, we performed a text-based analysis of their posts and verify that they tend to talk about topics which are not relevant to politics. In summary, we can conclude that our method is effective when modeling the topic interests of Twitter users.

For future work, we propose for further research to evaluate our approach with other probabilistic topic models like LDA and test its performance at topic assignment for short text.

References

1. Arthur, D., Vassilvitskii, S.: K-means++: the advantages of careful seeding. In: Proceedings of the 18 ACM-SIAM Symposium on Discrete Algorithms, ser. SODA 2007, Philadelphia, PA, USA, Society for Industrial and Applied Mathematics, pp. 1027–1035 (2007)
2. Blei, D.M., Ng, A.Y., Jordan, M.I.: Latent dirichlet allocation. J. Mach. Learn. Res. **3**, 993–1022 (2003)
3. Boratto, L., Carta, S.: State-of-the-art in group recommendation and new approaches for automatic identification of groups. In: Soro, A., Vargiu, E., Armano, G., Paddeu, G. (eds.) Information Retrieval and Mining in Distributed Environments, vol. 324, pp. 1–20. Springer, Berlin (2011). https://doi.org/10.1007/978-3-642-16089-9_1
4. Chen, J., Nairn, R., Nelson, L., Bernstein, M., Chi, E.: Short and Tweet: experiments on recommending content from information streams. In: Proceedings of the SIGCHI Conference on Human Factors in Computing Systems, Ser. CHI 2010, pp. 1185–1194. ACM, New York (2010)

5. Chen, K., Chen, T., Zheng, G., Jin, O., Yao, E., Yu, Y.: Collaborative personalized tweet recommendation. In: Proceedings of the 35th International ACM SIGIR Conference on Research and Development in Information Retrieval, pp. 661–670. ACM (2012)

6. Dempster, A.P., Laird, N.M., Rubin, D.B.: Maximum likelihood from incomplete data via the EM algorithm. J. Roy. Stat. Soc.: Ser. B (Methodol.) **39**(1), 1–38 (1977)

7. Freund, Y., Schapire, R.E.: Experiments with a new boosting algorithm. In: Proceedings of the Thirteenth International Conference on International Conference on Machine Learning, Ser. ICML 1996, pp. 148–156. Morgan Kaufmann Publishers Inc., San Francisco (1996)

8. Godin, F., Slavkovikj, V., De Neve, W., Schrauwen, B., Van de Walle, R.: Using topic models for Twitter hashtag recommendation. In: Proceedings of the 22nd International Conference on World Wide Web, Ser. WWW 2013 Companion, pp. 593–596. ACM, New York (2013)

9. Guy, I.: Social Recommender Systems. In: Ricci, F., Rokach, L., Shapira, B. (eds.) Recommender Systems Handbook, pp. 511–543. Springer, Boston, MA (2015). https://doi.org/10.1007/978-1-4899-7637-6_15

10. Iman, Z., Sanner, S., Bouadjenek, M.R., Xie, L.: A longitudinal study of topic classification on Twitter. In: Proceedings of the Eleventh International AAAI Conference on Web and Social Media, Ser. ICWSM 2017, pp. 552–555 (2017)

11. Lai, L.S.L., Turban, E.: Groups formation and operations in the Web 2.0 environment and social networks. Group Decis. Negot. **17**(5), 387–402 (2008)

12. Low, Y., Gonzalez, J., Kyrola, A., Bickson, D., Guestrin, C., Hellerstein, J.M.: Graphlab: a new framework for parallel machine learning. CoRR, vol. abs/1006.4990 (2010)

13. Macqueen, J.: Some methods for classification and analysis of multivariate observations. In: 5th Berkeley Symposium on Mathematical Statistics and Probability, pp. 281–297 (1967)

14. Mikolov, T., Sutskever, I., Chen, K., Corrado, G.S., Dean, J.: Distributed representations of words and phrases and their compositionality. In: Burges, C.J.C., Bottou, L., Ghahramani, Z., Weinberger, K.Q. (eds.) Advances in Neural Information Processing Systems 26: 27th Annual Conference on Neural Information Processing Systems 2013, Proceedings of a Meeting Held 5–8 December 2013, Lake Tahoe, Nevada, United States, pp. 3111–3119 (2013)

15. Recalde, L., Mendieta, J., Boratto, L., Teran, L., Vaca, C., Baquerizo, G.: Who you should not follow: extracting word embeddings from Tweets to identify groups of interest and Hijackers in demonstrations. IEEE Trans. Emerg. Topics Comput. **7**, 206–217 (2017)

16. Recalde, L., Kaskina, A.: Who is Suitable to Be Followed Back when You Are a Twitter interested in politics? In: Proceedings of the 18th Annual International Conference on Digital Government Research, Ser. DG.O 2017, pp. 94–99. ACM, New York (2017)

17. Salton, G., Buckley, C.: Term-weighting approaches in automatic text retrieval. Inf. Process. Manage. **24**(5), 513–523 (1988)

18. Sriram, B., Fuhry, D., Demir, E., Ferhatosmanoglu, H., Demirbas, M.: Short text classification in Twitter to improve information filtering. In: Proceedings of the 33rd International ACM SIGIR Conference on Research and Development in Information Retrieval, Ser. SIGIR 2010, pp. 841–842. ACM, New York (2010)

19. Thorndike, R.L.: Who belongs in the family. Psychometrika, 267–276 (1953)

20. Verbeek, J.J., Vlassis, N., Kröse, B.: Efficient greedy learning of gaussian mixture models. Neural Comput. **15**(2), 469–485 (2003)
21. Weng, J., Lim, E.-P., Jiang, J., He, Q.: TwitterRank: finding topic-sensitive influential Twitterers. In: Proceedings of the Third ACM International Conference on Web Search and Data Mining, Ser. WSDM 2010, pp. 261–270. ACM, New York (2010)
22. Yang, S.-H., Kolcz, A., Schlaikjer, A., Gupta, P.: Large-scale high-precision topic modeling on Twitter. In: Proceedings of the 20th ACM SIGKDD International Conference on Knowledge Discovery and Data Mining, Ser. KDD 2014, pp. 1907–1916. ACM, New York (2014)
23. Yang, Y.: A study of thresholding strategies for text categorization. In: Proceedings of the 24th Annual International ACM SIGIR Conference on Research and Development in Information Retrieval, Ser. SIGIR 2001, pp. 137–145. ACM, New York (2001)

Venue Suggestion Using Social-Centric Scores

Mohammad Aliannejadi[1]([envelope]) and Fabio Crestani[2]

[1] University of Amsterdam, Amsterdam, The Netherlands
m.aliannejadi@uva.nl
[2] Università della Svizzera italiana, Lugano, Switzerland
fabio.crestani@usi.ch

Abstract. User modeling is a very important task for making relevant suggestions of venues to the users. These suggestions are often based on matching the venues' features with the users' preferences, which can be collected from previously visited locations. In this paper, we present a set of relevance scores for making personalized suggestions of points of interest. These scores model each user by focusing on the different types of information extracted from venues that they have previously visited. In particular, we focus on scores extracted from social information available on location-based social networks. Our experiments, conducted on the dataset of the TREC Contextual Suggestion Track, show that social scores are more effective than scores based venues' content.

1 Introduction

Recent years have witnessed an increasing use of location-based social networks (LBSNs) such as Yelp, TripAdvisor, and Foursquare. These social networks collect valuable information about users' mobility records, which often consist of their check-in data and may also include users' ratings and reviews. Therefore, being able to provide personalized suggestions to users plays a key role in satisfying the user needs on such social networks. Moreover, LBSNs collect very valuable information from social interactions of users. For instance, the rating history of a user's friends on a social network can be leveraged to improve a recommender system's performance [31]. Other works have shown that the recommendation can be improved using information from LBSN users who are not in a particular user's friendship network [39]. Also, Foursquare has developed some algorithms to extract informative keywords (called *venue taste keywords*) from users' online reviews. These keywords can be used not only for browsing the reviews more effectively, but also for modeling users. For example, in our previous work [12], we proposed a frequency-based score incorporating venue taste keywords while modeling users.

Work done while Mohammad Aliannejadi was affiliated with Università della Svizzera italiana (USI).

L. Boratto et al. (Eds.): BIAS 2020, CCIS 1245, pp. 127–142, 2020.
https://doi.org/10.1007/978-3-030-52485-2_12

Recent research has focused on recommending venues using collaborative-filtering technique [14,23], where the system recommends venues based on users whose preferences are similar to those of the target user (i.e., the user who receives the recommendations). Collaborative-filtering approaches are very effective, but they suffer from the cold-start (i.e., they need to collect enough information about a user for making recommendations) and the data-sparseness problems. Furthermore, these approaches mostly rely on check-in data to learn the preferences of users, and such information is insufficient to get a complete picture of what the user likes or dislikes about a specific venue (e.g., the food, the view). In order to overcome this limitation, we model the users by performing a deeper analysis on users' past ratings as well as their reviews. In addition, following the principle of collaborative filtering, we exploit the reviews from different users with similar preferences.

In this paper, we present a set of similarity scores for suggesting venues to users, where the users are modeled based on venues' content as well as social information. Venues' categories are considered as content and online reviews on LBSNs are considered as social information. Mining social reviews help a system understand the reasons behind a rating: was it for the quality of food, for the good service, for the cozy environment, or for the location? In cases where we lack reviews from some of the users (e.g., they have rated a venue but chose not to review it), we cannot extract opinions, we apply the collaborative filtering principle and we use reviews from other users with similar interests and tastes. Our intuition is that a user's opinion regarding an attraction could be learned based on the opinions of others who expressed the same or similar rating for the same venue. To do this we exploit information from multiple sources and combine them to gain better performance.

This paper extends our previous works [5,8,12] focusing on the social aspects of user modeling. In particular, we have extended the experiments and discussions where we study the impact of using multiple social-centric scores on the performance. The remainder of the paper is organized as follows. Section 2 reviews related work. Then, we present our methodology in Sect. 3. Section 4 describes our experiments. Finally, Sect. 5 is a short conclusion and description of future work.

2   Related Work

Recommender systems try to predict the users' preferences in order to help them find interesting items. Research on recommender systems was first conducted in the 90s [20], and since then it has attracted a lot of attention for recommending products in e-commerce websites or information [18,24] (e.g., news, tweets). Recently, due to the availability of the Internet access on mobile devices [6] and based on the fact that users interact with LBSNs more often, researchers have been focusing their interest in analyzing social aspects while recommending venues.

Much work has been carried out in this area based on the core idea that users with similar behavioral history tend to act similarly [25]. This is the underlying idea of collaborative filtering based (CF-based) approaches [26,41]. CF can be divided into two categories: memory-based and model-based. Memory-based approaches consider user rating as a similarity measure between users or items [37]. Model-based approaches, on the other hand, employ techniques like matrix factorization [28,32]. However, CF-based approaches often suffer from data sparsity since there are a lot of available locations, and a single user can visit only a few of them. As a consequence, the user-item matrix of CF becomes very sparse, leading to poor performance in cases where there is no significant association between users and items. Many studies have tried to address the data sparsity problem of CF by incorporating additional information into the model [40,43]. More specifically, Ye et al. [40] argued that users check-in behavior is affected by the spatial influence of locations and proposed a unified location recommender system incorporating spatial and social influence to address the data sparsity problem. Yin et al. [41] proposed a model that captures user interests as well as local preferences to recommend locations or events to users when they are visiting a new city.

Yuan et al. [44] proposed to consider both geographical and temporal influences while recommending venues to the users via a geographical-temporal influence-aware graph. They proposed to propagate these influences using a breadth-first strategy. Also, Rahmani et al. [33] introduced joint temporal-geographical activity centers and used them to improve the performance of matric factorization. Ference et al. [22] took into consideration user preference, geographical proximity, and social influences for venue recommendation. Zhang and Chow [46] exploited geographical, social, and categorical correlations. They modeled the geographical correlation using a kernel estimation method and the categorical correlation by applying the bias of a user on a venue category. The social check-in frequency or rating was modeled as a power-law distribution to employ the social correlations between users. Rahmani et al. [34] trained a neural model to learn category embeddings and used them to enhance venue recommendation. Zhang et al. [45] considered three travel-related constraints (i.e., uncertain traveling time, diversity of the venues, and venue availability) and use them to prune the search space. Griesner et al. [26] also proposed an approach integrating temporal and geographic influences into matrix factorization. In a more recent work, Li et al. [29] introduced a fourth-order tensor factorization-based recommendation system considering users' time-varying behavioral trends while capturing their long-term and short-term preferences simultaneously. Aliannejadi et al. [12] proposed a probabilistic mapping approach to determine the most salient information from a venue's content to reduce the dimensionality of data, and extended it to consider the appropriateness of a venue, given a user's context while ranking the venues [3,11]. Yuan et al. [42] addressed the data sparsity problem assuming that users tend to rank higher the venues that are geographically closer to the one that they have already visited.

Another line of research focuses on enhancing recommendation using users' reviews on LBSNs. When a user writes a review about a venue, there is a wealth of information which reveals the reasons why that particular user is interested in a venue or not. Chen et al. [21] state three main reasons for which the reviews can be beneficial for a recommender system: (1) extra information that can be extracted from reviews enables a system to deal with large data sparsity problem; (2) reviews have been proven to be helpful to deal with the cold-start problem; (3) even in cases when the data is dense, they can be used to determine the quality of the ratings or to extract user's contextual information. Also, research has shown that venue reviews are effective in determining how similar are two venues [4,13] Zhang et al. [47] fused virtual ratings derived from online reviews into CF. Yang and Fang [38] demonstrated how it is possible to get improved recommendations by modeling a user with the reviews of other users' whose tastes are similar to the ones of the target user. In particular, they modeled users by extracting positive and negative reviews to create positive and negative profiles for users and venues. The recommendation is then made by measuring and combining the similarity scores between all pairs of profiles. The effectiveness of online reviews was also shown in more recent works [9].

In this paper, we focus on modeling users based on available information on LBSNs. While the available information also includes venues' content (e.g., opening hours), the majority of it is the information left by active users on these social networks. We demonstrate how this type of information helps a recommender system and how a recommender system can leverage it to improve its effectiveness.

3   Venue Suggestion

In this section, we first describe the frequency-based scores based on the venues' categories and keywords extracted from Foursquare reviews. Then, we present how to leverage online reviews for venue suggestion.

3.1   Frequency-Based Score

We base the frequency-based scores on the assumption that users prefer the type of locations that they like more frequently and rate them positively[1]. Therefore, we create positive and negative profiles considering the content of locations in the user's check-in history and calculate the normalized frequencies as they appear in their profile. Then we compute a similarity score between the user's profile and a new location. For simplicity, we only explain how to calculate the frequency-based score using venue keywords. The method can be easily generalized to calculate the score for venue categories.

Let u be a user and $h_u = \{v_1, \ldots, v_n\}$ their history of check-ins. Each location has a list of keywords $C(v_i) = \{c_1, \ldots, c_k\}$. We define the user category profile as follows:

---

[1] We consider reviews with rating [4,5] as positive, 3 as neutral, and [1,2] as negative.

Definition 1. *A **Positive Keyword Profile** is the set of all unique keywords belonging to venues that user u has previously rated positively. A **Negative Keyword Profile** is defined analogously for venues that are rated negatively.*

Each keyword in the positive/negative keyword profile is assigned with a user-level normalized frequency. We define the user-level normalized frequency for a keyword as follows:

Definition 2. *A **User-level Normalized Frequency** for an item (e.g., keyword) in a profile (e.g., positive keyword profile) for user u is defined as:*

$$\mathrm{cf}_u^+(c_i) = \frac{\sum_{v_k \in h_u^+} \sum_{c_j \in C(v_k), c_j = c_i} 1}{\sum_{v_k \in h_u} \sum_{c_j \in C(v_k)} 1},$$

where h_u^+ is the set of locations that u rated positively. We calculate user-level normalized frequency for negative keywords, cf_u^-, analogously.

Foursquare Taste Keywords. Foursquare automatically extracts a list of keywords, also known as "tastes" to better describe a venue. These keywords are extracted from online reviews of users who visit a venue. As an example, "Central Park" in "New York City" is described by these taste terms: *picnics, biking, trails, park, scenic views*, etc. Such keywords are very informative, since they often express characteristics of a venue, and they can be considered as a complementary source of information for venue categories.

Table 1 shows all taste keywords and categories for a sample restaurant on Foursquare. As we can see, the taste keywords represent much more details about the venue compared to categories. The average number of taste keywords for venues (8.73) is much higher than the average number of categories for venues (2.8). It suggests that these keywords could describe a venue in more details compared to categories.

We create positive and negative keyword profiles for each user based on Definitions 1 and 2. Given a user u and candidate venue v, the frequency-based similarity score based on venue keywords, $S_{key}(u, v)$, is calculated as follows:

$$S_{key}(u, v) = \sum_{c_i \in C(v)} \mathrm{cf}_u^+(c_i) - \mathrm{cf}_u^-(c_i). \tag{1}$$

Venue Categories. Here we aim to exploit the categories of the venues a user liked in the past. Such information represents an important information that can be used to infer what kind of places a user may enjoy visiting. In some cases, categories are the only source of information. For example, a venue that has not received many online reviews. We adopt the same frequency-based approach as we did for venue taste keywords. Thus, we create positive and negative category profiles for user considering venue categories, based on Definitions 1 and 2. Then, we compute the category similarity score, $S_{cat}(u, v)$, as we did for the keyword-based score (see Eq. (1)).

Table 1. A sample of taste keywords and categories for a restaurant

Taste keywords	Pizza, lively, cozy, good for dates, authentic, casual, pasta, desserts good for a late night, family-friendly, good for groups, ravioli, lasagna, salads, wine, vodka, tagliatelle, cocktails, bruschetta
Categories	Pizza place, italian restaurant

3.2   Review-Based Score

Modeling a user only on locations' content is general and does not determine why the user enjoyed or disliked a venue. The content of locations is often used to infer "which type" of venues, a user likes. On the other hand, reviews express the reasons for users' ratings. Since there could be a lack of explicit reviews from the user, we tackle this sparsity problem using reviews of other users who gave a similar rating to the location. In particular, we calculate the review-based score using a binary classifier.

We model this problem as binary classification since a user, before visiting a new city or location, would get a positive or negative impression of the location after reading the online reviews of other users. We assume that a user would measure the characteristics of a location according to their expectations and interests. These characteristics are mainly inferred from the existing online reviews of other users. The user would be convinced to visit a particular location if the reviews satisfy their expectations up to a certain point. An alternative to binary classification would be a regression model, however, we assume that users behave like a binary classifier when they read online reviews in order to make a decision on whether to visit a venue or not. For example, assume a user reads a few positive and negative online reviews about a venue and measures how similar the mentioned qualities are to their expectations. Finally, depending on the balance between the positive remarks and the negative ones, they make a binary decision (i.e., whether to go or not). We see this behavioral pattern similar to that of a binary classifier: it learns from the positive and negative samples and compares the learned parameters with a test sample and assigns its label accordingly. Furthermore, due to data sparsity, grouping ratings as positive and negative aids us to model users more effectively.

For each user, we train a binary classifier using the reviews from the locations in a user's check-in history. The positive classification training samples for user u are positive reviews of locations that were liked by u. Likewise, the negative reviews of locations that u disliked constitute the negative training samples. We decided to ignore the negative reviews of liked locations and positive reviews of disliked locations since they are not supposed to contain any useful information.

After removing the stop words, we consider the TF-IDF score of terms in reviews as features. We trained many classifiers but linear SVM outperformed all other models. Therefore, we choose linear SVM and consider the value of the its decision function as the review-based score and refer to it as $S_{rev}(u, v)$. The decision function gives us an idea on how relevant a location is to a user profile.

We used the scikit-learn[2] implementation of SVM with default parameters (i.e., penalization: $l2$-norm, loss function: squared hinge, c = 1.0).

3.3   Location Ranking

After defining the mentioned relevance scores, here we explain how we combine them. Given a user and a list of candidate locations, we calculate the mentioned scores for each location and combine them to create a ranked list of locations. We adopt several learning to rank[3] techniques to rank the candidate locations since they have proven to be effective for similar tasks [30]. In particular, we examine the following learning to rank techniques: AdaRank, Coordinate Ascent (aka. CAscent), RankBoost, MART, λ-MART, RandomForest, RankNet, and ListNet. We study the performance of different five models using different combinations of the scores as follows:

- **LTR-All**: This model consists of all proposed relevance scores: S_{cat} (from both Yelp and Foursquare), S_{rev}, and S_{key}.
- **LTR-S**: It consists only of the social-centric scores: S_{rev} and S_{key}.
- **LTR-C**: It includes only of non social scores: S_{cat} (from both Yelp and Foursquare).
- **LTR-Y**: We only include the scores calculated using Yelp: S_{cat} (only from Yelp) and S_{rev}.
- **LTR-F**: Information from Foursquare is only considered for this model: S_{cat} (only from Foursquare) and S_{key}.

4   Experiments

This section describes the dataset, the experimental setup for assessing the performance of our methodology, and the experimental results.

4.1   Experimental Setup

Dataset. Our experiments were conducted on the collection provided by the Text REtrieval Conference (TREC) for the Batch Experiments of the 2015 Contextual Suggestion Track[4]. This track was originally introduced by the National Institute of Standards and Technology (NIST) in 2012 to provide a common evaluation framework for participants that are interested in dealing with the challenging problem of contextual suggestions and venue recommendation. In short, given a set of example places as user's preferences (profile) and contextual information (e.g., the *city* where the venues should be recommended), the task consists in returning a ranked list of 30 candidate places which match the user's

---

[2] http://scikit-learn.org/.

[3] We use RankLib implementation of learning to rank: https://sourceforge.net/p/lemur/wiki/RankLib/.

[4] https://sites.google.com/site/treccontext/trec-2015.

profile. The ratings range between 0 (very uninterested) and 4 (very interested). The collection, provided by TREC, consists of a total $9K$ distinct venues and 211 users. For each user, the contextual information plus a history of 60 previously rated attractions are provided. Additionally, for our experiments, we used the additional crawled information released by [10].

Evaluation Metrics. We use the official evaluation metrics of TREC for this task which are P@5 (Precision at 5), nDCG@5 (Normalized Discounted Cumulative Gain at 5), and MRR (Mean Reciprocal Rank). In order to find the optimum setting of learning to rank techniques, we conducted a 5-fold cross validation with respect to nDCG@5. We determine the statistically significant differences using the two-tailed paired t-test at a 95% confidence interval ($p < 0.05$).

Compared Methods. We compare our proposed method with state-of-the-art context-aware and social-based venue recommendation methods.

– *LinearCatRev* [1] is the best performing model of TREC 2015. It extracts information from different LBSNs and uses it to calculate category-based and review-based scores. Then, it combines the scores using linear interpolation. We choose this baseline for two reasons, firstly because it is the best performing system of TREC 2015, and secondly because it also uses scores derived from different LBSNs.
– *GeoSoCa* exploits geographical, social, and categorical correlations for venue recommendation [46]. GeoSoCa models the geographical correlation using a kernel estimation method with an adaptive bandwidth determining a personalized check-in distribution. It models the categorical correlation by applying the bias of a user on a venue category to weigh the popularity of a venue in the corresponding category modeling the weighted popularity as a power-law distribution. It models the social ratings as a power-law distribution employing the social correlations between users.
– *n-Dimensional Tensor Factorization (nDTF)* [27] generalizes matrix factorization to allow for integrating multiple contextual features into the model. Regarding the features, we included two types of features: (1) venue-based: category, keywords, average rating on Yelp, and the number of ratings on Yelp (as an indicator of its popularity); (2) user-based: age group and gender.

4.2   Results and Discussions

In this section, we present a set of experiments in order to demonstrate the effectiveness of our approach. Then, we study the effect of social features on the performance.

Performance Evaluation Against Compared Methods. Table 2 demonstrates the performance of our approach against the compared methods. We

Table 2. Performance evaluation on TREC 2015. Bold values denote the best scores and the superscript * denotes significant differences compared to LinearCatRev. Δ values (%) express the relative difference, compared to LinearCatRev.

	P@5	$\Delta(\%)$	nDCG@5	$\Delta(\%)$	MRR	$\Delta(\%)$
LinearCatRev	0.5858	–	0.6055	–	0.7404	–
GeoSoCa	0.5147*	−12.14	0.5404*	−10.75	0.6918*	−6.56
nDTF	0.5232*	−10.96	0.5351*	−11.63	0.6707*	−9.41
LTR-All	0.5913	0.94	0.6087	0.53	0.7411	0.10
LTR-S	**0.6038***	3.07	**0.6235***	2.98	**0.7419**	0.21
LTR-C	0.5376*	−8.22	0.5408*	−10.69	0.6643*	−10.28
LTR-Y	0.5323*	−9.13	0.5334*	−11.91	0.6500*	−12.20
LTR-F	0.5558*	−5.11	0.5784*	−4.47	0.7261	−1.93

chose to report the results obtained by RankNet because it exhibited the best performance among all other learning to rank techniques (see Table 3). Table 2 shows that LTR-S outperforms the competitors with respect to the three evaluation metrics. This shows that using social-centric features can effectively model users on LBSNs leading to higher recommendation performance. Note that LTR-S also outperforms LTR-All which consists of both social- and content-based scores, indicating that category scores are not as effective as social scores. This is also evident in the results obtained by LTR-C, where only category scores are included in the model and the results are much lower than of LinearCatRev. Table 2 also illustrates the performance of our model when using the scores obtained from only one source of information. In particular, LTR-Y and LTR-F are trained using the scores computed only on Yelp and Foursquare data, respectively. As we can see, they both perform worse than LinearCatRev, suggesting that combining cross-platform social information is critical while recommending venues to users. Finally, we see that GeoSoCa and nDTF exhibit the worst performance among all compared methods. This happens mainly because these methods rely on user-venue check-in associations among the training and test sets. In other words, there should be enough common venues appearing in both the training and test sets, otherwise, they fail to recommend unseen venues. Hence, they suffer from the high level of the sparsity of the dataset. In fact, the intersection of venues in the training and test sets is 771 (out of 8,794).

To train the review-based classifier, we used various classifiers such as Naïve Bayes and k-NN; however, the SVM classifier exhibited a better performance by a large margin. The SVM classifier is a better fit for this problem since it is more suitable for text classification, which is a linear problem with weighted high dimensional feature vectors. Also, we observed a significant difference between the number of positive reviews and negative reviews per location. Generally, locations receive more positive reviews than negative reviews and, in our case, this results in an unbalanced training set. Most of the classification algorithms

Table 3. Effect on nDCG@5 for different learning to rank techniques on TREC 2015. Bold values denote the best scores per model and the superscript * denotes significant differences compared to LinearCatRev. Δ values (%) express the relative difference, compared to LinearCatRev (nDCG@5 = 0.6055).

	LTR-All	Δ	LTR-S	Δ	LTR-C	Δ	LTR-Y	Δ	LTR-F	Δ
MART	0.5899*	−2.57	0.5995	−1.00	0.5575*	−7.93	0.6023	−0.53	0.5691*	−6.01
RankNet	0.6087	0.53	**0.6235***	2.98	0.5408*	−10.69	0.5334*	−11.91	0.5784*	−4.47
RankBoost	0.5924*	−2.17	0.5980	−1.23	0.5573*	−7.96	0.5891*	−2.70	0.5529*	−8.69
AdaRank	0.6074	0.32	0.6180	2.06	0.5762*	−4.84	0.6009	−0.76	0.5735*	−5.28
CAscent	**0.6089**	0.57	0.6160	1.74	**0.5763***	−4.82	0.6037	−0.30	0.5768*	−4.73
λ-MART	0.6065	0.17	0.6134	1.31	0.5645*	−6.77	0.5987	−1.12	0.5724*	−5.47
ListNet	0.6068	0.21	0.6198	2.36	0.5762*	−4.84	**0.6066**	0.18	**0.5787***	−4.42

fail to deal with the problem of unbalanced data. This is mainly due to the fact that those classifiers try to minimize an overall error rate. Therefore, given an unbalanced training set, the classifier is usually trained in favor of the dominant class to minimize the overall error rate. However, SVM does not suffer from this, since it does not try to directly minimize the error rate but instead tries to separate the two classes using a hyperplane maximizing the margin. This makes SVM more intolerant of the relative size of each class. Another advantage of linear SVM is that the execution time is very low and there are very few parameters to tune.

Impact of Different Learning to Rank Techniques. In this experiment, we aim to show how the recommendation effectiveness is affected by applying different learning to rank techniques to combine the scores. Table 3 reports nDCG@5 applying different learning to rank techniques for TREC 2015. We report the performance for LTR-All, LTR-S, LTR-C, LTR-Y, and LTR-F. As we can see, RankNet outperforms other learning to rank techniques when using only social-centric features (LTR-S). It is worth noting that RankNet and ListNet are both based on artificial neural networks, and they perform best considering most of the models. As we can observe, applying different learning to rank techniques can potentially have a big impact on recommendation results. Therefore, it is critical to apply the best technique according to the scores.

Impact of Number of Reviews. Here we show how the recommendation effectiveness is affected by the number of online reviews used to compute the review-based score. Users leave a massive number of reviews about venues on LBSNs, making it very difficult for a system to consider all the reviews while modeling users. Figure 1a illustrates the distribution of reviews per venue, showing that a considerable number venues receive many reviews. Therefore, it is crucial to study the impact of the number of reviews on the performance of our model.

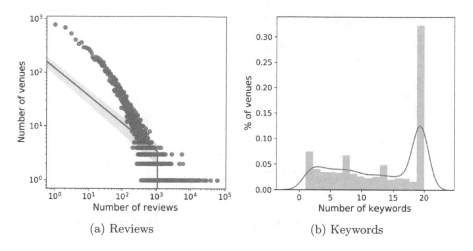

(a) Reviews   (b) Keywords

Fig. 1. Distribution of the number reviews and keywords per venue.

Figure 2 shows the performance of LTR-S as we change the number of reviews while building user profiles. We follow three criteria as we vary the number of reviews:

- *LTR-S-Random* selects k reviews per venue randomly. To prevent random bias, we ran this model 5 times and report the average performance.
- *LTR-S-Recent* includes the k most recent reviews in the user profile. Here, we are interested in exploring the temporal effect of reviews.
- *LTR-S-Active* builds the review profiles considering the reviews from top k active users. A user activity is measured by the total number of reviews that they have written on Yelp. Here, we are interested in finding out if the users level of activity can be used to determine the credibility of their reviews.

As we can see, results are comparable to LTR-S when we use only 230 reviews, showing that the model converges after a certain number of reviews. Moreover, using more reviews can potentially have a negative impact, because the model will be biased towards the venues that have a higher number of reviews (i.e., more popular venues). The results of LTR-S-Random exhibit the least consistency as we increase k, showing that a random selection of reviews is not as effective as other criteria. We see that both LTR-S-Recent and LTR-S-Active show less consistency with lower k's, but improve as k grows. Specifically, LTR-S-Recent achieves its best performance with $k = 190$ (nDCG@5 = 0.6271) and LTR-S-Active with $k = 230$ (nDCG@5 = 0.6273), both outperforming LTR-S. This indicates that pruning reviews based on time and user activity improves not only the system's efficiency but also its effectiveness.

Impact of Number of Keywords. In this experiment we study how the recommendation effectiveness is affected by the number of venue taste keywords in

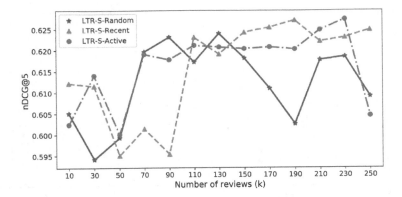

Fig. 2. Performance of LTR-S in terms of nDCG@5 using different number of reviews
(k).

user profiles. As discussed in [12], venue taste keywords are very sparse because
they are automatically extracted from user reviews and contain various senti-
mental tags. Moreover, as we can see in Fig. 1b, venue profiles on Foursquare are
featured with many keywords and it is crucial to reduce the dimensionality of
keywords such that less important keywords are removed from the profiles. We
follow three criteria as we vary the number of keywords in the profiles:

- *LTR-SKey-VRand* randomly selects k keywords for each venue and creates
  user profiles using those keywords. Note that since the maximum number of
  keywords per venue is 20, we vary k from 0 to 20.
- *LTR-SKey-URand* creates the user profiles using the full list of keywords but
  considers only k randomly selected keywords from the user's profile, when
  computing the relevance score. We vary k from 0 to 300.
- *LTR-SKey-UPop* creates the user profiles using the full list of keywords but
  computes the relevance scores using only k keywords with highest frequencies.
  We vary k from 0 to 300.

As we can see in Fig. 3, the performance of LTR-SKey-VRand increases as
we increase the number of randomly selected keywords per venue. LTR-SKey-
URand, on the other hand, shows a different behavior. We see that while in
general having more keywords in the user's profile benefits the model, selecting
k keywords from the profile in a random order results in an inconsistent behavior
of the model. For example, we observe that even in some cases (e.g., $k = 10$)
the performance of the model is lower than a model trained with no keywords.
LTR-SKey-UPop behaves differently and, generally, its performance improves as
we increase k. This shows that the popularity of a keyword in a user's profile
is a good indicator of its importance to the user. We also see that the best
performance is achieved when $k = 160$, suggesting that applying a dimensionality
reduction on the keywords space can help us model the users more effectively,
something that we studied in [12].

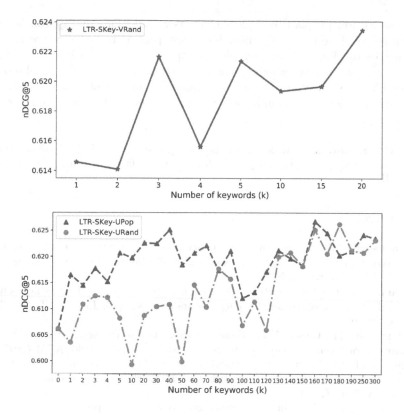

Fig. 3. Performance of LTR-S in terms of nDCG@5 using different number of keywords (k).

5   Conclusions and Future Work

In this paper we proposed a set of similarity scores for recommending venues based on content- and social-based information. As content, we used a frequency-based strategy to model venue categories. Social-centric scores consisted of online reviews on LBSNs and keywords that are automatically extracted from online reviews. We modeled the reviews using a classifier per user and used the same frequency-based strategy to model the keywords. Experimental results corroborated the effectiveness of our approach and showed that combining social-centric scores outperforms all other scores combinations, as well as the baselines. Moreover, we studied the impact of the number of reviews and keywords per venue on the system's performance. Our results showed that selecting a certain number of reviews based on their timestamp or author's activity improves a system's efficiency and effectiveness. Also, selecting the k most repeated keywords in a user's profile improves the efficiency of our model, indicating that reducing the dimensionality of venue taste keywords in a smarter way can be beneficial, something that we explored in [12].

In the future, we plan to explore other keyword modeling approaches such as average word embedding, which has been proven to be effective in other domains [15,16]. Furthermore, we plan to study this problem in other domains such as conversational search and recommendation [2,17,35] and mental disorder analysis [36]. Also, the availability of a massive number of online reviews has motivated us to leverage them to perform semi-supervised learning of the review classifier [7,19].

Acknowledgment. This work was partially supported by the Swiss National Science Foundation (SNSF) under the project "Relevance Criteria Combination for Mobile IR (RelMobIR)."

References

1. Aliannejadi, M., Bahrainian, S.A., Giachanou, A., Crestani, F.: University of Lugano at TREC 2015: contextual suggestion and temporal summarization tracks. In: TREC 2015. NIST (2015)
2. Aliannejadi, M., Chakraborty, M., Ríssola, E.A., Crestani, F.: Harnessing evolution of multi-turn conversations for effective answer retrieval. In: CHIIR, pp. 33–42. ACM (2020)
3. Aliannejadi, M., Crestani, F.: Venue appropriateness prediction for personalized context-aware venue suggestion. In: SIGIR 2017, pp. 1177–1180. ACM (2017)
4. Aliannejadi, M., Crestani, F.: A collaborative ranking model with contextual similarities for venue suggestion. In: IIR. CEUR Workshop Proceedings, vol. 2140. CEUR-WS.org (2018)
5. Aliannejadi, M., Crestani, F.: Personalized context-aware point of interest recommendation. ACM Trans. Inf. Syst. $36(4)$, 45:1–45:28 (2018)
6. Aliannejadi, M., Harvey, M., Costa, L., Pointon, M., Crestani, F.: Understanding mobile search task relevance and user behaviour in context. In: CHIIR, pp. 143–151. ACM (2019)
7. Aliannejadi, M., Kiaeeha, M., Khadivi, S., Ghidary, S.S.: Graph-based semi-supervised conditional random fields for spoken language understanding using unaligned data. In: ALTA 2014, pp. 98–103. ACL (2014)
8. Aliannejadi, M., Mele, I., Crestani, F.: User model enrichment for venue recommendation. In: Ma, S., et al. (eds.) AIRS 2016. LNCS, vol. 9994, pp. 212–223. Springer, Cham (2016). https://doi.org/10.1007/978-3-319-48051-0_16
9. Aliannejadi, M., Mele, I., Crestani, F.: Venue appropriateness prediction for contextual suggestion. In: TREC 2016. NIST (2016)
10. Aliannejadi, M., Mele, I., Crestani, F.: A cross-platform collection for contextual suggestion. In: SIGIR 2017, pp. 1269–1272. ACM (2017)
11. Aliannejadi, M., Mele, I., Crestani, F.: Personalized ranking for context-aware venue suggestion. In: SAC 2017, pp. 960–962. ACM (2017)
12. Aliannejadi, M., Rafailidis, D., Crestani, F.: Personalized keyword boosting for venue suggestion based on multiple LBSNs. In: Jose, J.M., et al. (eds.) ECIR 2017. LNCS, vol. 10193, pp. 291–303. Springer, Cham (2017). https://doi.org/10.1007/978-3-319-56608-5_23
13. Aliannejadi, M., Rafailidis, D., Crestani, F.: A collaborative ranking model with multiple location-based similarities for venue suggestion. In: ICTIR, pp. 19–26. ACM (2018)

14. Aliannejadi, M., Rafailidis, D., Crestani, F.: A joint two-phase time-sensitive regularized collaborative ranking model for point of interest recommendation. IEEE Trans. Knowl. Data Eng. **32**(6), 1050–1063 (2019)
15. Aliannejadi, M., Zamani, H., Crestani, F., Croft, W.B.: In situ and context-aware target apps selection for unified mobile search. In: CIKM, pp. 1383–1392. ACM (2018)
16. Aliannejadi, M., Zamani, H., Crestani, F., Croft, W.B.: Target apps selection: towards a unified search framework for mobile devices. In: SIGIR, pp. 215–224. ACM (2018)
17. Aliannejadi, M., Zamani, H., Crestani, F., Croft, W.B.: Asking clarifying questions in open-domain information-seeking conversations. In: SIGIR, pp. 475–484. ACM (2019)
18. Bahrainian, S.A., Bahrainian, S.M., Salarinasab, M., Dengel, A.: Implementation of an intelligent product recommender system in an e-Store. In: An, A., Lingras, P., Petty, S., Huang, R. (eds.) AMT 2010. LNCS, vol. 6335, pp. 174–182. Springer, Heidelberg (2010). https://doi.org/10.1007/978-3-642-15470-6_19
19. Bennett, K.P., Demiriz, A.: Semi-supervised support vector machines. In: NIPS, pp. 368–374. The MIT Press (1998)
20. Breese, J.S., Heckerman, D., Kadie, C.M.: Empirical analysis of predictive algorithms for collaborative filtering. In: UAI 1998, pp. 43–52. Morgan Kaufmann (1998)
21. Chen, L., Chen, G., Wang, F.: Recommender systems based on user reviews: the state of the art. User Model. User-Adap. Inter. **25**(2), 99–154 (2015). https://doi.org/10.1007/s11257-015-9155-5
22. Ference, G., Ye, M., Lee, W.: Location recommendation for out-of-town users in location-based social networks. In: CIKM 2013, pp. 721–726. ACM (2013)
23. Gao, H., Tang, J., Hu, X., Liu, H.: Exploring temporal effects for location recommendation on location-based social networks. In: RecSys 2013, pp. 93–100. ACM (2013)
24. Giachanou, A., Crestani, F.: Like it or not: a survey of twitter sentiment analysis methods. ACM Comput. Surv. **49**(2), 28:1–28:41 (2016)
25. Goldberg, D., Nichols, D.A., Oki, B.M., Terry, D.B.: Using collaborative filtering to weave an information tapestry. Commun. ACM **35**(12), 61–70 (1992)
26. Griesner, J., Abdessalem, T., Naacke, H.: POI recommendation: towards fused matrix factorization with geographical and temporal influences. In: RecSys 2015, pp. 301–304. ACM (2015)
27. Karatzoglou, A., Amatriain, X., Baltrunas, L., Oliver, N.: Multiverse recommendation: n-dimensional tensor factorization for context-aware collaborative filtering. In: RecSys 2010, pp. 79–86. ACM (2010)
28. Koren, Y.: Factorization meets the neighborhood: a multifaceted collaborative filtering model. In: SIGKDD 2008, pp. 426–434. ACM (2008)
29. Li, X., Jiang, M., Hong, H., Liao, L.: A time-aware personalized point-of-interest recommendation via high-order tensor factorization. ACM Trans. Inf. Syst. **35**(4), 31:1–31:23 (2017)
30. Liu, T.: Learning to rank for information retrieval. Found. Trends Inf. Retr. **3**(3), 225–331 (2009)
31. Rafailidis, D., Crestani, F.: Joint collaborative ranking with social relationships in top-n recommendation. In: CIKM 2016, pp. 1393–1402. ACM (2016)

32. Rahmani, H.A., Aliannejadi, M., Ahmadian, S., Baratchi, M., Afsharchi, M., Crestani, F.: LGLMF: local geographical based logistic matrix factorization model for POI recommendation. In: Wang, F., et al. (eds.) AIRS 2019. LNCS, vol. 12004, pp. 66–78. Springer, Cham (2020). https://doi.org/10.1007/978-3-030-42835-8_7

33. Rahmani, H.A., Aliannejadi, M., Baratchi, M., Crestani, F.: Joint geographical and temporal modeling based on matrix factorization for point-of-interest recommendation. In: Jose, J.M., et al. (eds.) ECIR 2020, Part I. LNCS, vol. 12035, pp. 205–219. Springer, Cham (2020). https://doi.org/10.1007/978-3-030-45439-5_14

34. Rahmani, H.A., Aliannejadi, M., Zadeh, R.M., Baratchi, M., Afsharchi, M., Crestani, F.: Category-aware location embedding for point-of-interest recommendation. In: ICTIR, pp. 173–176. ACM (2019)

35. Ríssola, E.A., Chakraborty, M., Crestani, F., Aliannejadi, M.: Predicting relevant conversation turns for improved retrieval in multi-turn conversational search. In: TREC. NIST Special Publication, vol. 1250. National Institute of Standards and Technology (NIST) (2019)

36. Ríssola, E.A., Aliannejadi, M., Crestani, F.: Beyond modelling: understanding mental disorders in online social media. In: Jose, J.M., et al. (eds.) ECIR 2020, Part I. LNCS, vol. 12035, pp. 296–310. Springer, Cham (2020). https://doi.org/10.1007/978-3-030-45439-5_20

37. Sarwar, B.M., Karypis, G., Konstan, J.A., Riedl, J.: Item-based collaborative filtering recommendation algorithms. In: WWW 2001, pp. 285–295. ACM (2001)

38. Yang, P., Fang, H.: University of Delaware at TREC 2015: combining opinion profile modeling with complex context filtering for contextual suggestion. In: TREC 2015. NIST (2015)

39. Yang, P., Wang, H., Fang, H., Cai, D.: Opinions matter: a general approach to user profile modeling for contextual suggestion. Inf. Retrieval J. **18**(6), 586–610 (2015). https://doi.org/10.1007/s10791-015-9278-7

40. Ye, M., Yin, P., Lee, W., Lee, D.L.: Exploiting geographical influence for collaborative point-of-interest recommendation. In: SIGIR 2011, pp. 325–334. ACM (2011)

41. Yin, H., Cui, B., Sun, Y., Hu, Z., Chen, L.: LCARS: a spatial item recommender system. ACM TOIS **32**(3), 11:1–11:37 (2014)

42. Yuan, F., Jose, J.M., Guo, G., Chen, L., Yu, H., Alkhawaldeh, R.S.: Joint geospatial preference and pairwise ranking for point-of-interest recommendation. In: ICTAI 2016, pp. 46–53. IEEE (2016)

43. Yuan, Q., Cong, G., Ma, Z., Sun, A., Magnenat-Thalmann, N.: Time-aware point-of-interest recommendation. In: SIGIR 2013, pp. 363–372. ACM (2013)

44. Yuan, Q., Cong, G., Sun, A.: Graph-based point-of-interest recommendation with geographical and temporal influences. In: CIKM 2014, pp. 659–668. ACM (2014)

45. Zhang, C., Liang, H., Wang, K.: Trip recommendation meets real-world constraints: POI availability, diversity, and traveling time uncertainty. ACM Trans. Inf. Syst. **35**(1), 5:1–5:28 (2016)

46. Zhang, J., Chow, C.: GeoSoCa: exploiting geographical, social and categorical correlations for point-of-interest recommendations. In: SIGIR 2015, pp. 443–452. ACM (2015)

47. Zhang, W., Ding, G., Chen, L., Li, C., Zhang, C.: Generating virtual ratings from Chinese reviews to augment online recommendations. ACM TIST **4**(1), 9:1–9:17 (2013)

The Impact of Foursquare Checkins on Users' Emotions on Twitter

Seyed Amin Mirlohi Falavarjani[✉], Hawre Hosseini, and Ebrahim Bagheri

Laboratory for Systems, Software and Semantics (LS³), Ryerson University,
Toronto, Canada
smirlohi@ryerson.ca

Abstract. Performing observational studies based on social network content has recently gained attraction where the impact of various types of interruptions has been studied on users' behavior. There has been recent work that have focused on how online social network behavior and activity can impact users' offline behavior. In this paper, we study the inverse where we focus on whether users' offline behavior captured through their check-ins at different venues on Foursquare can impact users' online emotion expression as depicted in their tweets. We show that users' offline activity can impact users' online emotions; however, the type of activity determines the extent to which a user's emotions will be impacted.

Keywords: Observational studies · Causal effect · Behavioral patterns · Twitter · Foursquare

1 Introduction

The recent decade has witnessed the expansion of the availability of social network platforms where users have had a growing opportunity to share abundant content of various types including, but not limited to, textual data, social interaction behavior including follower-followee relationships, and geographical information. These behaviors retain patterned features with a potential to be mined. Furthermore, they result in unconscious and conscious involvement of users in the process of mutual influence. The promise of social networks and generated content thereby have turned them into a large-scale sensor that can provide insights into people's activities, behaviors, thoughts, emotions and health [5]. As a result, the study of human behavioral patterns leveraging those online sources of information has been a dominant topic in numerous recent studies whose results have found application in such fields such as healthcare [12], advertising [15], and customer care [21], to name but a few.

Specifically, there is a growing attention to find the relation between linguistic analysis of users' activity on social media and their behavior, e.g., text analysis has been used to find the transition from mental illness to suicide ideation [9]. Variety of measures such as language, emotion, and user engagement has been

© Springer Nature Switzerland AG 2020
L. Boratto et al. (Eds.): BIAS 2020, CCIS 1245, pp. 143–151, 2020.
https://doi.org/10.1007/978-3-030-52485-2_13

derived from Twitter to characterize depressive behavior and consequently predict likelihood of depression of individuals in future [6]. Similarly, in [4,18,19],
linguistic analysis has been used to identify psychological disorders such as anxi-
ety and depression. Additionally, some studies are trying to understand how users
involve in their community by analyzing their social media activities. Authors in
[3] define activity in social media as action in response to societal needs. Based
on [1] social media can be considered as an arena for closing the information
divide between countries.

Observational studies provide a relaxed way of experimentation in order to
extract the causal effect where the assignment of users to treated and control
groups is not random and investigators do not have control over the assignment.
Relying on the power of observational studies and equipped with the potentially
viable sources of information from social networks, numerous studies have been
performed addressing a variety of issues. Studies have been done on observational
studies over social media and social networks through the linguistic analysis of
the users' textual content to discover causal knowledge from observational data
[17] in the context of health [9] in a range of issues including mental health [8],
nutrition [10], weight loss issues [7], to name but a few. The aforementioned
works provide some great examples of the promise of social media application
and particularly Twitter for the purpose of observational studies. There have
been studies focused on assessing user personality aspects by examining their
online behavior . Most of these works use supervised methods and are based on
the big five personality traits including openness, conscientiousness, extraver-
sion, agreeableness and neuroticism. Researchers have shown that these big five
dimensions can be extracted through linguistic analysis of the users' generated
textual content [22]. There are works which exploit the findings in a variety
of fields including improvement of recommendations [13,20] and rating systems
[14], location recommendation [23], improving rating prediction systems [16],
just to name a few.

User behavioral traces are embodied in either *offline activities* which refer
to activities users do in their real life, or *online activities* which refer to the
actions users do on the Internet, such as expressing their ideas on social networks.
Different patterns of offline activities and online actions could impact user's
behavior differently. Recently, authors in [2] studied the influence of online social
networks on users' online and offline behavior. Our work is the dual to the same
problem; we attempt to study the effect of offline activities on users' online
actions. To that aim, we design an observational study framework making use of
two famous social networks, namely Twitter and Foursquare. In our framework,
Foursquare check-ins are used to track users' offline activities, whereas Twitter
posts represent users' online actions. More specifically, our research problem is to
investigate how engaging in different offline activities, such as exercising and/or
visiting a bar, impact users' emotions over time. The locations users visit and
post on Foursquare enable us to track their offline activities. In order to track
users' emotions, we define a metric called *Emotion Conformity*, whereby we

measure users' emotional attitude towards active topics on Twitter compared to the broader community emotions towards the same topics.

2 Proposed Approach

2.1 Problem Definition

The objective of our work is to answer the question of whether engaging in an offline activity can impact user's online behavior and also the way different offline activities impact her behavior. More specifically, we aim at estimating how users' emotion conformity evolves as caused by engagement in an offline activity. To this end, we perform a cross-social network observational study in which user's posts on Twitter are considered as representative of users' online behavior and checkins on Foursquare represent their offline activities. We extract a given user's interests through modelling her interest in active Twitter topics and denote it as the *User Interest Profile*. Also, we extract user's emotions towards the topics she contributes to and is interested in denoted as *User Emotion Profile*, which is a representation of user online behavior and is core to our framework.

A topic s is assumed to be active if it is subject to extensive attention from users. We do not make any specific assumption on topic representations and thus a topic can be represented as a multinomial distribution over the vocabulary of unique terms mentioned in the collection of tweets, as follows:

Definition 1 (Active Topic). *Let C be the collection of tweets that is broadcast in time interval T and $\mathbb{V}$ be the set of all unique terms mentioned in C. We build a vector of N weights for each topic s, i.e., $w^s(v_1), ..., w^s(v_N)$, where $w^s(v_N)$ denotes the contribution importance of the word $v_N \in \mathbb{V}$ to topic s.*

As mentioned later in the experiments, the set of active topics can be extracted using existing LDA-based topic modeling techniques. In a specific time interval t with M active topics $S = \{s_1, s_2, ..., s_M\}$, we define interest profile for each user $u \in \mathbb{U}$ denoted by $UIP^t(u)$, as follows:

Definition 2 (User Interest Profile). *The user interest profile of user $u \in \mathbb{U}$ denoted by $UIP^t(u)$ is modeled by forming a vector of weights for each of M active topics, i.e., $(f_u^t(s_1), ..., f_u^t(s_M))$, where $f_u^t(s_M))$ indicates u's interest in topic $s_M \in S$. A user interest profile is normalized so that the sum of all weights in a profile equals to 1.*

We also extract user's emotions. A tweet's emotion is calculated as the difference between positive emotion and negative emotion. Thus, besides the active topics which every tweet belongs to, we calculate the emotion of every tweet as well. In a specific time interval t with M active topics $S = \{s_1, s_2, ..., s_M\}$, we define emotion profile for each user $u \in \mathbb{U}$ denoted by $UEP^t(u)$, as follows:

Definition 3 (User Emotion Profile). *The user emotion profile of user $u \in \mathbb{U}$ in time interval t, denoted by $UEP^t(u)$ is modeled by forming a vector of weights for each of M active topics, i.e., $(g_u^t(s_1), ..., g_u^t(s_M))$, where $g_u^t(s_M))$*

denotes the average emotion of user u with respect to topic $s_M \in S$. A user emotion profile is normalized so that $0 < h(s_M) \leqslant 1$.

In order to measure emotion conformity, we need to be measure users' emotions within the context of the larger community. To this end, we extend Definitions 2 and 3 as follows:

Definition 4 (Community Interest Profile)). Let U denote the set of users. The community Interest Profile, denoted by CIP^t, is represented by a vector of weights over the M topics, i.e., $(h^t(s_1), ..., h^t(s_M))$ as such CIP^t represents the normalized topic distribution for all tweets published in time t.

Moreover, we define a community emotion profile to show the emotion of the general population towards each topic.

Definition 5 (Community Emotion Profile)). The community emotion profile in time interval t, denoted as CEP^t, is represented by a vector of weights over the M topics, i.e., $(k^t(s_1), ..., k^t(s_M))$ where $k^t(s_i)$ denotes the average Emotion of users with respect to topic $s_m \in S$ and is normalized such that $0 < k^t(s_i) \leqslant 1$.

2.2 Metric Definition

By contrasting user-level measures from Definitions 2 and 3 with community-level measures of Definitions 4 and 5, we can now define the dependent variables corresponding how degrees of conformity change during time.

The user behavioral pattern that we are interested to study is user's conformity with general population's emotions. In our model, we define conformity as the degree to which a user aligns with and shares tweets bearing similar emotions towards the interests of the community. We measure emotional conformity as the degree to which the user exhibits the same emotions towards topics as does the general population. For example, a user who shows positive polarity towards the release of a new iPhone given the dominant emotion towards this topic is positive in the whole social network, has a high degree of emotion conformity (EF). On this basis, we calculate emotion conformity as follows:

$$EF^t(u) = UEP^t(u) - CEP^t. \tag{1}$$

2.3 Methodology

Here, we describe the approach taken to distinguish potential users to be selected as treated group and control group participants for our experiments. To this end, users who change their offline activities by 'starting' to visit a specific venue are nominated to form the treated group. We also draw upon the method used to distinguish the matched users for treated group members, i.e., control group participants.

Detecting Potential Users. We identify two different groups of users, who are active both on Twitter and Foursquare. In this analysis, users are separated into 2 groups; the treated group and the control group. The treated group U_T consists of users who start to visit a specific location which is hypothesized to have effect on the user u, and the control group U_C includes users who are different from the treated group in terms of the place they start to visit. The condition, also referred to as 'the interruption', for users in both groups is a point in time where a user begins to visit a specific venue (e.g., gym or bar) which she would not visit prior to that time. The reason to use the condition based model is to:

1. Eliminate the effect of external parameters which can cause uncertainty in concluding whether visiting a specific venue has an effect on the user's online behavior; and,
2. To filter out the users and make the database more admissible and relevant.

The parameter of significance is the difference between the effect on the user in the treated group with a user in the control group. This parameter gives important information about the effect of visiting different specific locations and is denoted by T_u. The effect can easily be calculated using the equation: $T_u = CIE_{u,T} - CIE_{u,C}$ where $CIE_{u,C}$ and $CIE_{u,T}$ are the mean results of the two groups [11].

Matching Through Propensity Score Matching. An observational study differs from RCT (randomized control trial) in that the subjects are not randomly assigned to treated and control groups. This experimental methodology relieves the effect of confounding parameters. In order to eliminate confounding effects, statistical matching is executed in order to reduce the effect of confounding variables. We use a standard approach of matching called *Propensity Score Matching* (PSM). In PSM method, users in the treated and control groups are matched across the groups based on their propensity scores. Propensity score is defined as the probability of assigning a particular treatment to a user given a set of observed confounding variables and is obtained using the logistic regression. The propensity score can be defined Prob(T = 1 — X = x) where T is a binary variable showing user is in the treatment group and X is the set of confounding variables. We employ number of tweets, number of twitter followers, number of Twitter friends, Gender and number of Foursquare checkins as the variables in PSM with a median absolute standard mean difference of 0.12. We exploited PSM in order to rule out any radical parameters that could possibly yield uncertain results. We match a given user from the treated group with one in control group with similar propensity scores.

3 Experiments

3.1 Dataset Description and Experimental Setup

We build our dataset with data collected from users who are active on both Twitter and Foursquare. These social networks provide us with complete and comprehensive information about user online and offline behavior, with Twitter representing the online actions of users and Foursquare providing the data about users' offline actions. Users active on both Twitter and Foursquare social networks are found through recognizing Twitter users who share their Foursquare check-ins using the Swarm application. Swarm is a mobile application provided by Foursquare that lets users share the places they visit by posting on user's Twitter timeline.

In our experiments, we extract recent tweets for 17,220 users who are active on both Twitter and Foursquare using Twitter API. In order to calculate Emotion Conformity values for each user we implement TwitterLDA to extract active topics and we use LIWC 2015 to extract user's emotions. After dividing users' tweets into monthly time intervals, we determine the Emotion Conformity for each user by calculating the differences of emotion distributions for user and community in the same time intervals. For the treated group, we distinguish users who do not check-in at any bar related venues for two months but start going to a bar related venue weekly after an interruption and continue this behavior for the next 8 months. For the control group, we find users who do not check-in at any gyms or fitness centres but start going to a gym related venue weekly for at least 8 months after the interruption. We match each user from the treated group with a user in the control group using propensity score matching.

3.2   Study Findings

Our findings are summarized in Fig. 1. As seen in the figure, the three groups of users, those in the control group as well as those in the treated groups of going to the bar and going to the gym where fully matched in the first two months of the study, meaning that the both the propensity scores for the users as well as their emotion conformity was the same. This indicates that the users in the these

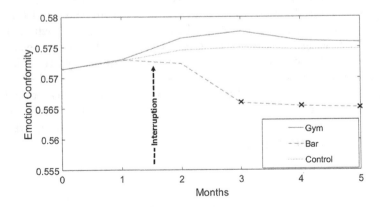

Fig. 1. The results of experiments for treated and control groups comparison in terms of Emotion Conformity.

three groups are comparable and any behavior change after the application of the treatment is attributable to the observed offline activity.

We find that the emotion conformity of the users in the control group does not change beyond the second month as the users in this group do not experience any new offline activity. On the other hand, those users who embark on going to the gym, have an increased emotion conformity. However, the increase is not statistically significant. In contrast, those users who start to go to a bar after the second month and consistently go to the bar, as mentioned earlier, at least once a week, experience a reduced emotion conformity. The observed changes in emotion conformity is also statistically significant over both the control group as well as the treated group who went to the gym. This means that the observed change in the behavior of those users who went to the bar consistently cannot be attributed to chance and can be attributed to their offline behavior. So our findings can be summarized as follows:

- Information collected from different social networks can be collected and aligned to extract insight about both users' online and offline activities;
- While it was shown in previous studies that online behavior can be have impact on users' offline activities, we have also shown preliminary results that indicate that users' offline activities can impact their online activities;
- We have demonstrated that some offline activities have a higher potential to more significantly disrupt the users' regular online behavior. For instance in our study, while going to the gym does insignificantly change a users emotion conformity, the impact is removed with time; on the other hand, the impact of going to the bar is significant and sustained over time.

As future work, we are interested in studying this phenomenon more extensively by covering a wider range of offline activities and a broader user set.

References

1. Ali, A.H.: The power of social media in developing nations: new tools for closing the global digital divide and beyond. Harv. Hum. Rts. J. **24**, 185 (2011)
2. Althoff, T., Jindal, P., Leskovec, J.: Online actions with offline impact: how online social networks influence online and offline user behavior. In: Proceedings of the Tenth ACM International Conference on Web Search and Data Mining, pp. 537–546. ACM (2017)
3. Brandtzæg, P.B.: Social networking sites: their users and social implications–a longitudinal study. J. Comput.-Mediated Commun. **17**(4), 467–488 (2012)
4. Bucci, W., Freedman, N.: The language of depression. Bull. Menninger Clin. **45**(4), 334 (1981)
5. Choudhury, M.D., Counts, S., Horvitz, E.: Predicting postpartum changes in emotion and behavior via social media. In: 2013 ACM SIGCHI Conference on Human Factors in Computing Systems, CHI 2013, Paris, France, 27 April–2 May 2013, pp. 3267–3276 (2013)

6. Choudhury, M.D., Gamon, M., Counts, S., Horvitz, E.: Predicting depression via social media. In: Proceedings of the Seventh International Conference on Weblogs and Social Media, ICWSM 2013, Cambridge, Massachusetts, USA, 8–11 July 2013 (2013)

7. Cunha, T., Weber, I., Pappa, G.: A warm welcome matters!: the link between social feedback and weight loss in /r/loseit. In Proceedings of the 26th International Conference on World Wide Web Companion, pp. 1063–1072. International World Wide Web Conferences Steering Committee (2017)

8. De Choudhury, M., Kıcıman, E.: The language of social support in social media and its effect on suicidal ideation risk. In: Proceedings of the International AAAI Conference on Weblogs and Social Media. International AAAI Conference on Weblogs and Social Media, vol. 2017, p. 32. NIH Public Access (2017)

9. De Choudhury, M., Kiciman, E., Dredze, M., Coppersmith, G., Kumar, M.: Discovering shifts to suicidal ideation from mental health content in social media. In: Proceedings of the 2016 CHI Conference on Human Factors in Computing Systems, pp. 2098–2110. ACM (2016)

10. De Choudhury, M., Sharma, S., Kiciman, E.: Characterizing dietary choices, nutrition, and language in food deserts via social media. In: Proceedings of the 19th ACM Conference on Computer-Supported Cooperative Work & Social Computing, pp. 1157–1170. ACM (2016)

11. Dos Reis, V.L., Culotta, A.: Using matched samples to estimate the effects of exercise on mental health from twitter. In: Proceedings of the Twenty-Ninth AAAI Conference on Artificial Intelligence, pp. 182–188 (2015)

12. Greaves, F., Ramirez-Cano, D., Millett, C., Darzi, A., Donaldson, L.: Harnessing the cloud of patient experience: using social media to detect poor quality healthcare. BMJ Qual. Saf. **22**(3), 251–255 (2013)

13. Hu, R., Pu, P.: Enhancing collaborative filtering systems with personality information. In: Proceedings of the Fifth ACM Conference on Recommender Systems, pp. 197–204. ACM (2011)

14. Karumur, R.P., Nguyen, T.T., Konstan, J.A.: Exploring the value of personality in predicting rating behaviors: a study of category preferences on movielens. In: Proceedings of the 10th ACM Conference on Recommender Systems, pp. 139–142. ACM (2016)

15. Li, C., Lu, Y., Mei, Q., Wang, D., Pandey, S.: Click-through prediction for advertising in twitter timeline. In: Proceedings of the 21th ACM SIGKDD International Conference on Knowledge Discovery and Data Mining, Sydney, NSW, Australia, 10–13 August 2015, pp. 1959–1968 (2015)

16. Liu, Y., Cao, X., Yu, Y.: Are you influenced by others when rating?: improve rating prediction by conformity modeling. In: Proceedings of the 10th ACM Conference on Recommender Systems, pp. 269–272. ACM (2016)

17. Oktay, H., Taylor, B.J., Jensen, D.D.: Causal discovery in social media using quasi-experimental designs. In: Proceedings of the First Workshop on Social Media Analytics, pp. 1–9. ACM (2010)

18. Oxman, T.E., Rosenberg, S.D., Tucker, G.J.: The language of paranoia. Am. J. Psychiatry **139**(3), 275–282 (1982). https://doi.org/10.1176/ajp.139.3.275

19. Pennebaker, J.W., Mehl, M.R., Niederhoffer, K.G.: Psychological aspects of natural language use: our words, our selves. Ann. Rev. Psychol. **54**(1), 547–577 (2003)

20. Roshchina, A., Cardiff, J., Rosso, P.: User profile construction in the twin personality-based recommender system (2011)

21. Sulistya, A., Sharma, A., Lo, D.: Spiteful, one-off, and kind: predicting customer feedback behavior on Twitter. In: Spiro, E., Ahn, Y.-Y. (eds.) SocInfo 2016. LNCS, vol. 10047, pp. 368–381. Springer, Cham (2016). https://doi.org/10.1007/978-3-319-47874-6_26
22. Tausczik, Y.R., Pennebaker, J.W.: The psychological meaning of words: LIWC and computerized text analysis methods. J. Lang. Soc. Psychol. **29**(1), 24–54 (2010)
23. Yang, S., Sklar, M.: Detecting trending venues using foursquare's data. In: RecSys Posters (2016)

Improving News Personalization Through Search Logs

Xiao Bai[1], B. Barla Cambazoglu[2], Francesco Gullo[3(✉)], Amin Mantrach[4], and Fabrizio Silvestri[5]

[1] Yahoo Research, Sunnyvale, USA
xbai@oath.com
[2] RMIT University, Melbourne, Australia
barla.cambazoglu@rmit.edu.au
[3] R&D Department, UniCredit, Rome, Italy
gullof@acm.org
[4] Criteo Research, Palo Alto, USA
a.mantrach@criteo.com
[5] Facebook, London, UK
fsilvestri@fb.com

Abstract. Content personalization is a long-standing problem for online news services. In most personalization approaches users are represented by topical interest profiles that are matched with news articles in order to properly decide which articles are to be recommended. When constructing user profiles, existing personalization methods exploit the user activity observed within the news service itself without incorporating information from other sources.

In this paper we study the problem of news personalization by leveraging usage information that is external to the news service. We propose a novel approach that relies on the concept of "search profiles", which are user profiles that are built based on the past interactions of the user with a web search engine. We extensively test our proposal on real-world datasets obtained from Yahoo. We explore various dimensions and granularities at which search profiles can be built. Experimental results show that, compared to a basic strategy that does not exploit the search activity of users, our approach is able to boost the clicks on news articles shown at the top positions of a ranked result list.

1 Introduction

Online news services have dramatically changed the way people access information. Nowadays, the Web has plenty of news sites. While this plethora of resources provides a fruitful source of information for professionals, it may create a problem for normal end users who typically want to reach the desired pieces of information quickly.

A number of today's online new services, such as Google News, aim at aggregating different news sources and presenting them to their end users in an organic way. During

---

An extended version of this paper appeared in [3]. Most of the work was done while all the authors were affiliated with Yahoo Labs, Barcelona, Spain.

© Springer Nature Switzerland AG 2020
L. Boratto et al. (Eds.): BIAS 2020, CCIS 1245, pp. 152–166, 2020.
https://doi.org/10.1007/978-3-030-52485-2_14

a session on these news aggregators, users expect to be provided with content that they consider relevant, useful, or interesting. Since every single user has her own set of interests, *personalization* of presented news results becomes an important requirement.

Personalization of a news service is a long-standing challenge. Traditional approaches consist of ranking news articles based on how well they match the user's interests [1,5,12–14,17–19,24,27]. Inferring the interests of a specific user (i.e., building a *user profile*) is a critical aspect that heavily affects the quality of a news personalization system. While earlier systems explicitly asked users to specify their profiles [5,33], it is common today to develop automated user-profiling strategies that do not require any manual effort on the user side [1,14,17].

One of the most valuable information sources used to automatically build user profiles is the online behavior exhibited by users during their interaction with online services. In general, the online behavior can be obtained from endogenous or exogenous sources. In the context of news personalization, endogenous information refers to the interaction of users with the news service itself (e.g., news articles they have read in the past), while exogenous information consists of the user activity that is performed on services other than the news service.

In most existing news personalization systems user profiles are built using endogenous information [9,22,23,26,30]. The rationale is that a news article read by a user represents a clear evidence of her interests. While endogenous information is undoubtedly the most reliable source for discovering user interests, it may not tell us the whole story about the user. Indeed, most users interact with several online services, each serving a different purpose. It is not uncommon that the interaction with a service reflects user interests that are related to that specific service only and, as such, cannot be unveiled by other services. This means that user interests arising only from endogenous information may correspond to a limited portion of the overall user interests. In this context exogenous information constitutes a precious source of additional knowledge to complete user profiles and improve the quality of a news personalization system.

As an example, consider a user from Europe who is used to access an online news service mainly for football news. Suppose that this user is planning a trip to the US and starts interacting with a web search engine to look for flights and accommodation, thus leaving a clear trace in web search logs about her current interest in the US country. Now assume that, while she is still planning her trip, a news about significant changes in the rules for European citizens to enter the US becomes public. This news is clearly interesting for the user, as it might even preclude her access to the country she is planning to visit. In this example a news personalization system relying only on endogenous information would not be able to recognize such news as relevant or useful, as the news content does not match the user's interest about football (the only interest manifested during the user's past interactions with the news service). On the contrary, this news would be recognized as interesting and probably recommended to the user if the system relied on exogenous information derived from web search logs.

Contributions. In this paper we study the novel problem of news personalization by leveraging search logs. To the best of our knowledge, the problem of studying the impact of such an exogenous source on news personalization has never been considered.

Our claim is that the endogenous information provided by the interaction of users with the news portal can be enriched by exogenous information extracted from web search query logs in order to improve the overall news personalization experience. Specifically, our goal is to understand what kind of information in query logs should be considered to build more complete and higher quality user profiles. This is orthogonal to the specific methods used for constructing user profiles and combining profiles from different sources. In this work we show that very basic methods already suffice to significantly improve the quality of news recommendation, thus attesting that a clear signal on the impact of the web-search source on news personalization exists regardless of the complexity of the employed models. More sophisticated models are clearly expected to be even more effective. For instance, running a topic model on top of search and news profiles together would lead to simultaneously finding latent relationships between the two types of profiles, with consequent benefit with respect to considering each type of profile in isolation. Devising the best ways of building profiles from query logs and combining them with endogenous profiles is however an interesting open problem that we defer to future work.

Our approach focuses on users who have used both the online news service and the search service. For each user, we record the terms contained in the queries that the user issued to the search engine and, for every query of the user, we record the terms contained in the titles and abstracts of the top 10 results returned by the search engine as answers to the query. These terms altogether constitute what we call the *search profile* of the user. For the personalization task, we consider the search profile of a user coupled with her *news profile*, which is the basic profile built based only on the past interactions of the user with the news service. More precisely, for a given user, both her search profile and her news profile are used to score the news articles, by computing: (1) the cosine similarity between the vector representing the search profile and the vector representing the news content, and (2) the cosine similarity between the news profile vector and the news content vector. We then produce a unified ranking that takes into account both the search profile score and the news profile score by resorting to two alternative methods traditionally used in the literature: (*i*) *score aggregation*, where the two initial scores are combined into a new single score that is eventually used for producing the ultimate ranking, and (*ii*) *rank aggregation*, where the two initial rankings are aggregated into a single ranking through a voting strategy.

We conduct a thorough experimental evaluation to verify whether and when such a combination of search profiles and news profiles can improve the quality of the news personalization task compared to using news profiles in isolation. The main findings arising from our experimental evaluation are as follows:

- The combination of search profiles with news profiles considerably improves upon using news profiles only, and the score aggregation method outperforms the rank aggregation method.
- Using search profiles consisting of query terms and the terms within the titles of the top 10 search results leads to a significant improvement, while including the terms contained in the top 10 abstracts does not increase the quality further.
- Employing search profiles leads to improvement for both active users (expected) and inactive users (positively surprising).

- The quality of search profiles depends on the number of queries used to build the profiles. In our experiments we observe an improvement upon the strategy that relies only on news profiles when a user issues no less than 300 queries in a period of 3 months, i.e., when a user issues around 3 queries per day, on average.
- Building search profiles using three months of search history consistently improves the quality of personalization upon the case where the search history spans a shorter period. On the other hand, extending the time period further (e.g., 4–6 months) does not bring additional improvement upon the three-month case.

Roadmap. The rest of the paper is organized as follows. Section 2 introduces how we build search profiles and combine them with news profiles. Section 3 reports on our experiments. Section 4 discusses related work. Section 5 concludes the paper.

2   Search-Enhanced News Personalization

Constructing Search Profiles. We construct the search profile of a user by using the information extracted from the query logs of a web search engine. Query logs record all actions that users perform on the search service. Specifically, they keep track of the time a query was issued, by whom, and the top-k result web pages returned by the search engine as answers to the query. For each result web page, we have access to its URL, title, and an abstract summarizing the content of the page.

Previous work has shown that queries are a good proxy for representing user interests, especially in a personalization task [15]. In general, however, queries on their own contain very few terms and, as a consequence, search profiles built by considering only query terms may easily suffer from a sparsity issue. A possible solution is to exploit the additional information contained in the top results of a query. The fact that such web pages are returned as an answer to the query by the underlying search engine is an implicit evidence that their content is likely to be relevant to the query and they can thus be safely exploited to expand the query-term-only search profiles. In particular, we enrich the search profiles by considering titles and abstracts of the top result pages. We hereinafter refer to search profiles built using only query terms, query terms plus title, and query terms plus title and abstract as, *query-based*, *title-enriched*, and *abstract-enriched* search profiles, respectively.

More formally, we construct a user profile as follows. Given a topic space $\mathcal{T}$ of dimensionality N_f, a user profile is represented as an N_f-dimensional numerical vector, where each element i denotes the degree of user interest in the topic i in $\mathcal{T}$. In this work we resort to the basic bag-of-words model to define the topic space, therefore N_f corresponds to the number of distinct terms (i.e., 1-grams) that form the vocabulary. The degree of user interest in the topic (term) i is computed by employing a standard TF-IDF strategy, whose details are provided next.

Let N_u be the total number of users and N_q be the total number of queries issued to the search engine by all users in a selected time period. The terms of the complete set of queries can be represented as an $(N_q \times N_f)$-dimensional integer matrix $\mathbf{Qw}$, where each entry Qw_{ij} stores the number of times term j appears in query i. The title terms and the abstract terms of the top results of each query can be represented in an analogous way by $(N_q \times N_f)$-dimensional matrices $\mathbf{Tw}$ and $\mathbf{Aw}$, respectively. Matrices $\mathbf{Qw}$, $\mathbf{Tw}$, and $\mathbf{Aw}$ basically keep track of the TF part. The information about the queries issued by the various users is instead stored in a binary matrix $\mathbf{Qu}$ of size $N_q \times N_u$, where $Qu_{ij} = 1$ if and only if user j issued query i.

Using the above notation, the query-based search profiles of the selected users are represented as an $(N_u \times N_f)$-dimensional matrix $\mathbf{Uq}$ defined as $\mathbf{Uq} = \mathbf{Qu}^T \mathbf{Qw}$. Similarly, the title-enriched search profiles are given by the matrix $\mathbf{Ut} = \mathbf{Qu}^T (\mathbf{Qw} + \mathbf{Tw})$, while the matrix $\mathbf{Ua} = \mathbf{Qu}^T (\mathbf{Qw} + \mathbf{Tw} + \mathbf{Aw})$ corresponds to the abstract-enriched search profiles. To properly account for term importance, the entries of the three matrices $\mathbf{Uq}$, $\mathbf{Ut}$, and $\mathbf{Ua}$ are scaled using an IDF function computed on the corresponding user profiles. Specifically, each count in $\mathbf{Uq}$, $\mathbf{Ut}$, and $\mathbf{Ua}$ is multiplied by a scaling term computed as the logarithm of the ratio between the total number of queries in the log and the number of queries where the corresponding term appears. IDF is just one among many possible functions that can be used to alleviate the shortcomings of excessively frequent terms.

Note that matrices $\mathbf{Uq}$, $\mathbf{Ut}$, and $\mathbf{Ua}$ contain the search profiles of all users in the selected set: the profile of a single user i can be obtained by simply selecting the i-th row of the matrix of interest.

Combining Search Profiles with News Profiles. In a real news recommender system every time a user j accesses the system, she is provided with a ranked list of n news articles. Each news article a_l is assigned a relevance score se_{jl} that expresses how relevant a_l is for user j. Specifically, the score se_{jl} reflects how well news a_l matches the news profile of user j. A common approach to compute this relevance score is to set it equal to the cosine similarity between the news profile vector and the news vector. The scores $\{se_{jl}\}_{l=1}^n$ determine the ranking positions $\{pe_{jl}\}_{l=1}^n$ ($pe_{jl} \in [1..n]$) associated with the articles in the list: higher scores correspond to lower ranking positions.

To leverage search profiles, we associate each news article a_l with a further relevance score ss_{jl}, computed as the cosine similarity between the search profile of user j and news a_l. The relevance scores $\{ss_{jl}\}_{l=1}^n$ in turn yield a further ranking $\{ps_{jl}\}_{l=1}^n$.

In order to combine relevance scores and/or ranking positions given by search profiles and news profiles, we rely on two basic strategies, namely *score aggregation* (denoted SP_Score, where SP stands for search profiles) and *rank aggregation* (denoted SP_Rank). The difference between the two approaches is that SP_Score combines the two relevance scores and uses this combined score to infer a news ranking, whereas SP_Rank directly combines the two rankings to derive the ultimate ranking. Specifically, the combined score Ss_{jl} provided by SP_Score is a linear combination of the min-max-normalized se_{jl} and ss_{jl} scores (normalization performed to project the two rankings onto a common $[0, 1]$ range). We experiment with various values of the parameter used to control the combination. More details on this are in Sect. 3. The final ranking produced by the SP_Rank method is computed by applying the well-known Borda-count election method to the two rankings $\{pe_{jl}\}_{l=1}^n$ and $\{ps_{jl}\}_{l=1}^n$.

3   Experiments

Dataset. We use the click logs of Yahoo News and the query logs from Yahoo Web Search.[1] We rely on the news click logs of a random day and build search profiles by using the queries that were issued at most six months before that day. We restrict our evaluation to a sample of the users who clicked on at least one news article on the test day and issued at least 1000 queries during the three-month period before the test day. This results in a set of about 70K users, for whom a total number of 140K independent news recommendations have been produced during the test day.

Methods. We implement the proposed SP_Score and SP_Rank as discussed in Sect. 2. As far as the SP_Score method, we set the parameter that controls the linear combination between the search profile score and the news profile score to 0.5, as we empirically observed that this value gives good results in most cases.

The main goal of the evaluation is to compare SP_Score and SP_Rank to a baseline method that relies on news profiles only, where the news profiles shared by the proposed methods and the baseline are built by keeping track of the content of the past news read by a user. In particular, the baseline method is a hybrid news-personalization system that exploits only news profiles. More precisely, for each user u and term t in the vocabulary, a weight w_{ut} is computed as the number of times user u has clicked on a news article containing term t. The ultimate news profile vector of user u corresponds to an N-dimensional real-valued vector v_u (where N is the vocabulary size), whose entries $v_u(t)$, for each term t, are computed as the logarithm of the ratio between w_{ut} and the number of clicks on the same term t of other users who have clicked on news articles similar to those clicked by u. This way news profiles rely on both content-based information (weights w_{ut}) and collaborative filtering (scaling given by the weights of other similar users). Recommendations are made by ranking news articles by a combination of cosine similarity between news profiles and news vectors and popularity (in terms of absolute number of clicks) of the article.

As a further baseline, we consider a recency-based approach that is quite popular in the context of news personalization. Specifically, according to this method the news articles in each pageview are re-ranked in descending order of their publishing time. For details about the notion of pageview please see blow. We refer to this recency-based approach as TimeB.

Performance Assessment. The interaction between a user and the news site is as follows. Every time a user accesses the system, she receives a list of 20 news articles, which are primarily ranked by the baseline method exploiting news profiles only. We refer to a pair ⟨user, news list⟩ as a *pageview*. Our goal is to re-rank the 20 news articles in each pageview by employing the proposed SP_Score and SP_Rank methods.

We evaluate the quality of the news rankings produced by our methods by resorting to the *Normalized Discounted Cumulative Gain* (NDCG) metric [2,28]. NDCG measures the quality of a ranked list of items/documents by giving more importance to the items ranked at the top positions of the list. If the user is not satisfied with what is immediately proposed to her, she will need to scroll down with the risk of loosing attention.

The NDCG measures this phenomenon, by discounting the recommendations at lower positions of the ranking. This conforms with the news-personalization context, where, regardless of the device, only a few slots are available to display recommendations.

The main goal of our evaluation is to assess whether the proposed search-profile-based methods yield higher $NDCG$ values than the baseline. Specifically, in each set of experiments, we focus on the average $NDCG$ value (i.e., averaged over all pageviews), on the cumulative distribution of $NDCG$ values, as well as on assessing whether the difference between two overall sets of $NDCG$ values (i.e., for all pageviews) is statistically significant. In particular, we assess statistical significance by employing the Wilcoxon signed rank test [10]. This choice is motivated since (i) the Wilcoxon test does not require for the statistics to be tested to follow any specific distribution, and (ii) it is a paired test, which is needed in our context as, for any set of experiments, we compare pairs of observations coming from two competing methods (i.e., NDCG values obtained for a specific pageview).

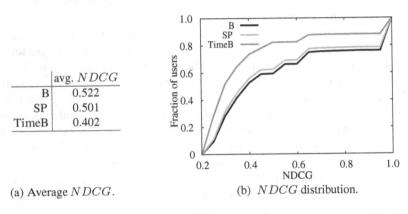

	avg. $NDCG$
B	0.522
SP	0.501
TimeB	0.402

(a) Average $NDCG$.   (b) $NDCG$ distribution.

Fig. 1. $NDCG$ of the news-profile-only baseline (B), the recency-based baseline (TimeB) and a strategy based on search profiles only (title-enriched search profiles, 3-month training period).

3.1   Results

In the following we report and discuss the main experimental findings observed with our empirical evaluation. Particularly, we are interested in evaluating six critical aspects: (1) usefulness of search profiles both in isolation and in combination with news profiles, (2) important features at the base of search profiles, (3) benefits of search profiles for active and inactive users, (4) volume of search queries needed for building satisfactory search profiles, (5) time horizon to be considered for constructing search profiles, (6) impact of recency on the quality of search profiles. In the following we provide detailed discussions on each of these aspects.

1. Do search profiles improve the quality of news personalization? First of all, even though our proposal considers search profiles in combination with news profiles, we believe it is anyway worth taking a look at the performance while using search profiles in isolation. We report this experiment in Fig. 1 and we observe that the results confirm what is suggested by common sense: the search-profile-only strategy is not enough to outperform the news-profile-only strategy (denoted as B in the figure). This was expected, as past interactions with the news service is the primary source of information to discover user interests in news. What is more interesting is that the difference between the two strategies is tangible but not particularly evident. This suggests that there is a good chance of observing consistent improvements when combining search profiles with news profiles. The experiments below confirm this claim. Before moving to that, we point out that Fig. 1 also reports on the results of the recency-based baseline TimeB, which recommends news based on their recency. Such a baseline performs evidently worse than the news-profile-only baseline B, and even worse than the search-profile-only strategy. Thus, we avoid reporting its results in the rest of the experiments. For easiness of presentation, we hereinafter use "news-profile-only baseline" and "baseline" interchangeably to refer to the news-profile-only baseline.

In Fig. 2 we compare the $NDCG$ results achieved by the proposed SP_Score and SP_Rank methods to the baseline. The results of our methods reported here refer to search profiles built considering a 3-month training period and exploiting terms from each query issued along with the title of its top-10 result web pages (i.e., title-enhanced search profiles given by the matrix Ut defined in Sect. 2). The figure shows that our methods clearly outperform the news-profile-only baseline in terms of both average $NDCG$ and overall distribution of $NDCG$ values. Importantly, as reported in Fig. 2(a), the differences between the proposed methods and the baseline are statistically significant. Among the two proposed methods, SP_Score exhibits in general better accuracy: this is motivated by the fact that its profile-combining strategy is more fine-grained than SP_Rank (see Sect. 2).

Therefore, based on the findings above, we can state that it is possible to improve the quality of news personalization by exploiting the web search history of a user.

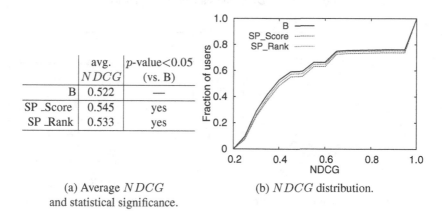

	avg. $NDCG$	p-value<0.05 (vs. B)
B	0.522	—
SP _Score	0.545	yes
SP _Rank	0.533	yes

(a) Average $NDCG$ and statistical significance.

(b) $NDCG$ distribution.

Fig. 2. $NDCG$ results of the baseline (B) and the proposed SP_Score and SP_Rank methods (title-enriched search profiles, 3-month training period).

2. What are the important features to be considered in a search profile? To answer this question, we study the impact of building search profiles at different granularities, i.e., by considering query terms only (i.e., query-based search profiles given by the matrix U_q defined in Sect. 2), or including information from titles (i.e., title-enhanced search profiles given by the matrix U_t in Sect. 2) or titles plus abstracts (i.e., abstract-enhanced search profiles given by the matrix U_a in Sect. 2) of the top-10 web pages returned as results to the query by the underlying search engine.

The results of this experiment are reported in Fig. 3. The first finding is that query terms alone are too sparse to allow any method to obtain a clear improvement upon the news-profile-only baseline. In fact, using query terms only, our SP_Score method slightly outperforms the baseline, but the difference is not statistically significant. Instead, augmenting the search profiles with both queries and titles (Q+T) gives much better results: the differences with respect to the baseline are statistically significant for both SP_Score and SP_Rank.

Further enriching the search profiles with terms in the abstracts clearly keeps the difference from the baseline statistically significant and leads to a slight ulterior improvement with respect to using Q+T terms. The improvement is however not that evident: the average $NDCG$ only slightly increases (0.07% for SP_Score and 0.11%

		avg. $NDCG$	p-value<0.05 (vs. B)
	B	0.5217	—
SP_Score	Q	0.5259	no
	Q+T	0.5449	yes
	Q+T+A	0.5453	yes
SP_Rank	Q	0.5155	no
	Q+T	0.5328	yes
	Q+T+A	0.5334	yes

(a) Average $NDCG$ and statistical significance.

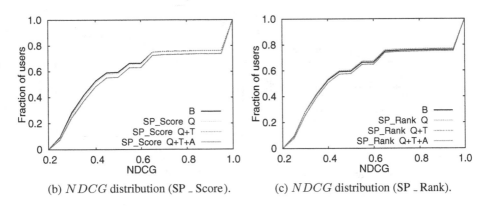

(b) $NDCG$ distribution (SP_Score).   (c) $NDCG$ distribution (SP_Rank).

Fig. 3. $NDCG$ results of the baseline (B) and the proposed SP_Score and SP_Rank with different information considered to build the search profiles: query-based search profiles (Q), title-enriched search profiles (Q+T), abstract-enriched search profiles (Q+T+A).

	all users		active users		inactive users	
	avg. $NDCG$	p-value<0.05 (vs. B)	avg. $NDCG$	p-value<0.05 (vs. B)	avg. $NDCG$	p-value<0.05 (vs. B)
B	0.522	—	0.522	—	0.522	—
SP_Score	0.545	yes	0.588	yes	0.538	yes
SP_Rank	0.533	yes	0.573	yes	0.526	yes

(a) Average $NDCG$ and statistical significance

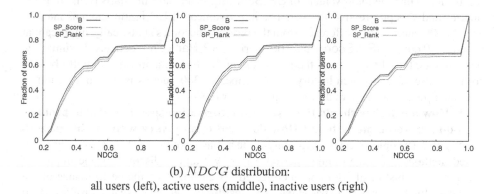

(b) $NDCG$ distribution:
all users (left), active users (middle), inactive users (right)

Fig. 4. $NDCG$ results of the baseline (B) and the proposed SP_Score and SP_Rank methods for different users (title-enriched search profiles, 3-month training period).

for SP_Rank), and the difference between the Q+T $NDCG$ values and the Q+T+A $NDCG$ values is not statistically significant. A possible explanation is that the terms contained in the abstract but not in the title are usually contextual terms that add only little information to what is already provided by the query+title terms themselves.

Considering the increased dimensionality of the resulting search profiles when using abstracts, we can thus conclude that building search profiles using query+title terms is perhaps the best choice in terms of trade-off among accuracy, computational effort, and space needed to store the profiles.

3. Is there any difference between active and inactive users? The next aspect we focus on is to which extent the improvement exhibited by our search-profile-based methods distinctly affect users who are active/inactive in the news site. We define active and inactive users as those who clicked on at least 100 and less than 100 news articles during a 3-month training period, respectively. The ultimate goal is to understand whether our strategy is valid also for users who have a weaker interaction with the news site, i.e., users who have less than 100 clicks on the news website during the 3-month training period. The results are reported in Fig. 4. According to the figure, for either active or inactive users, both SP_Score and SP_Rank methods achieve better $NDCG$ results than the news-profile-only baseline, and the differences are statistically significant. The impact of this finding is noteworthy, as it clearly assesses that the proposed methods leveraging exogenous information improve the quality of news recommendation, even for those users who exhibit weak interaction with the news site.

4. How many search queries are needed when building a search profile in order to observe quality improvements? We now shift the attention to the problem of assessing how much web search history is actually needed for observing an improvement in the quality of news personalization. In Fig. 5 we report the results achieved by aggregating title-enriched search profiles at different granularities (in terms of number of queries): from 200 to 1000 queries. The queries we consider in the various samples are randomly selected from the ones issued by each user during a three-month period. The figure shows that the improvement of SP_Score upon the baseline starts right after 200 queries and gets progressively larger. The improvement of SP_Rank happens later: at around 600 queries. The difference from the baseline becomes statistically significant at around 300 queries (SP_Score) and 700 queries (SP_Rank), respectively. In summary, we can state that the quality of the news personalization system can evidently benefit from the use of web search history for a number of 300 queries issued in a period of 3 months (i.e., an average of around 3 queries per day).

5. How much time should the historical information span in order to produce high-quality recommendations? How does the quality vary with the increase in time span? The objective here is to analyze the behavior of the proposed search-profile-based methods when the training period varies. We aim at discovering the impact of the amount of historical information collected for each user on the performance of the search profile for that user. In particular, we consider title-enriched search profiles based on queries issued on a time period spanning one month, two months, ..., up to six months before the test day.

Figure 6 shows the distribution of the size of search profiles, computed as the number of queries issued by a user divided by the maximum number of queries among all users. The distributions for search profiles based on queries issued during four and five months are not reported for the sake of readability of the figure. Results of our methods are instead reported in Fig. 7.

For all time periods considered, the figure shows that both SP_Score and SP_Rank are significantly better than the news-profile-only baseline, and increasing the training period always leads to better accuracy, although the improvement tends to decrease with

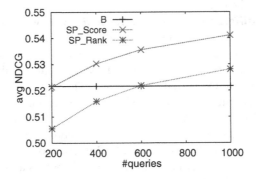

Fig. 5. $NDCG$ results of the baseline (B) and the two proposed methods (SP_Score and SP_Rank) with varying the number of queries issued (title-enriched search profiles).

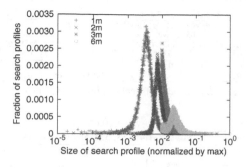

Fig. 6. Distribution of profile size.

increasing time period. Indeed, in Fig. 7(b), where we report whether the difference between the results of two consecutive time periods is statistically significant, we can see that this observation only holds for the time periods of up to three months, while for the remaining time periods the differences are not statistically significant. Based on this finding, we can therefore conclude that the richer the search profile is, the more useful the search signal is in the news personalization task, at least up to a three-month time period. Considering time periods larger than three months does not lead to any consistent performance improvement.

4 Related Work

News personalization has become an extremely active research area in the last years [20]. Existing approaches are usually broadly classified into *collaborative filtering* [32], *content-based* [25], and *hybrid* [6]. Collaborative-filtering-based news-personalization systems [9,31] recommend news to any specific user based on the ratings of other users who share similar interests with her. In content-based systems [1,4,5,13,14,17,19,34] a user profile is built which is based on the user's past activity on the news website and recommend news based on how well they match that profile. Collaborative filtering and content-based systems are also combined together into the so-called hybrid news-personalization systems [8,16,21–23,35].

The problem of exploiting web-search information, such as query logs, click-through data, or session data, for personalization of online services has been extensively studied in the literature. However, this body of research has focused on personalization of services that are inherent to web search itself, such as type resolution of entities in a web-search query [29], enrichment of web-search queries by query expansion [7] or web-search results [11]. Our work instead exploits information from web-search queries to improve personalization of an external service, i.e., a news portal.

	1 month		2 months		3 months		4 months		5 months		6 months	
	avg. $NDCG$	p-value <0.05 (vs. B)	avg. $NDCG$	p-value <0.05 (vs. B)	avg. $NDCG$	p-value <0.05 (vs. B)	avg. $NDCG$	p-value <0.05 (vs. B)	avg. $NDCG$	p-value <0.05 (vs. B)	avg. $NDCG$	p-value <0.05 (vs. B)
B	0.522	—	0.522	—	0.522	—	0.522	—	0.522	—	0.522	—
SP_Score	0.540	yes	0.543	yes	0.545	yes	0.546	yes	0.548	yes	0.549	yes
SP_Rank	0.524	yes	0.530	yes	0.533	yes	0.534	yes	0.536	yes	0.537	yes

(a) Average $NDCG$ and statistical significance vs. the baseline.

p-value <0.05

	2M vs. 1M	3M vs. 2M	4M vs. 3M	5M vs. 4M	6M vs. 5M
SP_Score	yes	yes	no	no	no
SP_Rank	yes	yes	no	no	no

(b) Statistical significance among the various time periods.

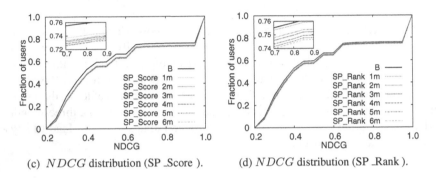

(c) $NDCG$ distribution (SP_Score).   (d) $NDCG$ distribution (SP_Rank).

Fig. 7. $NDCG$ results of the baseline (B) and the proposed SP_Score and SP_Rank with different training periods to build the search profiles (title-enriched search profiles).

5   Conclusions

We addressed the problem of news personalization by leveraging information extracted from web search query logs. We devised a method that represents the interests of a users based on the web search queries she issued, the titles of the pages returned as a result to the queries, as well as the displayed snippets. We evaluated two strategies for combining personalized news rankings obtained by exploiting web search history with news rankings obtained through common user interactions with the news site. Our experiments indicate that exploiting search profiles leads to considerable improvements upon using traditional news-interaction-based profiles only.

In the future we plan to dig into the methods used for building search profiles and to combine search profiles and news profiles. In particular, as a first attempt, we will study the impact of using topic model on top of search and news profiles, so as to better capture the latent relationships between the two types of profile. We also plan to apply our idea to other services that may provide user-interaction data (e.g., social networks).

References

1. Ahn, J.w., Brusilovsky, P., Grady, J., He, D., Syn, S.Y.: Open user profiles for adaptive news systems: help or harm? In: Proceedings of International Conference on World Wide Web (WWW), pp. 11–20 (2007)
2. Baeza-Yates, R., Ribeiro-Neto, B., et al.: Modern Information Retrieval, vol. 463. ACM Press, New York (1999)
3. Bai, X., Cambazoglu, B.B., Gullo, F., Mantrach, A., Silvestri, F.: Exploiting search history of users for news personalization. Inf. Sci. **385–386**, 125–137 (2017)
4. Bansal, T., Das, M., Bhattacharyya, C.: Content driven user profiling for comment-worthy recommendations of news and blog articles. In: Proceedings of International ACM Conference on Recommender Systems (RecSys), pp. 195–202 (2015)
5. Billsus, D., Pazzani, M.J.: A hybrid user model for news story classification. In: Kay, J. (ed.) UM99 User Modeling. CICMS, vol. 407, pp. 99–108. Springer, Vienna (1999). https://doi.org/10.1007/978-3-7091-2490-1_10
6. Burke, R.: Hybrid recommender systems: survey and experiments. User Model. User-Adap. Inter. **12**(4), 331–370 (2002). https://doi.org/10.1023/A:1021240730564
7. Chirita, P.A., Firan, C.S., Nejdl, W.: Personalized query expansion for the web. In: Proceedings of International ACM SIGIR Conference on Research and Development in Information Retrieval, pp. 7–14 (2007)
8. Chu, W., Park, S.T.: Personalized recommendation on dynamic content using predictive bilinear models. In: Proceedings of International Conference on World Wide Web (WWW), pp. 691–700 (2009)
9. Das, A.S., Datar, M., Garg, A., Rajaram, S.: Google news personalization: scalable online collaborative filtering. In: Proceedings of International Conference on World Wide Web (WWW), pp. 271–280 (2007)
10. Demšar, J.: Statistical comparisons of classifiers over multiple data sets. J. Mach. Learn. Res. (JMLR) **7**, 1–30 (2006)
11. Dou, Z., Song, R., Wen, J.R.: A large-scale evaluation and analysis of personalized search strategies. In: Proceedings of International Conference on World Wide Web (WWW), pp. 581–590 (2007)
12. Fetahu, B., Markert, K., Anand, A.: Automated news suggestions for populating wikipedia entity pages. In: Proceedings of ACM International Conference on Information and Knowledge Management (CIKM), pp. 323–332 (2015)
13. Gabrilovich, E., Dumais, S., Horvitz, E.: Newsjunkie: providing personalized newsfeeds via analysis of information novelty. In: Proceedings of International Conference on World Wide Web (WWW), pp. 482–490 (2004)
14. Garcin, F., Dimitrakakis, C., Faltings, B.: Personalized news recommendation with context trees. In: Proceedings of International ACM Conference on Recommender Systems (RecSys), pp. 105–112 (2013)
15. Harvey, M., Crestani, F., Carman, M.J.: Building user profiles from topic models for personalised search. In: Proceedings of ACM International Conference on Information and Knowledge Management (CIKM), pp. 2309–2314 (2013)
16. Hsieh, C.K., Yang, L., Wei, H., Naaman, M., Estrin, D.: Immersive recommendation: news and event recommendations using personal digital traces. In: Proceedings of International Conference on World Wide Web (WWW), pp. 51–62 (2016)
17. Husin, H., Thom, J., Zhang, X.: News recommendation based on web usage and web content mining. In: ICDE Workshops, pp. 326–329 (2013)
18. Lagun, D., Lalmas, M.: Understanding user attention and engagement in online news reading. In: Proceedings of International Conference on Web Search and Data Mining (WSDM), pp. 113–122 (2016)

19. Lang, K.: NewsWeeder: learning to filter netnews. In: Proceedings of International Conference on Machine Learning (ICML), pp. 331–339 (1995)
20. Li, L., Wang, D.D., Zhu, S.Z., Li, T.: Personalized news recommendation: a review and an experimental investigation. J. Comput. Sci. Technol. **26**(5), 754–766 (2011). https://doi.org/10.1007/s11390-011-0175-2
21. Li, L., Wang, D., Li, T., Knox, D., Padmanabhan, B.: Scene: a scalable two-stage personalized news recommendation system. In: Proceedings of International Conference on Research and Development in Information Retrieval (SIGIR), pp. 125–134 (2011)
22. Li, L., Chu, W., Langford, J., Schapire, R.E.: A contextual-bandit approach to personalized news article recommendation. In: Proceedings of International Conference on World Wide Web (WWW), pp. 661–670 (2010)
23. Liu, J., Dolan, P., Pedersen, E.R.: Personalized news recommendation based on click behavior. In: Proceedings of International Conference on Intelligent User Interfaces (IUI), pp. 31–40 (2010)
24. Lommatzsch, A.: Real-time news recommendation using context-aware ensembles. In: de Rijke, M., et al. (eds.) ECIR 2014. LNCS, vol. 8416, pp. 51–62. Springer, Cham (2014). https://doi.org/10.1007/978-3-319-06028-6_5
25. Lops, P., de Gemmis, M., Semeraro, G.: Content-based recommender systems: state of the art and trends. In: Ricci, F., Rokach, L., Shapira, B., Kantor, P.B. (eds.) Recommender Systems Handbook, pp. 73–105. Springer, Boston (2011). https://doi.org/10.1007/978-0-387-85820-3_3
26. Ma, H., Liu, X., Shen, Z.: User fatigue in online news recommendation. In: Proceedings of International Conference on World Wide Web (WWW), pp. 1363–1372 (2016)
27. Maksai, A., Garcin, F., Faltings, B.: Predicting online performance of news recommender systems through richer evaluation metrics. In: Proceedings of International ACM Conference on Recommender Systems (RecSys), pp. 179–186 (2015)
28. Manning, C.D., Raghavan, P., Schütze, H., et al.: Introduction to Information Retrieval, vol. 1. Cambridge University Press, Cambridge (2008)
29. Pantel, P., Lin, T., Gamon, M.: Mining entity types from query logs via user intent modeling. In: Proceedings of Annual Meeting of the Association for Computational Linguistics (ACL), pp. 563–571 (2012)
30. Park, S.T., Pennock, D., Madani, O., Good, N., DeCoste, D.: Naïve filterbots for robust cold-start recommendations. In: Proceedings of ACM SIGKDD International Conference on Knowledge Discovery and Data Mining (KDD), pp. 699–705 (2006)
31. Resnick, P., Iacovou, N., Suchak, M., Bergstrom, P., Riedl, J.: Grouplens: an open architecture for collaborative filtering of netnews. In: Proceedings of ACM Conference on Computer-Supported Cooperative Work and Social Computing (CSCW), pp. 175–186 (1994)
32. Su, X., Khoshgoftaar, T.M.: A survey of collaborative filtering techniques. In: Advances in Artificial Intelligence 2009, p. 4:2 (2009)
33. Tan, A.H., Teo, C.: Learning user profiles for personalized information dissemination. In: Proceedings of IEEE International Joint Conference on Neural Networks (IJCNN), vol. 1, pp. 183–188 (1998)
34. Trevisiol, M., Aiello, L.M., Schifanella, R., Jaimes, A.: Cold-start news recommendation with domain-dependent browse graph. In: Proceedings of International ACM Conference on Recommender Systems (RecSys), pp. 81–88 (2014)
35. Wen, H., Fang, L., Guan, L.: A hybrid approach for personalized recommendation of news on the web. Expert Syst. Appl. **39**(5), 5806–5814 (2012)

Analyzing the Interaction of Users with News Articles to Create Personalization Services

Alessandro Celi[1]($\boxtimes$), Alejandro Piad[2]($\boxtimes$), Jósval Díaz Blanco[3]($\boxtimes$), and Romina Eramo[1]($\boxtimes$)

[1] University of L'Aquila, L'Aquila, Italy
{alessandro.celi,romina.eramo}@univaq.it
[2] University of Havana, Havana, Cuba
apiad@matcom.uh.cu
[3] University of Matanzas, Matanzas, Cuba
josval.diaz@umcc.cu

Abstract. News personalization technologies aim at providing contents tailored to the users preferences. While recommender systems provide suggestions to users by taking advantage of individual preferences, content of news portals can be tailored on the bases of sociological aspects (e.g., the demographics of the users or the region in which they live) elicited from user interactions with the news. This allows to generate personalization with a coarse granularity; however, no study has ever shown a large-scale analysis of how the users interact with the news, focusing on different user segments. This paper uses the Yahoo News Feed dataset, a corpus that contains more than 101 billion examples of interactions between users and news items. The data present in the corpus spans for a range of 4 months, and was extracted from real user interactions with news items in the Yahoo Web portal. The dataset has been analyzed in order to understand users behaviors and their relations with sociological aspects. Thanks to our analysis, different forms of personalization can be generated.

Keywords: User interaction · News · Personalization

1 Introduction

News portals are characterized by the overwhelming amount of content they can offer. Finding ways to present news items to users is not trivial. Indeed, the amount of topics that are usually covered by a news portal is very large and might not always meet the interest of the users, and the life of a piece of news is very short (the traffic of around 80% of articles decreases monotonically after 12 h [7]). Personalized news recommendation [10, 13, 17] might allow to tailor the provided content to the individual preferences of the users. However, no information about the individual preferences of a user might be available or it might be good to

© Springer Nature Switzerland AG 2020
L. Boratto et al. (Eds.): BIAS 2020, CCIS 1245, pp. 167–180, 2020.
https://doi.org/10.1007/978-3-030-52485-2_15

tailor the structure of a news portal on inherent characteristics of a segment of users (e.g., the users of a certain geographic area might be very interested in politics, while those that live in a different area might be more interested in sports). Therefore, analyzing how the users interact with news articles and trying to find correlations between their interest and specific sociological characteristics (e.g., their demographics or the geographic area) is essential in order to provide high-level forms of personalization that might fit the interests of a specific user segment.

The interaction of the users with news articles are a form of implicit feedback that the users provide, which generates large amounts of data that is not trivial to analyze. Recent years have seen the birth and development of the "big data" world, a collection of tools, techniques and systems designed to make sense and efficiently process the impressive amounts of data generated daily. Besides the algorithms, systems and tools, one important resource are datasets or corpus of this data, collected, formatted and prepared to be used by the machine learning and statistical analysis tools [8].

As a confirmation of the incredible amount of data that is generated by the users when they interact with news articles, on January 2016 the Internet company Yahoo[1] released *Yahoo News Feed*, a massive dataset of interactions between users and news items. This is one the largest news corpus available to the research community.

This work is dedicated to the analysis of the interactions between users that expose commons sociological characteristics and news articles. Characterizing users' interests is the key to generate personalizations in news portals. This study represent a base-block to the development of coarse-grain forms of personalizations for the selected users' segments (e.g., group recommendations [4–6], or targeted ads [16]).

We can summarize the main contributions of the paper as follows:

- study users' reading preferences and interactions highlighting sociological aspects;
- perform analysis on the huge News Feed dataset that captures geographically-distributed user interactions;
- severals type of analysis are performed in different fields: (*i*) demographics, (*ii*) time evolving, (*iii*) semantics.

The rest of the paper is organized as follows: in Sect. 2 we present related work, Sect. 3 introduces the Yahoo News Feed dataset, Sect. 4 describe some specific analysis. Finally, Sect. 5 draws some conclusions and presents related work.

2   Related Work

In the last decade, news personalization has become an important research area [14], as advocated by many techniques that have been proposed to tackle personalized news recommendation. These include content-based [15], collaborative

---

[1] Yahoo Webscope Program: https://webscope.sandbox.yahoo.com/.

filtering system [18] an hybrid approaches. In addition, a novel approach that relies on the concept of "search profiles" has been proposed; user profiles are built on the base of the past user interactions with a web search engine [2]. News recommendation is a problem widely-studied in the literature. Google News [10] generates recommendations using three approaches: collaborative filtering using MinHash clustering, Probabilistic Latent Semantic Indexing (PLSI), and co-visitation counts. O'Banion et al. [17] model user interests based on Twitter and propose a content-based approach for news recommendation. Goosen et al. [13] provide news recommendations by adapting TF-IDF with the semantics of a domain ontology, resulting in Concept Frequency - Inverse Document Frequency (CF-IDF). The analysis of the interests of the users can also be useful to provide recommendations to journalists. On this purpose, Cucchiarelli et al. [9] present a recommender system, What To Write and Why, capable of suggesting to a journalist, for a given event, the aspects still uncovered in news articles on which the readers focus their interest.

Regarding the analysis of the interaction of the users with the news, Castillo et al. [7] characterize the life cycle of online news stories, relating it to social media reactions; results show that it is possible to model the overall traffic articles will receive, by observing the first ten to twenty minutes of social media reactions. Dezso et al. [11] perform an analysis of the visits to a Hungarian news portal, showing they are distributed according to a power-law across a broad range, with a mean of 36 h. Agarwal et al. [1] study the actions users perform after reading an article, like their printing, commenting, rating, and sharing through e-mail or social media. The authors perform personalized recommendations, but also uncover that article topics have an effect on the probability of each performed action. In [3], an analysis of the reading behavior of the users in a mobile digital publishing platform is performed. The authors develop a tool that allows the human editors to analyze the reading behavior of the users, by providing analytics that show how the users read magazine issues.

As it is possible to notice analyzing the literature, no previous study perform a large-scale analysis of the interaction between news articles of a specific topic and users who exhibit common sociological characteristics.

3 Methodology

In this section, we present the methodology followed in this study. Section 3.1 will provide an overview of the aspects we analyzed, while Sect. 3.2 will present the considered dataset.

3.1 Analyzed Aspects

The performed analysis of the dataset is designed to better understand the structure of the data, and also to provide a hints into how to best exploit such data for personalization and information retrieval tasks. To achieve this goal, we are going to analyze the dataset from severals points of view:

- **Demographics analysis:** we measure the relative percentages of users divided by gender, age, and geographical location.
- **Time sensitive users' interests analysis:** we analyze the evolution of users' reading behavior over time.
- **Semantic analysis:** we analyze users' needs, considering the semantic content of the news.

3.2 Description of the Used Dataset

For our study, we used the Yahoo News Feed dataset R10. R10 is a massive collection of data, which compressed rounds about 1.5 TB and uncompressed a total of 13.5 TB of information. It is based on a sample of user's interaction with the news stream on the Yahoo Homepage, Yahoo Sports, Yahoo Finance, Yahoo Entertainment, Yahoo News, and Yahoo Real Estate. To build the dataset, a random sample of 17 million active Yahoo users was selected in June 2015. Then their historical news item interaction data from February 2015 through May 2015 was obtained and processed to remove all identifiable properties. This results in a set of over 6 million news items, and 101 billion user-news interaction examples.

Users are represented as meaningless, anonymous ids, so that no identifying information is revealed. For some of the anonymized users, binary gender label (male or female), an age-range label and the city from which the user event originated are also available. For the news items, the dataset provides content information such as the Yahoo generated summary of the news article and some key phrases that were extracted from the article. Each user-item interaction is also marked up with a timestamp of that event and the position of the article in the stream.

The dataset is divided into 3 different sub-collections: *users*, *items*, and *events* data. Each of these sub-collections actually consists of a large number of tab-separated text files with an item per line. Table 1 shows a description of each sub-collection in terms of size, number of files, columns and number of entries present (total lines in all the files of the corresponding collection).

Table 1. Description of the collections present in the dataset.

Collection	Files	Entries	Columns	Total size
Users	9	17 168 169	3	266 MB
Items	30	6 188 322	2	1 200 MB
Events	11 502	101 253 173 240	11	1 021 GB

The collections present in the dataset are described as follows:

- *Users collection*, contains one entry per user, with three fields: *user-id*, *age* and *gender*;

– *Items collection* contains one entry per news item, with two fields: *item-id*
  and *content* field, which is a JSON encoded object storing metadata about
  the corresponding news (*category*, *concepts*, *summary* and *title*); finally
– *Event collection* table links together news items and users. Every entry corresponds to a possible interaction of a user with a news item. It contains
  the following fields: *user-id*, *event-id*, *timestamp*, *item-id*, *city*, *state*, *property*
  and other fields that describe user's surfing characteristic on respect to the
  specific triple item-event-user.

The next section presents different analysis we performed on the dataset.

4   Results of the Performed Analyses

This section with present the outcome of our analyses from the previously presented points of view. Indeed, we will analyze how users belonging to different
demographic segments interact with the news, how time impact the user interactions, and what roles semantics play in these interactions.

4.1   Demographic Analysis

Table 2 shows the number of users in the dataset distributed by age and gender.

Table 2. Number of users present in the dataset grouped by gender and age rank.

Age	Cat.	Gender			Total	Pop. %
		?	F	M		
?	–	7 818 138	1 018 794	1 481 237	10 318 169	
20–30	1	16 854	647 040	706 106	1 370 000	13,9
31–40	2	14 683	577 624	777 693	1 370 000	12,8
41–50	3	15 791	545 645	808 564	1 370 000	13,4
51–60	4	14 950	533 777	821 273	1 370 000	13,9
>60	5	17 413	521 624	830 963	1 370 000	19,5
Total	–	7 897 829	3 844 504	5 425 836	17 168 169	

These results indicate some interesting facts. The number of users per age
group is not a uniformly sampled from the entire population. Furthermore,
each age category was intentionally constructed with the same number of users
(1 370 000). To obtain statistically meaningful results we group users by age.
This kind of grouping allows us to understand much better the preferred news
categories. Whereas, users with unknown age should be used for statistics not
relating to age, in order to avoid inaccurate results.

Table 3. Ranking by amount of click in each state per week.

State	Weeks 2015						Average
	08–14/02	22–28/03	05–11/04	12–18/04	03–09/05	17–23/05	
California	12628361	16750676	17562015	18340115	21686666	25283357	18708532
Texas	6958839	9128672	9845583	10165255	12288211	14781145	10527951
Florida	4151990	5487830	5782849	5904961	6725293	7769069	5970332
New York	4014744	5472156	5693252	5780038	6832485	7837484	5938360
Illinois	3909767	5210135	5533416	5505726	6298431	6964390	5570311
Ohio	2951334	3778020	4029340	3994779	4554748	5159533	4077959
Pennsylvania	2726420	3869379	4089724	4058708	4572868	5113939	4071840
Georgia	2485115	3390382	3427918	3664585	3916488	4269934	3525737
Michigan	2241276	2918808	2985416	3019034	3587861	4109264	3143610
New Jersey	2099044	2908997	3018337	3074663	3559773	4079558	3123395
Virginia	1802021	2457482	2587490	2647360	3129446	3691275	2719179
North Carolina	1829820	2328877	2450054	2541477	2966764	3487608	2600767
Washington	1771836	2313846	2351611	2440713	2620226	2890338	2398095
Arizona	1543711	2089149	2195809	2273011	2640599	2984960	2287873
Massachusetts	1558221	2101291	2206015	2176547	2515628	2906974	2244113
Maryland	1436326	1939900	2030456	2067143	2531702	2960047	2160929
Missouri	1391344	1847733	1949688	1945819	2423141	2859216	2069490
Wisconsin	1350840	1834865	1966431	1850343	2178282	2406014	1931129
Colorado	1215368	1587792	1692209	1759584	2071591	2372721	1783211
Indiana	1116255	1459043	1603107	1584994	1944684	2325577	1672277
Tennessee	1179118	1537475	1642172	1684078	1837171	2078625	1659773
Minnesota	1051855	1463824	1547159	1519691	1797758	2043864	1570692
Connecticut	898696	1182508	1251986	1187262	1446408	1716601	1280577
Alabama	827597	1070515	1172805	1226080	1395105	1621240	1218890
Oregon	855713	1082729	1186545	1178846	1387517	1618314	1218277
Louisiana	729980	958948	995279	1075050	1342774	1710831	1135477
South Carolina	774323	999895	1051324	1093256	1239661	1437055	1099252
Nevada	700110	912868	983402	997410	1208333	1404022	1034358
Oklahoma	656134	867105	921299	946605	1241783	1567160	1033348
Kentucky	687300	912193	947857	942827	1127812	1343589	993596
Kansas	636398	871342	925857	940382	1068706	1206756	941574
Arkansas	561402	661798	734725	758577	908294	1104709	788251
Iowa	480282	654843	698916	680914	825150	943715	713970
Utah	399924	543035	575983	593470	695452	821341	604868
Mississippi	406880	523816	548923	575856	639132	755523	575022
Nebraska	346392	482186	511278	518654	593295	663725	519255
Hawaii	304044	371760	555584	575536	570162	574618	491951
New Mexico	334354	431056	459525	476482	573034	671408	490977
District of Columbia	311936	431946	460413	464699	520813	543831	455606
West Virginia	285131	387346	405263	403272	428260	480819	398349
New Hampshire	281710	360981	381970	369508	431011	512867	389675
Idaho	245484	312924	347451	340526	395642	468450	351746
Maine	249662	325564	343232	324086	380563	447576	345114
Rhode Island	202301	251263	267641	263427	313629	370572	278139
Montana	171979	227789	238279	236851	280722	330601	247704
Delaware	147203	200510	205392	211151	273766	348623	231108
Alaska	149576	204097	220408	220475	254274	285884	222452
North Dakota	139740	194281	198648	193758	232640	258261	202888
South Dakota	136227	183734	189670	191768	217025	241691	193353
Vermont	130001	159982	166463	156284	184291	215852	168812
Wyoming	104951	139674	146907	153029	181124	212510	156366

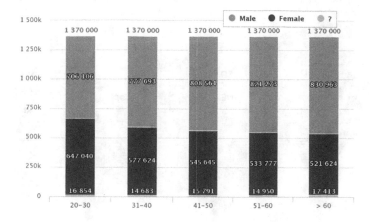

Fig. 1. Absolute number of users per age and gender.

Another interesting result is that the number of male users is significantly superior to the number of female users in the dataset, whereas in actual demographics is the other way around. This result confirm that into the online world male users are more than female users. Figure 1 illustrates gender statistics grouped by age.

Figure 2 shows the geographical distribution of the users in the United States. We obtained this information by analyzing on week of events (from April 5 to April 11, 2015) and counting the number of distinct users. We also test other five weeks (see Table 3 for the data), in order to validate the user/state distribution. Comparing these values with the actual population of the USA, obtained from [19], proves that users are distributed in the dataset exactly as the real population. We perform also a Pearson's χ^2 test for goodness of fit [12] of the relative frequencies (with p-value below the 0.001 significance level). We can conclude that, contrary to the results obtained for the distribution of age ranges (see Table 2), this dataset is suitable for studying news-related preferences according to geographical information.

Figure 3 shows the relative difference between the real population data and the actual number of users active on the week between April 5 and April 11, 2015. States are sorted in decreasing order of population. It can be seen that these relative values agree within at most a 5% error.

4.2 Time Sensitive Users' Interests Analysis

To understand how the users' behavior evolves over time, we analyze the number of interactions during each hour of the week that starts at April 5th and ends on April 11th of 2015.

Figure 4 represents the distribution of articles read throughout the week, separated by gender. The timestamps stored in the dataset do not have a timezone attached. It was necessary to normalize the dataset's timestamp according

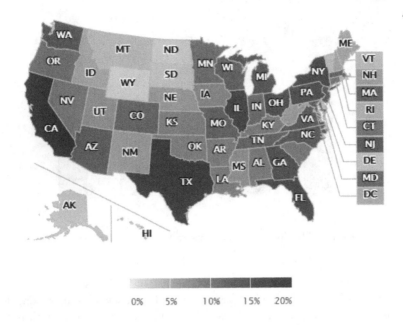

Fig. 2. Distribution of users by state.

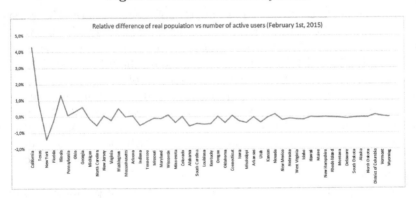

Fig. 3. Relative difference between the actual population and the number of active users per state.

to the timezone of the user's state. In total, there are 2 797 315 different male users and 1 777 408 different female users active a least once during this week. There are a total of 43 183 149 interactions for male users and 23 444 991 for female users. On average, each male user reads an average of 15, 43 news in the week, while female users read an average of 13, 19 news items.

Despite the difference in volume, the overall distribution of activity during the week is very similar for men and women. The general trend follows the

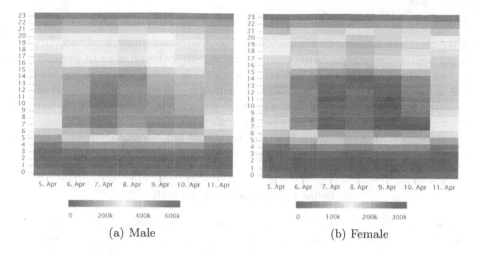

(a) Male   (b) Female

Fig. 4. Behavior by gender in the consultations for hours in a week.

expected distribution for the working days. 57.74% of activities are performed during regular working hours, i.e., from 8 am to 5 pm, from Monday until Friday. During the weekend, the volume of activity is considerably smaller. Also, there is a slight but evident diminishing of activity during the afternoon of Friday, and during lunch time in weekends.

However, most users are not active every day. Figure 5(a) shows the number of users that are active some specific number of days. On average a user is active 3.71 days of the week, but it can be seen there are users all over the spectrum. Figure 5(b) shows the number of users that perform that many interactions during the week. On average, a user reads 14.95 news during the week.

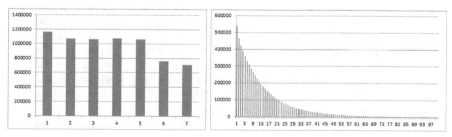

(a) Number of users active exactly X (b) Number of users with exactly X interac-
days.   tions.

Fig. 5. Histogram of users activity during the week.

4.3   Semantic Analysis

In this section, we present the results of the semantics analysis of the dataset. In particular, news topics are measured considering the number of interactions that exist in the dataset. We define the news topics based on the *keywords* field that is present in the news item. The identification of topics is a broad research area, and as such, many approaches exist for determining the topic of the natural language document. We decided, for generality, to resort to using the dataset's own definition of topics. Note that the *keywords* field is not a trivial keywords extraction from the news but it is a topic classifications of the news.

Table 4. Top concept by property.

Property	Top concept	Clicks	% Clicks	News	Clicks/news
RealEstate	Consumer Reports	99 026	1,699	1 632	60,678
	California	87 810	1,506	48 490	1,811
	Photograph	67 602	1,160	24 318	2,780
	Real estate	43 735	0,750	12 078	3,621
	The Wall Street Journal	40 358	0,692	20 658	1,954
News	Barack Obama	6 329 685	1,087	136 317	46,434
	Police officer	4 808 948	0,825	23 693	202,969
	United States	4 606 115	0,791	103 383	44,554
	California	3 135 266	0,538	20 738	151,185
	Russia	2 898 527	0,498	38 162	75,953
Sports	National Football League	2 318 411	1,326	98 225	23,603
	New England Patriots	1 600 424	0,915	42 802	37,391
	National Basketball Association	1 327 068	0,759	55 253	24,018
	Floyd Mayweather	1 015 839	0,581	20 460	49,650
	Manny Pacquiao	858 176	0,491	18 517	46,345
Finance	Retirement	1 569 266	0,984	10 215	153,624
	United States	1 557 934	0,977	103 383	15,070
	Price of oil	1 320 263	0,828	25 560	51,653
	Interest rate	1 100 735	0,690	26 649	41,305
	Apple Inc	974 509	0,611	18 880	51,616
FrontPage	Photograph	69 078 381	0,552	24 318	2840,628
	Barack Obama	65 533 045	0,523	136 317	480,740
	National Football League	64 443 853	0,515	98 225	656,084
	United States	44 778 198	0,358	103 383	433,129
	New England Patriots	36 214 872	0,289	42 802	846,102
Entertainment	Photograph	2 513 522	1,973	24 318	103,361
	Kim Kardashian	1 388 680	1,090	8 920	155,682
	Kanye West	941 771	0,739	11 276	83,520
	Bruce Jenner	919 419	0,722	7 021	130,953
	Whitney Houston	743 320	0,583	3 896	190,791

Table 4 shows the top 5 keywords (ranked by number of interactions) per property. As expected, the top keywords in each category are related to

State	Entertainment	Finance	News	RealEstate	Sports
California	10,0%	17,5%	57,1%	0,76%	14,8%
Texas	9,8%	15,5%	61,6%	0,73%	12,4%
New York	9,8%	20,4%	55,1%	0,63%	14,1%
Florida	9,3%	16,4%	60,1%	0,73%	13,4%
Illinois	9,9%	17,3%	57,5%	0,68%	14,7%
Ohio	10,1%	15,1%	57,8%	0,69%	16,4%
Pennsylvania	9,7%	19,0%	57,4%	0,63%	13,3%
Georgia	9,7%	14,0%	62,3%	0,65%	13,4%
Michigan	9,4%	15,3%	61,2%	0,67%	13,5%
New Jersey	9,6%	21,9%	54,3%	0,63%	13,5%
Virginia	9,3%	16,7%	59,6%	0,64%	13,7%
North Carolina	10,3%	15,6%	59,5%	0,72%	13,8%
Arizona	9,2%	16,3%	60,6%	0,73%	13,1%
Washington	7,8%	18,1%	60,7%	0,68%	12,6%
Maryland	9,8%	16,2%	59,8%	0,63%	13,5%
Massachusetts	9,5%	20,1%	55,0%	0,64%	14,7%
Missouri	10,0%	15,7%	60,9%	0,76%	12,6%
Wisconsin	9,6%	15,9%	60,1%	0,64%	13,8%
Colorado	7,8%	18,9%	60,2%	0,76%	12,2%
Indiana	10,5%	14,5%	59,6%	0,72%	14,7%
Tennessee	10,7%	13,9%	62,2%	0,73%	12,4%
Minnesota	8,3%	19,3%	57,4%	0,65%	14,4%
Connecticut	10,6%	18,7%	57,2%	0,72%	12,9%
Louisiana	11,0%	12,8%	63,1%	0,71%	12,4%
Alabama	9,5%	13,1%	64,2%	0,67%	12,5%
Oregon	7,9%	15,2%	63,8%	0,74%	12,4%
Oklahoma	10,2%	14,6%	63,9%	0,78%	10,4%
South Carolina	10,2%	14,3%	61,2%	0,74%	13,6%
Nevada	10,0%	14,0%	60,2%	0,80%	14,9%
Kentucky	10,8%	13,7%	62,1%	0,79%	12,6%
Kansas	9,6%	14,8%	62,6%	0,80%	12,2%
Arkansas	10,6%	12,5%	64,9%	0,82%	11,1%
Iowa	8,3%	18,4%	59,0%	0,70%	13,6%
Utah	10,1%	17,6%	58,1%	0,81%	13,4%
Mississippi	10,8%	11,6%	65,6%	0,68%	11,4%
Nebraska	8,9%	17,7%	61,1%	0,65%	11,6%
New Mexico	8,9%	12,7%	66,1%	0,74%	11,4%
Hawaii	8,6%	17,9%	56,5%	0,63%	16,3%
District of Columbia	9,8%	17,1%	58,2%	0,57%	14,3%
New Hampshire	8,8%	18,2%	57,8%	0,59%	14,5%
West Virginia	10,4%	12,3%	64,2%	0,68%	12,4%
Idaho	8,1%	13,8%	65,5%	0,75%	11,8%
Maine	8,9%	13,9%	62,6%	0,62%	14,1%
Rhode Island	10,7%	17,8%	55,8%	0,64%	15,1%
Delaware	10,0%	19,8%	57,1%	0,66%	12,5%
Montana	7,2%	14,1%	66,2%	0,70%	11,8%
Alaska	7,2%	12,2%	69,1%	0,66%	10,8%
North Dakota	8,0%	17,5%	58,5%	0,75%	15,2%
South Dakota	8,4%	15,4%	62,2%	0,68%	13,3%
Vermont	7,9%	13,9%	63,4%	0,62%	14,2%
Wyoming	7,0%	15,7%	65,6%	0,73%	10,9%

Fig. 6. Distribution of readings by state and category.

important personalities, events or institutions in every category. Interestingly, the keyword "Photograph" appears in the top of both *Front Page* and *Entertainment* and in 4th place in *Real State*. Rather than related to the art of photography itself, we believe this keyword indicates news that contains photos. This is an indication that such news attract more interest than others which only have feature text. Besides the number of interactions (clicks) we also report the percent of clicks each keyword received relative to the corresponding property, as well as the number of news items where that keyword appears, and the average ratio of clicks per news item. This last metric can be used to evaluate the "interest" that a particular topic attracts. Arguably, more interesting topics are those that get more interaction with fewer news.

Distribution of Readings by State and Category. Finally Fig. 6 illustrates the reading behavior of the users (grouped by state) with respect to the news categories. For instance, *New Jersey* is the state most interested in finance with a percentage of its users that read *Finance* articles equal to 21, 9%. Whereas, *Alaska*'s users are not interested in finance (only the 12, 2% of them read articles in this category), on the contrary the 69, 1% of them prefer reading *News*. Note that, the information obtained in this analysis can be used to tailor the *Front page* to the preferences of the users belong to a specific state.

5   Conclusions and Future Work

In this paper, we performed a large-scale analysis of the interactions between the users and the items in the Yahoo News Feed dataset. Extracting information from these interaction can be used to generate forms of personalization that are targeted to specific sets of users.

From the results, it emerges that, despite the difference in volume, the overall distribution of activity of women and men is very similar. Most of the activities are performed during the working days (especially in the working hours), whereas in the weekend the volume of activity is considerably smaller. The topics relevance is not only affected by the number of clicks, in fact a complete view is given by the average ratio of clicks per news item. The geographic interaction of the users with the content shows that the distribution of readers is in according to the real population; this makes the dataset suitable for studying news-related preferences according to geographical information. In fact, the geographic distribution of readers of specific categories helps in understanding users preferences (for instance, the *Front page* of each state could be personalized with respect to the most popular categories).

As future work we are interested in using this study as a baseline to analyze the collective attention of the news readers. Furthermore, human editors should be supported by tools that allow them to shape the content published by a news portal, based on the current users interests.

References

1. Agarwal, D., Chen, B.C., Wang, X.: Multi-faceted ranking of news articles using post-read actions. In: Proceedings of the 21st ACM International Conference on Information and Knowledge Management, CIKM 2012, pp. 694–703. ACM, New York (2012). https://doi.org/10.1145/2396761.2396850
2. Bai, X., Cambazoglu, B.B., Gullo, F., Mantrach, A., Silvestri, F.: Exploiting search history of users for news personalization. Inf. Sci. **385**, 125–137 (2017). https://doi.org/10.1016/j.ins.2016.12.038
3. Boratto, L., Cadeddu, M., Carta, S., Deplano, G., Mereu, F.: A tool to analyze the reading behavior of the users in a mobile digital publishing platform. In: Armano, G., Bozzon, A., Cristani, M., Giuliani, A. (eds.) Proceedings of the 2nd International Workshop on Knowledge Discovery on the WEB, KDWeb 2016. CEUR Workshop Proceedings, Cagliari, Italy, 8–10 September 2016, vol. 1748. CEUR-WS.org (2016). http://ceur-ws.org/Vol-1748/paper-01.pdf
4. Boratto, L., Carta, S.: Modeling the preferences of a group of users detected by clustering: a group recommendation case-study. In: Proceedings of the 4th International Conference on Web Intelligence, Mining and Semantics (WIMS 2014), pp. 16:1–16:7. ACM, New York (2014). https://doi.org/10.1145/2611040.2611073
5. Boratto, L., Carta, S.: ART: group recommendation approaches for automatically detected groups. Int. J. Mach. Learn. Cybern. **6**(6), 953–980 (2015). https://doi.org/10.1007/s13042-015-0371-4
6. Boratto, L., Carta, S.: The rating prediction task in a group recommender system that automatically detects groups: architectures, algorithms, and performance evaluation. J. Intell. Inf. Syst. **45**(2), 221–245 (2015). https://doi.org/10.1007/s10844-014-0346-z
7. Castillo, C., El-Haddad, M., Pfeffer, J., Stempeck, M.: Characterizing the life cycle of online news stories using social media reactions. In: Proceedings of the 17th ACM Conference on Computer Supported Cooperative Work & #38; Social Computing, CSCW 2014, pp. 211–223. ACM, New York (2014). https://doi.org/10.1145/2531602.2531623
8. Chen, H., Chiang, R.H., Storey, V.C.: Business intelligence and analytics: from big data to big impact. MIS Q. **36**(4), 1165–1188 (2012)
9. Cucchiarelli, A., Morbidoni, C., Stilo, G., Velardi, P.: What to write? A topic recommender for journalists. In: Popescu, O., Strapparava, C. (eds.) Proceedings of the 2017 Workshop: Natural Language Processing Meets Journalism, NLPmJ@EMNLP, Copenhagen, Denmark, 7 September 2017, pp. 19–24. Association for Computational Linguistics (2017). http://aclanthology.info/papers/W17-4204/w17-4204
10. Das, A.S., Datar, M., Garg, A., Rajaram, S.: Google news personalization: scalable online collaborative filtering. In: Proceedings of the 16th International Conference on World Wide Web, WWW 2007, pp. 271–280. ACM, New York (2007). https://doi.org/10.1145/1242572.1242610
11. Dezső, Z., Almaas, E., Lukács, A., Rácz, B., Szakadát, I., Barabási, A.L.: Dynamics of information access on the web. Phys. Rev. E **73**(6), 066132 (2006)
12. Pearson, K.: X. on the criterion that a given system of deviations from the probable in the case of a correlated system of variables is such that it can be reasonably supposed to have arisen from random sampling. Philos. Mag. Ser. 5 **50**(302), 157–175 (1900). https://doi.org/10.1080/14786440009463897

13. Goossen, F., IJntema, W., Frasincar, F., Hogenboom, F., Kaymak, U.: News personalization using the CF-IDF semantic recommender. In: Proceedings of the International Conference on Web Intelligence, Mining and Semantics, WIMS 2011, pp. 10:1–10:12. ACM, New York (2011). https://doi.org/10.1145/1988688.1988701

14. Li, L., Wang, D.D., Zhu, S.Z., Li, T.: Personalized news recommendation: a review and an experimental investigation. J. Comput. Sci. Technol. **26**(5), 754 (2011). https://doi.org/10.1007/s11390-011-0175-2

15. Lops, P., de Gemmis, M., Semeraro, G.: Content-based recommender systems: state of the art and trends. In: Ricci, F., Rokach, L., Shapira, B., Kantor, P.B. (eds.) Recommender Systems Handbook, pp. 73–105. Springer, Boston, MA (2011). https://doi.org/10.1007/978-0-387-85820-3_3

16. Malheiros, M., Jennett, C., Patel, S., Brostoff, S., Sasse, M.A.: Too close for comfort: a study of the effectiveness and acceptability of rich-media personalized advertising. In: Proceedings of the SIGCHI Conference on Human Factors in Computing Systems, CHI 2012, pp. 579–588. ACM, New York (2012). https://doi.org/10.1145/2207676.2207758

17. O'Banion, S., Birnbaum, L., Hammond, K.: Social media-driven news personalization. In: Proceedings of the 4th ACM RecSys Workshop on Recommender Systems and the Social Web, RSWeb 2012, pp. 45–52. ACM, New York (2012). https://doi.org/10.1145/2365934.2365943

18. Su, X., Khoshgoftaar, T.M.: A survey of collaborative filtering techniques. Adv. in Artif. Intell. **2009**, 4:2 (2009). https://doi.org/10.1155/2009/421425

19. P.D. U.S. Census Bureau: Annual estimates of the resident population for the United States, Regions, States, And Puerto Rico: April 1, 2010 to July 1, 2016 (nst-est2016-01) (2016). https://www2.census.gov/programs-surveys/popest/tables/2010-2016/state/totals/nst-est2016-01.xlsx

Using String-Comparison Measures to Improve and Evaluate Collaborative Filtering Recommender Systems

Luiz Mario Lustosa Pascoal[(⊠)], Hugo Alexandre Dantas do Nascimento, Thierson Couto Rosa, Edjalma Queiroz da Silva, and Everton Lima Aleixo

Institute of Informatics, Federal University of Goiás, Goiânia, Goiás, Brazil
{luizpascoal,hadn,thierson,edjalmasilva,evertonaleixo}ufg.br
http://inf.ufg.br/

Abstract. Recommender Systems are expert systems that utilize the user's interests in order to recommend different products. One of the main techniques employed in this type of system is the Collaborative Filtering which recommends products to users based on their interactions and on what items similar users have liked in the past. However, many traditional methods for determining similarity do not consider temporal information neither the rich information that is contained in sequentially-ordered user interactions. Therefore, the present work proposes the usage of traditional string comparison approaches for defining new similarity measures between pairs of users that take into consideration time-ordered data. The general idea is to model the similarity computation between users as an approximate string matching problem and to employ classical algorithms that solve it. Experiments conducted in different application domains demonstrate that the measures based on a string-comparison approach can improve accuracy. Furthermore, they represent a new way of evaluating the performance of sequence-based recommendation.

Keywords: String-comparison · Recommender Systems · Measures

1 Introduction

A Recommender system (RS) is a decision support system that can provide the desirable information to the customers as per their needs. Theses systems are able to handle large volumes of data in order to select different contents to be presented to the user as a way of recommendation [1]. Good recommendations allow the target-user[1] to quickly find items of interest without being overwhelmed by irrelevant information [19].

---

[1] User who will receive the recommendation generated by the system.

This work was supported by research grant from FAPEG (Goiás Research Foundation, Process Nr. 04/2015) as a PhD scholarship.

© Springer Nature Switzerland AG 2020
L. Boratto et al. (Eds.): BIAS 2020, CCIS 1245, pp. 181–194, 2020.
https://doi.org/10.1007/978-3-030-52485-2_16

One of the most used approach on recent RSs is the Collaborative Filtering (CF) technique, which recommends items to users according to the preferences of other similar users using collected information, such as: explicit rating or implicit interaction, regarding a set of items like movies, songs or books. Nonetheless, the CF have received great attention due to the flexibility of incorporating other computational models as described in the survey of [12,18].

An important component of the CF is the similarity function that determines how close a target-user is to other users. Traditionally, the history of the users' ratings is analyzed for discovering similarity between users, thus generating a neighborhood of similar users which is of utmost importance [4]. Most of CF techniques are entirely based on the user's rating of a given product. However, a well known limitation that has been reported in science is that users have made fewer and fewer evaluations of products. This directly influences the quality of any future suggestion that the system may offer since the similarity function depends on the ratings performed by different users [3,13].

In addition to the lack of ratings, the majority of CF implementations neglect the fact that the user "taste" may change over time. Also these systems are not designed to use the rich information that is contained in the sequentially-ordered user interactions that are often available in practical applications. Therefore, some researchers have studied the influence of time in Recommendation Systems with the aim of improving recommendation accuracy. A common approach to deal with such influence is to delete old ratings, or implementing a time decay function, or even disregard users who are only similar considering old reviews [21]. Other approaches include a session-based temporal graph, that create long and short-term interest models, as described in [19]. Nevertheless, how to properly use time information in order to discover the underlying dynamics of the user preferences, still remains a major research challenge [23].

Another open issue is how to correctly evaluate the recommendations generated by a model that considers the sequence of user actions as input. Quadrana, Cremonesi and Jannach [17] reported that previous works have employed several standard classification and ranking metrics to perform evaluation. However, when the application domain requires recommendations to fulfill an explicit or implicit order constraint, these metrics cannot fully inform us about the quality of the recommendations, since, in some situations, it is important to consider entire lists of recommended items, as there are application domains where the recommendation of one item (e.g., an accessory) only makes sense after some other object was purchased [7,8].

Therefore, this paper advances the research on the usage of time attributes in the RSs field by introducing an approach that uses string-comparison measures algorithms as similarity functions between users. Our assumption is that the order in which the users performed actions on a system (such as, for example, the order of the films they saw, the songs listened to and the read books) determines part of their personality and, therefore, their preferences during future activities in the same context. So, in our approach, we represent the sequences of actions performed by a user as a string that defines him/her, and then treat the similarity between users as a similarity between the strings that describe their actions.

Additionally, we propose to use these same string-comparison measures to evaluate the performance of traditional CF RSs. The proposed method employs various concepts that have already been shown in different CF solutions. In this aspect, the novelty of our method is the determination of similarity between users considering the sequentially ordering of user interaction, and two new approaches for evaluating the generated recommendation list that are more sensitive to the order in which the items are evaluated over time.

The remainder of this paper is organized as follows. Section 2 presents the theoretical foundation for understanding the work, including a brief introduction to CF Recommender Systems and a short review about string-comparison measures. Section 3 presents our proposed CF method. Next, in Sect. 4, we describe the experiments for testing our proposal, emphasizing the adopted evaluation metrics and the results obtained with them. Finally, we present the conclusions of our research and suggest ideas for future work.

2   Basic Concepts

2.1   Recommender Systems Based on Collaborative Filtering

The main goal of a Recommender System is to provide a user with a list of items that may be of his or her interest, by predicting how the user might evaluate each item. Among other approaches, the Collaborative Filtering (CF) technique was proved to be useful by a number of classical studies [1,3,4,13].

CF algorithms are based on records of preferences and actions collected on a daily basis for many users. This technique has received great attention from the academic community due to various practical applications that help users process large amounts of data and ensure a customized recommendation [3].

The idea behind collaboration is to cluster people based on a significant degree of similarity in order to provide recommendations [18]. To accomplish such clustering, knowledge about the users are needed. This can be obtained explicitly, by having the system asking the users to tell about their interests, generally through a rating task, and/or implicitly, by analysing the users' behavior registered during their interaction with the system [11].

Table 1 illustrates a Rating Matrix $(R_{m_x n})$ used as input in a typical RS. The m lines represent the list of users, $U = u_1, u_2, \ldots, u_m$, and the n columns refer to the list of items $I = i_1, i_2, \ldots, i_n$. Each element $r_{u,i} \in R$ indicates the rating of the user u to the item i. The value scale of the ratings depends on the application design. For Table 1, we used the rate interval $[1,5]$ where 1 is bad and 5 is excellent.

The task to be performed is to predict which rating the user would give to an item that has not yet been evaluated by him/her. Traditionally, RS based on CF identify users who have similar preferences when reviewing their history of ratings given by them in order to cluster the users appropriately [3].

The clustering of users is based on measures of similarity (or distance) between pairs of users regarding their previous ratings. These measures consider each row (user) of the Rating Matrix as a vector in the item (n-dimensional)

Table 1. Example of a Rating Matrix.

User/Item	I_1	I_2	I_3	I_4	...	I_n
U_1	2	4	5	4	...	*
U_2	1		4	3	...	*
U_3		4	5		...	*
U_4	5	2	3		...	*
U_5	2	4		1	...	*
...	...	...	...	...	...	*
U_m	*	*	*	*	...	*

space and evaluate the distance or similarity of two distinct users by comparing their correspondent vectors. The three classic measures are: a) the Cosine similarity function which measures the cosine of the angle between two user vectors, b) the Euclidean distance between two vectors, and c) the Pearson correlation [1]. The Pearson Correlation, used in our work, is shown in Eq. (1), where a and b represent two users and j represents an item; $v_{a,j}$ is then the rating of the user a to item j. The total average ratings performed by the user a in the system, given by $\overline{v}_a$ can be obtained through Eq. (2).

$$\omega(a,b) = \frac{\sum_j (v_{a,j} - \overline{v}_a)(v_{b,j} - \overline{v}_b)}{\sqrt{\sum_j (v_{a,j} - \overline{v}_a)^2 \sum_j (v_{b,j} - \overline{v}_b)^2}} \tag{1}$$

$$\overline{v}_a = \frac{1}{|I_a|} \sum_{j \in I_a} v_{a,j} \tag{2}$$

Although any of these measures may be used to find the $k - Nearest - Neighbors$ (kNN) with similar interests the most used measure in Collaborative Filtering is the Pearson correlation coefficient. Upon (kNN) of a given user, it is possible to predict the user's opinion in relation to other items [11]. In Eq. (3), the predicted evaluation of the user a for the item j is given by $P_{a,j}$ and can be calculated using the weighted average of all evaluations, and the average of all ratings performed by user a on other items, as $W_{(e,a)}$. The $Raters$ is the set of users who evaluated j [1].

$$P_{a,j} = \overline{v}_a + \frac{\sum_{e \in Raters}(v_{e,j} - \overline{v}_e)W_{(e,a)}}{\sum_{e \in Raters}|W_{(e,a)}|} \tag{3}$$

The likelihood of recommending the item j to user a is determined according to the predicted rating, in which higher values are more likely to be recommended to the user. In order to produce accurate prediction ratings, good similarity measures between users are important [4]. Therefore, we present a new mechanism to compute similarity between users based on string-comparison measures. String comparison is a very common problem in many domains. Algorithms for it are available and can be used on our context, as described in the next section.

2.2   String-Based Similarity Measures

Let $X[1, \cdots, p]$ and $Y[1, \cdots, q]$ be two input strings. A common subsequence (CS) $CS[1, \cdots, s]$ of $X[1, \cdots, p]$ and $Y[1, \cdots, q]$ is a set of symbols which occur in both strings in the same relative order, but not necessarily contiguous. The Longest Common Subsequence (LCS) of strings X and Y, given by $LCS(X, Y)$, is a common subsequence of maximal length. The traditional technique for finding the $LCS(X[1, \cdots, p], Y[1, \cdots, q])$ is to determine the longest common subsequence for all possible prefix combinations of the input strings. The recurrence relation for calculating the length of the LCS for each prefix pair $(X[1, \cdots, i], Y[1, \cdots, j])$ is presented in Eq. (4) [2]:

$$R[i,j]_{LCS} = \begin{cases} 0 & \text{if } i = 0 \text{ or } j = 0 \\ R[i-1, j-1]_{LCS} + 1 & \text{if } X[i] = Y[j] \\ max R[i-1, j]_{LCS}, R[i, j-1]_{LCS} & \text{if } X[i] \neq Y[j] \end{cases} \quad (4)$$

The length of the $LCS(X, Y)$ can be found by computing $R[p, q]_{LCS}$. The LCS string itself can be discovered by keeping an auxiliary data structure for holding information about the steps taken when computing R. A brute-force algorithm for the LCS, which checks every possible subsequence of X and compares it with Y, has exponential time $\mathcal{O}(2^p \times q)$. However, there is a tabular solution to this problem using dynamic programming with cost $\mathcal{O}(p \times q)$ [16], which makes it suitable for practical applications. Deeper analytic studies about the LCS problem and its methods are presented by Bergroth et al. [2].

The Levenshtein (Leven) [16] can be considered as a dissimilarity measure since it computes the number of edits necessary to transform the string X into Y. The operations used to perform the transformations are: insertion (adding a new character); deletion (deleting a character); and substitution (replace one character by another). The Levenshtein measure between the two strings X and Y is given by $R[p, q]_{Leven}$, is presented in Eq. (5).

$$R[i,j]_{Leven} = \begin{cases} \max(i,j) & \text{if } \min(i,j) = 0 \\ \min \begin{cases} R[i-1, j]_{Leven} + 1 \\ R[i, j-1]_{Leven} + 1 \\ R[i-1, j-1]_{Leven} + 1_{X[i] \neq Y[j]} \end{cases} & \text{otherwise} \end{cases} \quad (5)$$

Finally, the Jaro Similarity is a function based on the number and order of the common characters between two strings; it takes typical spelling deviations into account and is mainly used in the area of record linkage [16]. The Jaro algorithm measures the amount of characters in common, being no more than half the length of the longer string in distance, with consideration for transpositions. Therefore, the higher the Jaro measure is for two strings, the more similar the strings are. The Jaro Similarity between the two strings X and Y is given by $R[p, q]_{Leven}$, as presented in Eq. (6), which h is the number of matching characters and t is half the number of transpositions, which is the number of matching (but different sequence order) characters [6].

$$R[i,j]_{Jaro} = \begin{cases} 0 & \text{if } h = 0 \\ \frac{1}{3} \left(\frac{h}{|X|} + \frac{h}{|Y|} + \frac{h-t}{h} \right) & \text{otherwise} \end{cases} \quad (6)$$

In this paper, we use the string-comparison measures to compute the similarity between pairs of users. Each unique item in the database (for example a movie) is represented as a different character. A user characteristic string is simply a sequence of items purchased by him/her in the order it appears. Therefore, the simplest data structure to represent such strings is a vector, with each element having an unique ID and other information such as the date it was seen and a rating given by the user to the item. In the end, we order the vector to create the user's timeline according to their timestamps.

3   Proposed Recommender System Architecture

3.1   System Overview

Generally, a traditional User-based CF RS consists of two phases: a *Preprocessing phase* in which we compute the similarity between users based on the ratings previously given by them to the items (this also allows to define a neighborhood relation involving the users); and a *recommendation phase*, during which the ratings for items that were not evaluated yet are now predicted and the items with highest estimated ratings are recommended. For the first phase, it is necessary to use the available ratings provided by the users to the items. In the current work, we consider that each user has a rating timeline, consisting of a sequence of items that he or she saw and evaluated. We assume that two users are similar if their timelines are also alike. These two phases are embedded in the general architecture of the proposed method, as presented in Fig. 1.

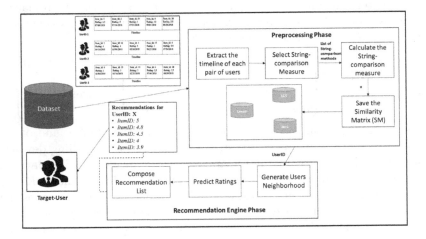

Fig. 1. Proposed CF-recommender system architecture.

It is noteworthy that the Preprocessing phase is performed before triggering the Recommendation engine. For each pair of users present in the dataset, we compute a chosen string-comparison measure for the given pair of users, and saves it on a $User \times User$ matrix (SM), in which, every cell $SM_{i,j}$ represents the similarity value between users i and j. Due to the number of users, a large volume of processing is required in order to produce this similarity matrix. However, the processing is executed only once, and the generated SM is then properly saved according to its string-comparison method. Table 2 shows an example of the SM matrix in which all values were normalized according to the MIN-MAX range.

Table 2. Example of a similarity matrix (SM).

	u_1	u_2	u_3	u_4		u_m
u_1	max	0.9	0.3	0.4	⋯	0.6
u_2	0.9	max	0.8	0.8	⋯	0.2
u_3	0.3	0.8	max	0.1	⋯	0.3
u_4	0.4	0.8	0.1	max	⋯	0.7
⋯	⋯	⋯	⋯	⋯	⋯	⋯
u_m	0,6	0.2	0.3	0.7	⋯	max

Once the SM matrix is saved, the recommendation engine searches the most similar users to every target-user and save them in a neighborhood list assigned to the target-user. These lists are then submitted to the Predict Rating module, which is responsible for predicting ratings on items that have not been rated by the target-users before. Finally, the items with highest predicted values are recommended to each target-user in the form of a recommendation list.

3.2   Methods to Determine the Similarity Function

In Sect. 2, we learned that the similarity function is crucial for the efficiency of the CF technique. Therefore, our paper presents methods to obtain the similarity between two users u and v using the LCS, Leven and Jaro string-comparison to generate the SM matrix.

For the LCS method, we implemented three variants that maintain the essence of the original metric but consider relevant strategies to the recommendation context. The first variant, named **LCS-P**, computes the similarity taking only the user's interaction with the system, regardless whether a rating was submitted or not. For each pair of users u, v, we calculate a coefficient of similarity $(sim_{LCS-P}(u,v))$, obtained from Eq. (7), in which L represents the size of the LCS extracted from the timelines H_u and H_v, related to users u and v respectively.

$$sim_{LCS-P}(u,v) = L = |LCS(H_u, H_v)| \tag{7}$$

The second variant of the LCS, named **LCS-W**, is presented in Eq. (8). In addition to the action, this method also considers the rating (explicit or implicit) given by users to different items. Therefore, $sim_{LCS-W}(u, v)$ is obtained by multiplying the length L by a factor that involves the weighted distance of the ratings given by users u and v for the items in LCS. The terms $R_u(k)$ and $R_v(k)$ are the normalized ratings (between 0 and 1) that the users u and v gave, respectively, to the k-th item of their LCS. This method explores the deterioration of ratings over time by weighting with a higher importance (with weight k) the rating difference of more recent items.

$$sim_{LCS-W}(u, v) = L \times \frac{1}{\sum_{k=1}^{L} \frac{k \times |R_u(k) - R_v(k)|}{\frac{(L+L^2)}{2}} + 1} \tag{8}$$

The last variant of the implemented LCS, named **LCS-R**, considers the existence of multiple common subsequences between the timelines of users u and v. Therefore, $sim_{LCS-R}(u, v)$ is obtained by successive applications of the LCS algorithm on the timelines of u and v. Once a LCS is computed, its length is added to the equation and the timelines of the two users are momentarily shortened by removing from them the occurrences of LCS items. The process is then repeated until the length of the resultant LCS is zero. Let k be the number of times the process is repeated. Equations (9) shows the LCS-R similarity measure.

$$sim_{LCS-R}(u, v) = \frac{\sum_{i=1}^{k} |s_i|}{\frac{(k+k^2)}{2}} \tag{9}$$

With:

$s_1 = LCS(Hu, Hv);$
$s_2 = LCS(Hu - s_1, Hv - s_1);$
$...$
$s_k = LCS(Hu - s_{k-1}, Hv - s_{k-1}).$

The next method, named **Leven**, uses the Leveshtein presented in Eq. (5), as $sim_{Leven}(u, v)$. However, since the Leveshtein is a dissimilarity measure, adjustments were necessary as presented in Eq. (10).

$$sim_{Leven}(u, v) = \frac{1}{1 + |Leven(H_u, H_v)|} \tag{10}$$

Finally, the last string-comparison method implemented was the **Jaro** Similarity previously presented in Eq. (6). Therefore, $sim_{Jaro}(u, v)$ is the similarity coefficient returned on the algorithm.

For all of the above methods, we use the different values of $sim(u, v)$ to fill each method respective SM matrix (Table 2) for all pair of users (u, v) in the dataset. For each target-user we keep a list of his/her neighbors properly ordered according to the computed similarity.

As means of comparison, we also implemented the traditional **Pearson** Correlation as similarity function, as described in Eq. (1).

4 Experiments

4.1 Setup

For this paper, we chose three appropriate datasets which contain rating times-tamps that record the precise moments when the users interacted with an item. The first dataset is the MovieLens1M [10]², which is a benchmark on the RSs field on the movies domain. The second is the 30Music dataset [20], which is a collection of listening and playlists data retrieved from Internet radio stations through Last.fm API³. Finally, we also prepared a simulated dataset generated randomly in order to verify the metrics behavior. Statistical detailed information on the datasets are presented in Table 3.

Table 3. Statistical information on used datasets.

Dataset	Users	Items	Ratings	Date range
MovieLens1M	6,040	3,952	1,000,209	4/2000–2/2003
30Music	28,724	10,000	3,408,683	1/2014–1/2015
Random	15,000	10,000	2,631,821	1/2010–1/2020

Different rating scale values were used in the chosen datasets. The MoviLens dataset uses a full star system from 1 to 5. The 30Music dataset presents the amount of time (in seconds) a user has listened to a set of songs. So, we considered that the longer the user listened to a song, the most he or she liked it. The Random dataset generated a random integer number also from 1 to 5. Therefore, we normalized all ratings into the $[0, 1]$ real interval.

The evaluation of a RS basically consists of verifying the performance of the recommendation algorithms in relation to user satisfaction. Generally, the dataset is split into Training and Test datasets. In the present work, the temporal aspect for division was considered. For each user, the first 80% of his/her ratings were taken as a Training dataset and the last 20% went used as the Test dataset. We adopted this strategy to validate our method performance on more recent users interactions.

The effectiveness of traditional CF methods, based on matrix completion, is usually evaluated with metrics based on prediction error, like Root Mean Square Error (RMSE) or Mean Average Error (MAE) [11]. These metrics assign the same relevance to the items in the recommendation lists which is not a good fit on sequence-based RS, where in almost all situations, is important to consider the entire list and the order the items in it, instead of only to assess the assertiveness in predicting a rating [22].

For different application domains, we can use standard classification metrics (precision and recall) since the recommendation problem can be visualized as

---

² https://grouplens.org/datasets/movielens/1m/.
³ https://www.last.fm/api/.

determining whether an item is or not in a recommendation list. So, in order to measure the system capability to recommend items in our context, we define two basic concepts: $relevant(u)$ is the set of items seen/evaluated by user u that appear in the test database; and $recommended\_relevant(u)$ is the set of items generated by the recommendation engine for u that also appear in $relevant(u)$. Using these concepts and following the notations adopted in other works [7,8,15, 23], we define *Precision* and *Recall* of a recommendation to a user u by Eqs. (11) and (12) respectively.

$$precision(u) = \frac{|recommended\_relevant(u)|}{|recommendation\_list(u)|} \qquad (11)$$

$$recall(u) = \frac{|recommended\_relevant(u)|}{|relevant(u)|} \qquad (12)$$

During the dataset splitting, it was observed that the number of items removed could vary between users. This would affect the reliability of precision and recall since some users have rated significantly less items than others. Thus, we also proposed the implementation of two new metrics that deal with this problem by normalizing precision and recall according to the number of ratings per user in the Test dataset. We named theses adaptations as *PrecisionNorm* and *RecallNorm*.

Furthermore, since we are studying sequences of rated items, it is worth not only to verify if we are capable of recommending the same set of expected items, but also if they can be generated in the same order in which they were saw and evaluated by the users [17]. Therefore, we advocate the usage of the *LCS* and *Levenstein* measures as new metrics for checking the quality of a recommendation. This implies in computing the LCS and Levenstein values considering the recommended sequences of items, outputted by our approach, and the known (correct) sequence of items in the users' timelines in the Test dataset. Note that higher values of LCS and inverted Levenshtein measures indicate that the recommender is capable of generating a sequence of items that is similar to the users' actual interactions.

For the same reason just mentioned above, we also decided to employ ranking metrics such as *MAP* and *NDCG*. The main difference is that MAP assumes binary relevance (an item is either of interest or not), while NDCG allows relevance scores in the form of real numbers. Even though the use of MAP has not been well seen in the Information Retrieval field [9], for the RS domain, where the order of occurrence of items is relevant, that metric may provide a valuable insight. Further elaboration on the usage of these metrics on the RSs field is presented at [5,11].

In order to run the experiments, we used the Apache Mahout[4] which is a Java framework very well documented and famous in Recommender Systems. Several adaptations on its source-code were needed in order to submit the list of neighbors for each target-user.

---

[4] Apache Mahout. WebSite: https://mahout.apache.org/users/recommender.

In total, we ran experiments using six methods on the three datasets. To comprehensively compare the results, the number of neighbors (the size of the neighborhood considered for every target-user) was set to 5, 8, 10, 15, 20, 25, 30, 40, 50 and 60. To ease understanding, the results presented are the mean value on these neighborhood sizes.

We also varied the size of the recommendation list created for the target-users. The aim was to analyze the accuracy of the method in recommending the next best items, and also the sequence in larger lists which can help detect interest drifts of individual users over time. The experimented recommendation-list sizes were 2, 5, 10, 15 and 20. This is shown at the X-axis of the charts in the next section.

4.2   Results

Figures 2 and 3 show the results obtained after the execution of all methods on the MovieLens1M and 30Music datasets respectively. A line chart is presented for every evaluation metric. Its X-axis refers to the size of the recommendation list and the Y-axis indicates the value of the given metric. The results of each method is presented using a different colored line.

The trends in the results for both datasets are very similar. The Leveshtein method presented the best results overall, indicating that few operations were needed to transform its generated recommendation list into the actual observed list. The second best result is obtained by the Jaro Similarity method. After a deeper comparison between the recommendation list and the test dataset, we learned that, for this method, its assertiveness is restricted to a few set of users. It is also worthy mentioning that the results of the Jaro and Pearson similarity functions appear to be more on regular in the PrecisionNorm chart than in Precision chart, in the last two figures, due to the normalization process.

From the metrics point of view, the precision and the recall behaved as expected, as the precision tendency is to decrease as the recommendation list increases, unlike the recall that is more likely to increase since it improves the chances of a Test dataset item to be in the recommendation list. The LCS charts follow the same pattern of the recall charts.

Finally, for the generated Random dataset, the results were very similar among all the implemented methods, and none of them were capable of generating good recommendation lists. The standard deviation across the recommendation list are <0.0001. It is also worth mentioning that our intention in creating this dataset was to verify if our methods were biased towards the Leveshtein metric (regardless of the dataset) and this showed not to be true.

Overall our results show that the precision metric, and particularly the recall metric allow a good comparison of the methods, describing a uniform trend in both charts. LCS is quite similar to recall, what needs further investigation as the LCS considers order while the other metric does not. MAP and NDCG provided different insights when we changed the dataset. Therefore, they also demand more studies for improving our understanding about which features of the datasets mostly affected these metrics. The Levenshtein was the most

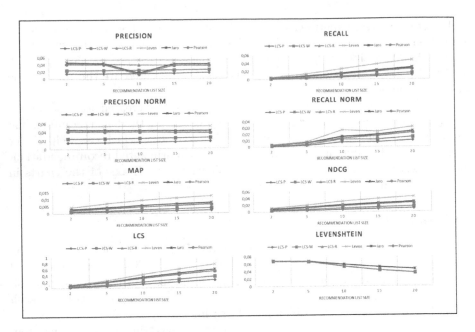

Fig. 2. Results obtained on the MovieLens1M dataset.

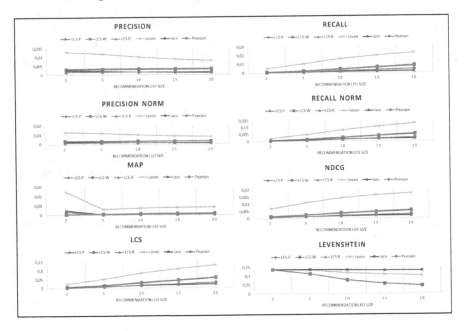

Fig. 3. Results obtained on the 30Music dataset.

surprisingly one, as some methods presented the same results in this metric (they appeared as overplaced lines in the chart).

Finally, we highlight the results produced by the string-comparison methods, used as similarity functions in replacement to the traditional Pearson correlation. Among the string-comparison methods, we encourage the usage of the **Leven** method since it obtained the best results on most metrics in both datasets.

5 Conclusion and Future Work

This paper introduced a new approach on the User-based CF RSs, that uses several string-comparison measures as similarity functions in order to find better users neighborhood and to improve recommendation effectiveness on sequential data. The conducted experiments showed, in general, the string-comparison based methods presented better results than the traditional Pearson correlation in all selected databases. And, among the string-comparison methods, we highlight the great performance of the Leven and Jaro Similarity methods.

We also introduced new approaches to measure the recommendation using the LCS and the Leveshtein algorithms. The results measured by these metrics indicate that they can be used to evaluate traditional RSs, but that they need further investigation. Overall, a general open issue in the RS field is the lack of "standard" metrics to assess quality criteria when recommendation lists as a whole needs to be evaluated [17].

Finally, as reported in other pieces of research, CF methods still present substantial room for improvement since some methods based on the *kNN* principle are still outperforming complex machine-learning based methods [14]. Therefore, as future work, we intend to implement a new recommender engine entirely based on the LCS problem which uses the users solely timeline to recommend. Also, we intend to implement a matrix factorization model and a deep learning model based on sequential information and test our proposals on new datasets from different domains.

References

1. Adomavicius, G., Tuzhilin, A.: Toward the next generation of recommender systems: a survey of the state-of-the-art and possible extensions. IEEE Trans. Knowl. Data Eng. **17**(6), 734–749 (2005)
2. Bergroth, L., Hakonen, H., Raita, T.: A survey of longest common subsequence algorithms. In: Seventh International Symposium on String Processing and Information Retrieval, SPIRE 2000. Proceedings, pp. 39–48. IEEE (2000)
3. Bobadilla, J., Ortega, F., Hernando, A., Gutiérrez, A.: Recommender systems survey. Knowl. Based Syst. **46**, 109–132 (2013)
4. Bobadilla, J., Serradilla, F., Bernal, J.: A new collaborative filtering metric that improves the behavior of recommender systems. Knowl. Based Syst. **23**(6), 520–528 (2010)
5. Bonnin, G., Jannach, D.: Evaluating the quality of playlists based on hand-crafted samples. In: Proceedings of ISMIR, pp. 263–268 (2013)

6. Cohen, W.W., Ravikumar, P., Fienberg, S.E., et al.: A comparison of string distance metrics for name-matching tasks. In: IIWeb, vol. 2003, pp. 73–78 (2003)
7. Cremonesi, P., Koren, Y., Turrin, R.: Performance of recommender algorithms on top-n recommendation tasks. In: Proceedings of the Fourth ACM Conference on Recommender Systems, pp. 39–46 (2010)
8. Feng, S., Li, X., Zeng, Y., Cong, G., Chee, Y.M., Yuan, Q.: Personalized ranking metric embedding for next new POI recommendation. In: Twenty-Fourth International Joint Conference on Artificial Intelligence (2015)
9. Fuhr, N.: Some common mistakes in IR evaluation, and how they can be avoided. In: ACM SIGIR Forum, vol. 51, pp. 32–41. ACM, New York (2018)
10. Harper, F.M., Konstan, J.A.: The movielens datasets: history and context. ACM Trans. Interact. Intell. Syst. (tiis) **5**(4), 1–19 (2015)
11. Herlocker, J.L., Konstan, J.A., Terveen, L.G., Riedl, J.T.: Evaluating collaborative filtering recommender systems. ACM Trans. Inform. Syst. (TOIS) **22**(1), 5–53 (2004)
12. Juan, W., Yue-xin, L., Chun-ying, W.: Survey of recommendation based on collaborative filtering. In: Journal of Physics: Conference Series, vol. 1314, p. 012078. IOP Publishing (2019)
13. Lü, L., Medo, M., Yeung, C.H., Zhang, Y.C., Zhang, Z.K., Zhou, T.: Recommender systems. Phys. Rep. **519**(1), 1–49 (2012)
14. Ludewig, M., Jannach, D.: Evaluation of session-based recommendation algorithms. User Model. User Adap. Inter. **28**, 331–390 (2018). https://doi.org/10.1007/s11257-018-9209-6
15. Mishra, R., Kumar, P., Bhasker, B.: A web recommendation system considering sequential information. Decis. Support Syst. **75**, 1–10 (2015)
16. Pikies, M., Ali, J.: String similarity algorithms for a ticket classification system. In: 2019 6th International Conference on Control, Decision and Information Technologies (CoDIT), pp. 36–41. IEEE (2019)
17. Quadrana, M., Cremonesi, P., Jannach, D.: Sequence-aware recommender systems. ACM Comput. Surv. (CSUR) **51**(4), 1–36 (2018)
18. Su, X., Khoshgoftaar, T.M.: A survey of collaborative filtering techniques. Adv. Artif. Intell. **2009**, 4 (2009)
19. Tuan, C.C., Hung, C.F., Wu, Z.H.: Collaborative location recommendations with dynamic time periods. Pervasive Mob. Comput. **35**, 1–14 (2017)
20. Turrin, R., Quadrana, M., Condorelli, A., Pagano, R., Cremonesi, P.: 30music listening and playlists dataset. In: RecSys Posters (2015)
21. Xiao, M., Yan, B.: Collaborative filtering recommendation algorithm based on shift of users' preferences. In: 2011 International Conference on Business Management and Electronic Information (BMEI), vol. 3, pp. 520–523. IEEE (2011)
22. Zhang, F., Gong, T., Lee, V.E., Zhao, G., Rong, C., Qu, G.: Fast algorithms to evaluate collaborative filtering recommender systems. Knowl. Based Syst. **96**, 96–103 (2016)
23. Zhang, J.D., Chow, C.Y., Li, Y.: Lore: exploiting sequential influence for location recommendations. In: Proceedings of the 22nd ACM SIGSPATIAL International Conference on Advances in Geographic Information Systems, pp. 103–112 (2014)

Enriching Product Catalogs
with User Opinions

Tiago de Melo[1]($\boxtimes$), Altigran S. da Silva[2], Edleno S. de Moura[2],
and Pável Calado[3]

[1] Universidade do Estado do Amazonas, Manaus, Brazil
tmelo@uea.edu.br
[2] Universidade Federal do Amazonas, Manaus, Brazil
{alti,edleno}@icomp.ufam.edu.br
[3] Universidade de Lisboa, Lisbon, Portugal
pavel.calado@tecnico.ulisboa.pt

Abstract. A large number of opinions on products and their features
are posted every day on e-commerce websites in user reviews. They
are a valuable source of knowledge for both manufacturers and customers. However, reviews often bring so much information that exceeds
the human capacity of reasoning and hampers their effective use. Thus,
researchers on how to organize a large number of opinions available on
the reviews in the Web play a substantial role. Traditional summarization methods group opinions around aspects, but they tend to generate
too many aspects groups that are generic and difficult to interpret. We
claim that the most important characteristics of the products correspond
to the attributes in product catalogs. Thus, these attributes should guide
the process of organizing opinions. This paper presents a summary of an
approach called *OpinionLink*, based on machine-learning techniques, to
enrich a product catalog with opinions extracted from product reviews.
The experimental results demonstrate the effectiveness of the proposed
approach.

Keywords: Data enrichment · Aspect-based summarization · Opinion
mining

1 Introduction

Thousands of people post reviews for all types of products offered online by
e-commerce websites. On this high volume of reviews, there is a large number
of opinions, which can be a valuable source of knowledge for decision-making,
for both manufacturers and customers – manufacturers can obtain immediate
feedback to improve the quality of their products and customers can obtain
assessments from other users prior to purchasing a product. As highlighted by
Knon *et al.* [7], the sheer volume of available reviews is such that it exceeds the
human processing capacity and can, thus, become a major barrier for its effective
use.

© Springer Nature Switzerland AG 2020
L. Boratto et al. (Eds.): BIAS 2020, CCIS 1245, pp. 195–204, 2020.
https://doi.org/10.1007/978-3-030-52485-2_17

Assume, for example, that a consumer is interested in the general user opinion on a particular cell phone's screen. To read all the reviews is impractical. A straightforward query containing the term *screen* is also not effective because people commonly write on different *aspects* of the screen, such as *resolution* or *contrast*, without using the actual word. Moreover, reviews are typically written by nontechnical users, and consequently, the text is not always correct and frequently contains misspellings and other typing errors. Thus, research on how to organize the otherwise unstructured user-provided reviews is a substantial challenge to both academia and industry.

A traditional method of organizing a large number of product reviews is to create an *opinion summary* [2,6]. However, current techniques to create opinion summarizations are inadequate to address customer queries on specific product characteristics, as illustrated by the aforementioned cell phone screen example [1,11,14]. This is because, in the current methods, opinions are arbitrarily clustered by aspects, causing these clusters to not necessarily align with the commonly expected product attributes. For example, there could be several clusters that refer to the screen: a cluster of opinions regarding resolution and color, another mixing glossiness with size, and numerous others. Thus, the customer must perform the nontrivial task of identifying what groups of aspects refer to the aspect of interest. Zha *et al.* [13] reported that for the *iPhone 3GS*, more than three hundred aspects were identified in the reviews. Summarizing this information can generate hundreds of clusters, without identifying what specific aspects refer to the actual cell phone screen. The question that arises then is how to structure opinions such that they can be effectively used by customers and manufacturers?

To address these issues, we make one important assumption: the most important product characteristics are represented by the attributes of the product catalogs, supplied by the manufacturers, and commonly made available to customers on e-commerce sites. According to Fensel et al. [4], product catalogs are designed for human readers and their function is to describe products to potential clients. Therefore, we argue that the process of organizing opinions should be guided by the attributes of these catalogs.

Grouping opinions around the attributes of the product catalog also allows the catalog to be enriched over time with these opinions. This makes the user reviews readily available without the requirement for further processing. Another advantage of this approach is that it allows one to easily compare people's opinions on products of the same category because they are all represented by the same attributes. Continuing our example, assuming that *cell phone screen* is one of the characteristics outlined in a product catalog for cell phones, one could easily discover what cell phone has more positive comments specifically regarding its screen. This comparison of opinions, although extremely useful to buyers, is not possible when using traditional methods of aspect-based opinion summarization because there is no guarantee of obtaining a single summary of opinions on this specific characteristic (the screen).

Motivated by the above observations, in this paper we presented an overview of *OpinionLink* [3], an approach we devised to *automatically map user opinions on a product to the attributes of its product catalog*. The ultimate goal of the proposed approach is to enrich the product catalog with opinions extracted from user reviews.

OpinionLink is divided into two phases: opinion extraction and opinion mapping. In the first phase, we use supervised classification to identify direct opinionated sentences (DOSs) in the reviews of a particular product, followed by standard methods to extract the corresponding opinions [12]. This phase is illustrated in Fig. 1 (top), where three opinions are extracted from a real user review. Notice that not all sentences are opinionated and therefore were discarded. Further, it is possible to have more than one opinion in a single sentence. The outcome of the first phase is a set of opinions on a product.

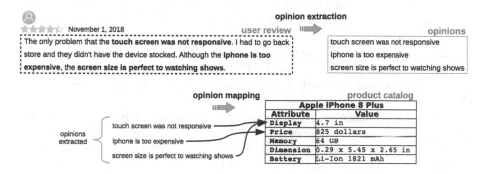

Fig. 1. Example of opinion extraction. First phase (top) and second phase (bottom).

In the second phase, we again use supervised classification to map the previously extracted opinions to attributes of the product catalog. This phase is illustrated in Fig. 1 (bottom), where each of the opinions extracted in the previous phase is mapped to one of the attributes of the product catalog.

The output of the second phase is an *enriched product catalog* where, for each product, each attribute of the catalog is enriched with a set of opinions regarding the attribute. In Fig. 2, we present the enriched product catalog with opinions extracted from user reviews of Fig. 1. The enriched product catalog will have, for each product, the objective values that are normally associated with its attributes and a new dimension with the *subjective values* represented by the user opinions. For simplicity, in this example, we assume that the opinions are represented by sentences. However, in the proposed approach, we adapted the definition of opinion established by Bing Liu [8], where opinions are represented by tuples whose components are, among other things, aspect expressions, and sentiment words.

To evaluate *OpinionLink*, we performed experiments considering two different scenarios. In the first scenario, we focused on the effectiveness of the proposed approach. Tests were performed using a set of product reviews on five categories

Apple iPhone 8 Plus		
Attribute	**Value**	**Opinions**
`Display`	`4.7 in`	touch screen was not responsive screen size is perfect to watching shows
`Price`	`825 dollars`	iPhone is too expensive
`Memory`	`64 GB`	
`Dimension`	`0.29 x 5.45 x 2.65 in`	
`Battery`	`Li-Ion 1821 mAh`	

Fig. 2. Enriched product catalog with opinions.

of electronic products collected from popular e-commerce websites[1]. We then evaluated the proposed method's performance on identifying opinionated sentences from the reviews. We also quantified the importance of each proposed feature through a feature ablation study. In this setting, we achieved an average of 0.87 in F_1. Next, we evaluated the proposed method's performance on the opinion-mapping task, where we achieved an average of 0.85 in F_1. Finally, we evaluated the quality of the *OpinionLink* full pipeline, functioning as an actual end-to-end catalog enrichment application. Results obtained indicate that we can use the proposed approach in a real application, achieving an average F_1 of 0.83.

In the second scenario, we evaluated the feasibility of using the proposed approach with a high volume of opinions. For this, we used a dataset of more than 600,000 real reviews, composed of more than four million sentences, and approximately 30,000 products in the same five categories of electronic products considered in the first scenario. The results allow us to state that it is possible to apply *OpinionLink* on a large scale.

The remainder of the paper is organized as follows. Section 2 presents the concepts and terminologies used in this paper. Section 3 includes an experimental evaluation of the proposed approach. Finally, Sect. 4 discusses our main conclusions.

2   *OpinionLink*: Overview

This section reviews the concepts and terminologies used in this paper. We consider a catalog as a set of products of the same category (e.g., *cell phones* or *laptops*), where each product is represented by its attributes and their corresponding values. More formally, we define the concept of product catalog as follows:

Definition 1. *A product catalog is a set of products $C = \{p_1, \ldots, p_n\}$, where each product is represented as $p = \{\langle A_1, v_1 \rangle, \ldots, \langle A_m, v_m \rangle\}$, and each pair $\langle A_i, v_i \rangle$ consists of an attribute name A_i paired with its value v_i for the corresponding product. The value v_i is a set that can be empty or contain one or more elements.*

---

[1] This data is available on request for future research.

A *review* is a text posted by a user on an e-commerce website, usually reporting their experience with a specific product, which we call the *target entity* of the review. Each review is composed of a set of *sentences*. Sentences that express factual information are called *objective* sentences, whereas sentences that express personal feelings or beliefs are called *subjective* or *opinionated* sentences. We are interested in the latter because they represent the reviewer's opinions of a product. As we have commented in the Introduction, a single sentence can have multiple opinions.

An opinionated sentence can be further classified as *comparative* or *direct*. A comparative sentence expresses a relation of similarities or differences between two or more products. The sentence *"the camera of the iPhone is much better than Galaxy"* is an example of a comparative sentence. A direct opinion sentence expresses an opinion directly on a characteristic or part of the product, or on the product as a whole. The sentence *"The camera of the iPhone is fantastic"* is an example of direct opinion. As our goal is to enrich each product of the catalog with the opinions of users regarding the specific product, we decided to eliminate comparative sentences. The definition of a DOS is more precisely stated as follows:

Definition 2. *A DOS is a sentence where an opinion is expressed directly on one or more characteristics of a product, or on the product as a whole.*

Opinions are represented by a sextuple $o = \langle a, w, s, st, h, t \rangle$, where a is the aspect of the target entity on which the opinion has been given, w is the sentiment words of the opinion, s is the sentiment polarity of the opinion toward aspect a, st is the sentence from where the opinion was extracted, h is the opinion holder, and t is the opinion posting time. This definition of opinion is derived from that presented in [8], although adapted to the context of this work.

We address the problem of enriching product catalogs with user opinions extracted from product reviews. Our main goal is to automatically map opinions to specific attributes. However, it is frequently the case that reviews also include opinions that do not refer to a specific attribute of a product. For instance, the sentence *"So far I'm really happy with this phone"* express a positive opinion for the product as a whole. Therefore, we should map this opinion to the target product. To enable this, we create a new attribute, called `General`. Furthermore, opinions can also target attributes that are not represented in the product catalog. For instance, the sentence *"The global warranty is pretty useful for me"* expresses an opinion for a characteristic of the product that is not represented as an attribute in the original product catalog. In order to handle this kind of opinion, we create an attribute called `Other`.

Considering these cases, given a product catalog C, our ultimate goal is to generate an *enriched catalog* C^+. More formally, we define the concept of an enriched product catalog as follows:

Definition 3. *An enriched product catalog is a set of enriched products* $C^+ = \{p_1^+, \ldots, p_n^+\}$, *where each enriched product is represented as* $p^+ = \{\langle A_1, v_1, O_1 \rangle, \ldots, \langle A_m, v_m, O_m \rangle\} \bigcup \{\langle \text{General}, v_G, O_G \rangle, \langle \text{Other}, v_O, O_O \rangle\}$, *where each A_i and v_i are the same attribute name and values from the original catalog C (as stated in Definition 1) and O_i is a set of opinions on attribute A_i. The triple $\langle \text{General}, v_G, O_G \rangle$ is added to handle opinions on the product as a whole, and $\langle \text{Other}, v_O, O_O \rangle$ is added to handle opinions on specific characteristics that are not represented in the other attributes.*

Notice that there are two main differences between a product p and its enriched version p^+. The first is that two new attributes have been added: General, to represent opinions regarding the product as a whole, and Other, to represent opinions relating to characteristics not initially represented in p. The second difference is that the enriched product specification considers that each attribute has, in addition to its value v, a set of opinions O regarding each attribute.

To accomplish the "opinion to attribute" mapping task that leads to the generation of the enriched catalog, we developed an approach called *OpinionLink*, based on machine-learning techniques. Further technical details on *OpinionLink* are described in [3].

3   Experiments Results

In our experiments, we used a dataset composed of user reviews and a product catalog from the BestBuy web site[2]. In this dataset, here called *BestBuy*, we consider products from five different categories: cameras (CAM), cell phones (CEL), DVD players (DVD), laptops (LAP) and routers (ROT). For each product, we randomly selected a set of reviews from those available in the web site. A summary of statistics from the dataset is presented in Table 1.

Table 1. Summary of statistics from the *BestBuy* dataset.

Category	#reviews	#sentences	#opinions
CAM	246	606	429
CEL	372	1,009	642
DVD	159	372	288
LAP	376	1,025	711
ROT	237	607	371
Total	**1,390**	**3,619**	**2,441**

---

[2] https://developer.bestbuy.com.

3.1   Identifying Direct Opinionated Sentences

To evaluate our method for the task of identifying direct opinionated sentences, we manually annotated each sentence from the reviews with the labels DOS, if the sentence is a *direct opinionated sentence*, and NDOS for other sentences.

We conducted the experiments using the following classifiers: Maximum Entropy (ME), Random Forest (RF), Support Vector Machines (SVM), and Gradient Boosting Trees (GBT). In all cases, sentences are represented by combining a traditional traditional "bag of words" (*BoW*) with the TF-IDF weighting schema and a set of nine features (*Feat*) linguistic features. These representation is called here *BoW+Feat*.

Table 2 shows the classifiers' performance in terms of precision (P), recall (R) and F_1 measure (F_1). The highest values for each category are marked in bold. In this experiment, each result denotes an average of 10-fold cross-validation.

Table 2. Experimental results of identifying directed opinionated sentences (DOS).

	CAM			CEL			DVD			LAP			ROT		
	P	R	F_1	P	R	F_1	P	R	F_1	P	R	F_1	P	R	F_1
ME$_{BoW+Feat}$	0.85	0.86	0.85	**0.94**	0.88	**0.91**	0.86	**0.86**	**0.86**	**0.90**	0.79	0.84	**0.91**	0.82	**0.86**
RF$_{BoW+Feat}$	0.82	**0.87**	0.85	0.93	0.87	0.90	0.85	0.84	0.84	0.86	0.79	0.82	0.89	0.82	0.85
GBT$_{BoW+Feat}$	0.85	0.86	**0.86**	0.92	0.87	0.89	0.87	**0.86**	**0.86**	0.84	**0.81**	0.83	0.89	**0.83**	**0.86**
SVM$_{BoW+Feat}$	**0.90**	0.83	**0.86**	0.92	**0.88**	**0.91**	**0.88**	0.84	**0.86**	0.89	**0.81**	**0.85**	0.89	**0.83**	**0.86**

The results in Table 2 reveal the best classifier is SVM$_{BoW+Feat}$ indicate that Support Vector Machines with *Bow+Feat* representation is the more appropriate solution for the direct opinionated sentence detection problem.

3.2   Opinion Mapping

To evaluate our opinion mapping method in isolation, we used as input manually identified direct opinionated sentences. We manually labeled each opinion o extracted from these DOS with the following labels: the *attribute name*, if o is an opinion on an attribute from the product catalog; *General*, if o is an opinion on the product as a whole; or *Other*, if o is an opinion on some product characteristic that is not represented as an attribute in the product catalog. The experiment was carried out using stratified 10-fold cross-validation, to ensure a balance in the proportion of classes within each partition.

The experimental results of our opinion mapping method are presented in Table 3. For the representations of sentences, we used the *Sentences Core Segments* strategy. As discussed in [3], this strategy is based on the observation that the core of an opinionated sentence corresponds only the segments of the sentence located between the aspect expressions and their sentiment words. For instance, in the sentence *"The only problem that the touch screen was not responsive"*, the core segment is *"touch screen was not responsive"*, where *"touch screen"* is the aspect expression and *"responsive"* is the sentiment word.

Table 3. Results for the opinion mapping task using the *Sentence Core Segments* strategy (*seg*).

	CAM			CEL			DVD			LAP			ROT		
	P	R	F_1	P	R	F_1	P	R	F_1	P	R	F_1	P	R	F_1
RF_{seg}	0.83	0.81	0.82	0.87	0.86	0.86	0.85	**0.87**	0.86	0.86	0.74	0.79	**0.91**	0.77	0.84
ME_{seg}	**0.84**	**0.86**	**0.85**	0.88	**0.89**	**0.88**	0.87	**0.87**	**0.87**	0.87	0.74	**0.80**	0.90	0.83	0.86
GBT_{seg}	0.82	0.80	0.81	0.87	0.83	0.85	**0.89**	0.85	**0.87**	0.84	0.75	0.79	0.86	0.84	0.85
SVM_{seg}	0.82	0.84	0.83	**0.89**	0.88	**0.88**	0.88	0.86	**0.87**	0.84	**0.77**	**0.80**	0.89	**0.86**	**0.88**

SVM_{seg} and ME_{seg} achieved the same average F_1 score (0.85) across all product categories. However, as observed by Morin and Bengio [10] and Goodman [5], a major weakness of Maximum Entropy is the very long training time. This leads us to conclude that using Sentence Core Segments and Support Vector Machines is the more appropriate solution for the opinion mapping task.

3.3   End-to-End Results

In this experiment, opinion extraction was performed using $SVM_{Bow+Feat}$ to identify DOS, as described in Sect. 3.1, and opinion mapping was performed using SVM_{seg}, as described in Sect. 3.2. We call this configuration $OpinionLink_{real}$. As a baseline, we used the best configuration from Sect. 3.2, that is, SVM_{seg} with DOS manually selected. We call this configuration $OpinionLink_{ideal}$.

Table 4 presents the performance of $OpinionLink_{ideal}$ in terms of F_1, compared to $OpinionLink_{real}$. As expected, $OpinionLink_{ideal}$ achieved better results in all categories, when compared to $OpinionLink_{real}$. The main reason is that the DOS that were incorrectly identified as factual in the first phase were not used for $OpinionLink_{real}$ and, as a consequence, recall was negatively affected. In addition, sentences that are not DOS but that were incorrectly classified as such, had a negative impact on precision. However, the difference in the results of the two methods is quite small (less than 0.02 on average), indicating that we can use our approach in a real application.

Table 4. Results of an end-to-end evaluation of *OpinionLink*.

	CAM	CEL	DVD	LAP	ROT
$OpinionLink_{ideal}$	0.83	0.88	0.87	0.80	0.88
$OpinionLink_{real}$	0.82	0.87	0.85	0.79	0.84

3.4   *OpinionLink* in Large Scale

We evaluate the feasibility of applying our method on a very large volume of opinions using an experimental dataset with data taken from the Amazon.com web site [9]³. This dataset has the same categories present in the *BestBuy* (CAM, CEL, DVD, LAP and ROT). A summary of the *Amazon* dataset is presented in Table 5(a).

Even after discarding the sentences that are not directly opinionated, the number of DOS to be processed is close to 3 million. Since it would be unfeasible to manually annotate all opinions found this huge volume of sentences, we created a random sample of 400 DOS from the whole set of reviews. This was enough to allow a confidence level of 95% in the results of our experiments.

For the opinion mapping task, we use the SVM classifier with our sentence segmentation strategy and train this classifier with the 400 DOS, using 10-fold cross-validation. Table 5(b) shows the classifiers' performance in terms of precision (P), recall (R), and F_1. As can be observed, the classifiers achieved good results in all product categories when applied to the task of mapping opinions to attributes.

Table 5. Experiments with *Amazon* dataset: (a) Summary of *Amazon* dataset and (b) Results.

Category	Products	Reviews	Sentences	
			Total	DOS
CAM	8,839	204,127	1,499,556	1,030,380
CEL	7,416	182,494	1,125,859	726,465
DVD	2,503	61,997	390,816	249,372
LAP	9,491	115,521	907,076	592,958
ROT	1,592	84,270	520,759	335,564
Total	**29,841**	**648,409**	**4,444,066**	**2,934,739**

(a)

	P	R	F_1
CAM	0.90	0.93	0.92
CEL	0.93	0.92	0.92
DVD	0.93	0.96	0.95
LAP	0.92	0.80	0.85
ROT	0.90	0.90	0.90

(b)

4   Conclusions

In this paper, we presented a summary of the approach named *OpinionLink* [3], whose aim is to automatically enriching product catalogs with user opinions. Opinions are extracted from reviews posted in e-commerce websites and associated with each individual product attribute. Experimental results have demonstrated the effectiveness of the proposed method and indicated that we can use this approach in a real application.

References

1. Amplayo, R.K., Song, M.: An adaptable fine-grained sentiment analysis for summarization of multiple short online reviews. DKE **110**, 54–67 (2017)

---

³ Available at http://jmcauley.ucsd.edu/data/amazon.

2. Condori, R.E.L., Pardo, T.A.S.: Opinion summarization methods: comparing and extending extractive and abstractive approaches. ESA **78**, 124–134 (2017)
3. de Melo, T., et al.: Opinionlink: leveraging user opinions for product catalog enrichment. IPM **56**(3), 823–843 (2019)
4. Fensel, D., et al.: Product data integration in B2B e-commerce. IEEE IS **16**(4), 54–59 (2001)
5. Goodman, J.: Classes for fast maximum entropy training. In: International Conference on Acoustics, Speech, and Signal Processing, vol. 1, pp. 561–564 (2001)
6. Hu, M., Liu, B.: Mining and summarizing customer reviews. In: Proceedings of the Tenth ACM SIGKDD International Conference on Knowledge Discovery and Data Mining, pp. 168–177. ACM (2004)
7. Kwon, B.C., et al.: Do people really experience information overload while reading online reviews? IJHCI **31**(12), 959–973 (2015)
8. Liu, B.: Sentiment Analysis: Mining Opinions, Sentiments, and Emotions. Cambridge University Press, Cambridge (2015)
9. McAuley, J.E.A.: Inferring networks of substitutable and complementary products. In: SIGKDD, pp. 785–794 (2015)
10. Morin, F., Bengio, Y.: Hierarchical probabilistic neural network language model. In: AISTATS, pp. 246–252 (2005)
11. Rakesh, V. et al.: A sparse topic model for extracting aspect-specific summaries from online reviews. In: International World Wide Web Conferences Steering Committee, WWW, pp. 1573–1582 (2018)
12. Schouten, K., Frasincar, F.: Survey on aspect-level sentiment analysis. TKDE **28**(3), 813–830 (2016)
13. Zha, Z., et al.: Product aspect ranking and its applications. TKDE **26**(5), 1211–1224 (2014)
14. Zhou, X., et al.: CMiner: opinion extraction and summarization for chinese microblogs. TKDE **28**(7), 1650–1663 (2016)

Correction to: *bias goggles*: Exploring the Bias of Web Domains Through the Eyes of Users

Giannis Konstantakis, Gianins Promponas, Manthos Dretakis, and Panagiotis Papadakos (iD)

Correction to:
Chapter "*bias goggles*: Exploring the Bias
of Web Domains Through the Eyes of Users" in:
L. Boratto et al. (Eds.): *Bias and Social Aspects in Search*
***and Recommendation*, CCIS 1245,**
https://doi.org/10.1007/978-3-030-52485-2_7

In the originally published version, the title of the paper starting on p. 66 contained a technical mistake. The title has been corrected as "bias goggles: Exploring the Bias of Web Domains Through the Eyes of Users".

The updated version of this chapter can be found at
https://doi.org/10.1007/978-3-030-52485-2_7

Author Index

Printed in the United States
By Bookmasters